Entrepreneurial Governance Neoliberal Era

CW00746950

Against the background of a growing tendency among state and local governments in the United States to vie against one another, spending public funds, and foregoing corporate tax revenues in order to attract private investment, this book offers an analysis of local economic development and business recruitment in the automotive industry. Asking why localities felt they could – and, more importantly, should – make deals with private capital in the first place, this book examines the shift toward entrepreneurial local governance from a global and historically informed perspective. Through a study of the 19 greenfield automotive assembly plants constructed in the United States during the neoliberal era, the author draws on interviews with corporate and government elites, to chart the connections between increasingly global competitive industry pressures and changing attitudes toward "incentivizing" private investment. Studying the development of an approach that has partially reoriented local governments away from managing localities and towards helping manage transnational capital flows by absorbing some of the increasing risk of long-term capital investment, *Entrepreneurial Governance in the Neoliberal Era* will appeal to scholars of sociology, politics, and urban studies with interests in globalization, the sociology of work and industry, the sociology of development, and neoliberal governance.

Oliver Cowart is Assistant Professor of Sociology at Paine College, U.S.A.

Routledge Studies in Urban Sociology

This series presents the latest research in urban sociology, welcoming both theoretical and empirical studies that focus on issues including urban conflict, politics and protest, social exclusion and social inclusion, urban regeneration and social class, and the ways in which these affect the social, economic, political, and cultural landscape of urban areas.

Titles in this series

For more information about this series, please visit: https://www.routledge.com/sociology/series/RSUS

Entrepreneurial Governance in the Neoliberal Era

Local Government and the Automotive Industry

Oliver Cowart

Routledge
Taylor & Francis Group

LONDON AND NEW YORK

First published 2022
by Routledge
2 Park Square, Milton Park, Abingdon, Oxon OX14 4RN

and by Routledge
605 Third Avenue, New York, NY 10158

Routledge is an imprint of the Taylor & Francis Group, an informa business

© 2022 Oliver Cowart

The right of Oliver Cowart to be identified as author of this work has been asserted by him in accordance with sections 77 and 78 of the Copyright, Designs and Patents Act 1988.

All rights reserved. No part of this book may be reprinted or reproduced or utilised in any form or by any electronic, mechanical, or other means, now known or hereafter invented, including photocopying and recording, or in any information storage or retrieval system, without permission in writing from the publishers.

Trademark notice: Product or corporate names may be trademarks or registered trademarks, and are used only for identification and explanation without intent to infringe.

British Library Cataloguing-in-Publication Data
A catalogue record for this book is available from the British Library

Library of Congress Cataloging-in-Publication Data
Names: Cowart, Oliver, 1984- author.
Title: Entrepreneurial governance in the neoliberal era: local government and the automotive industry/Oliver Cowart.
Description: Abingdon, Oxon; New York, NY: Routledge, 2021. | Series: Routledge studies in urban sociology | Includes bibliographical references and index.
Identifiers: LCCN 2021015427 (print) | LCCN 2021015428 (ebook) | ISBN 9780367620226 (hardback) | ISBN 9780367620233 (paperback) | ISBN 9781003107569 (ebook)
Subjects: LCSH: Automobile industry and trade--United States. | Industrial policy--United States. | Industrial promotion--United States. | Regional economics--United States. | Local government--United States. | Community 2 development, Urban--United States.
Classification: LCC HD9710.U52 C636 2021 (print) | LCC HD9710.U52 (ebook) | DDC 338.4/76292220973--dc23
LC record available at https://lccn.loc.gov/2021015427
LC ebook record available at https://lccn.loc.gov/2021015428

ISBN: 978-0-367-62022-6 (hbk)
ISBN: 978-0-367-62023-3 (pbk)
ISBN: 978-1-003-10756-9 (ebk)

DOI: 10.4324/9781003107569

Typeset in Times New Roman
by MPS Limited, Dehradun

This work is dedicated to my mother
Kathleen Boylan Cowart

Thank you for showing through your example and advocacy that intellectual pursuits are a worthy endeavor.

Contents

Acknowledgments

While this work is somewhat critical of the economic development efforts of governing officials and professionals in the southeastern United States, I am not directly critiquing the many professionals who shared their time and knowledge with me in the course of my research. All of my respondents were generous and helpful, and I am indebted to them for their contribution. I want to thank all the members of my dissertation committee, Alex Hicks, Rick Rubinson, John Boli, and Rick Doner, who encouraged me and offered constant advice that made this final product possible and put up with my occasional divagations into obscure Marxian ephemera. Thanks to Pat Hamilton for keeping it together. Thanks to those at Routledge who took on this book, particularly Neil Jordan and Alice Salt, my patient editorial team. Thanks to my supportive family, and thanks to Ryan, for his love, support, and extraordinary patience.

1 Introduction, context, and cases

In the early months of 2014, something strange happened in Chattanooga, Tennessee. Rumors had been circulating in trade journals and local papers that the German automaker Volkswagen was considering a plant expansion in North America to produce a new mid-sized sport utility vehicle, and the recently opened VW plant in Chattanooga was in the running along with another site in Mexico. However, a looming February vote by the Chattanooga plant employees on whether or not to accept United Auto Workers (UAW) organization was loudly denounced as threatening that site's chances for winning the new platform. These fulminations did not issue from the lips of VW executives; indeed, officials at the plant had already organized works' councils to deal with daily plant issues and had freely allowed UAW representatives to distribute literature to workers in the facility (Pare and Sher 2014). Rather, it was then Governor of Tennessee Bill Haslam and state and federal lawmakers who raised their voices against the specter of plant unionization. What is most surprising is that Tennessee lawmakers threatened to revoke their offer of incentives and subsidies to Volkswagen for the proposed expansion if unionization of the plant was approved – incentives that amounted to nearly half of the proposed $600 million dollar investment (Nelson 2014). Tennessee Senator "Todd Gardenhire said VW officials are 'in your face. It's their way or no way. They've decided by-golly they want the UAW here. They're not listening to the community'" (Pare 2015). In a face-off against efforts to organize workers in their trophy manufacturing plant, Tennessee politicians threatened disinvestment – in their own state.

If the state representatives in Tennessee were perhaps a bit more vocal and threatening than in most other cases of plant unionization efforts, the anti-union sentiment was not. Indeed, anti-labor attitudes are a perennial feature of southern culture and political society; as soon as the Taft–Hartley Act allowing them to do so passed in 1947, almost every state in the Confederate South rushed to adopt so-called "right to work" laws (bills or laws that ban obligatory union dues) (Cobb 1993; Hülsemann 2001). Nor were the incentives and subsidies offered out of the ordinary. As we will see this practice, known as industrial recruitment, has become increasingly commonplace in the United States since the 1980s. There are some curious little

DOI: 10.4324/9781003107569-1

puzzles here. If Tennessee recruited Volkswagen to create jobs in the first place, then how would allowing those workers at that plant to vote on unionization be ignoring the community? But local reporters have our answer for us: "Republican lawmakers, including Haslam and [US Senator] Bob Corker [Republican from Tennessee] complained loudly that the UAW would hinder economic development efforts"(Pare and Sher 2014). The community, it seems, is those most concerned with local economic development. In the end, tellingly, it was the workers themselves who decided the outcome by voting against unionization.

The states of the South have had a long history of being aggressive in trying to bring in industrial development and investment from capital, but in the past four decades or so, the efforts of these states to pursue development have changed in some critically important ways. As we will see, the strange kerfuffle over the Tennessee plant expansion encapsulates these changes quite well. Here, we see local governments vociferously decrying the political organization of labor, citing the harm it will do to efforts to pursue economic development, and to the community more broadly. And even though economic development efforts are nominally undertaken to bring jobs to that community, when the workers who *work* in those jobs contemplate organizing around their own political interests, governors and lawmakers say they are harming the community they constitute. Further, even though VW was publicly indifferent to unionization, the economic developers themselves protested it would have a negative impact on economic development efforts in the state. One might wonder just what local governments are doing here? I certainly did. This book is the result of the research and questions that have sought to dig beneath the surface of the economic development activities of local governments. I wanted to understand how these activities reflect fundamental changes in what government is and does, and how recruitment practices have altered relations between firms, localities, and workers.

When VW first came to Tennessee in 2008, the state offered up $577 million dollars in incentives for the plant, which were meant to make the state and locality more attractive to the global automotive producer than other competing locations. These incentives consisted of the suspension or abatements of various taxes by state and local governments as well as direct expenditures on the land for the plant site, worker training, and other up-front costs that go into starting a "greenfield" (or not previously developed) industrial project.[1] While very high profile projects such as Amazon's HQ2 debacles occasionally make the national news, today it is commonplace to open a local news app or paper to a story about a corporate headquarters, or sports stadium, or data processing center being won by a local town and state who work together to incentivize global corporations with lucrative agreements. While the complexity of such public–private agreements limits the quality of systematic analysis (much more on that in a moment), one attempt by the *New York Times* to track this kind of activity painted a stark picture:

A portrait arises of mayors and governors who are desperate to create jobs, outmatched by multinational corporations and short on tools to fact-check what companies tell them. Many of the officials said they feared that companies would move jobs overseas if they did not get subsidies in the United States...over the years, corporations have increasingly exploited that fear, creating a high-stakes bazaar where they pit local officials against one another to get the most lucrative packages. States compete with other states, cities compete with surrounding suburbs, and even small towns have entered the race with the goal of defeating their neighbors. (Story 2012)

The questions

Story begs the question here, are local leaders *really* desperate and short on resources, and whether this explains why New York City and its boroughs would shell out billions for a company that had *profits* worth more than 20 billion dollars in recent years? Scholars of development would note that the state in capitalist societies has a long history of acting as midwife to capitalist development, investment, and growth from imperialism (Chase–Dunn 1998; Wallerstein 1974) and the enclosures (Brenner 1977; Marx 1976) to the construction of interstate road systems and the formation of welfare regimes (Hicks 1999; O'Connor 1973). Moreover, critical geographers and political economists began to note in the 1980s that local governments – particularly in wealthy nations – started to behave in strange risky behaviors, getting thick with private partners, using the language of *entrepreneurialism* and competing much like the private companies that shared this vocabulary (Cox 2010; Harvey 1989; Peck and Tickell 1994, 2002). At the same time, the region where many automotive plants are located – the southeastern United States – has a long history of political elites being more aggressive than other local leaders in their attempts to lure industry, dating back to the textile industries moving to the South over the 1930s (Cobb 1993; Hülsemann 2001). All of these beg the questions of whether there is really a race to the bottom, and of whether there is actually anything new about these recruitment activities, and if there is anything new – what is it?

These questions lie at the heart of this book. At their core are issues of *social relations*: relations of governance between public agencies and private business; class relations between companies and their workers; and power relations among elites who make decisions, and whose knowledge matters most; and relations between these elites and the local communities and coalitions whose interests they ostensibly serve. To answer these questions, I turn to the comparative sociology of development and critical geographical literature and conduct a comparative case study of the recruitment of consumer automotive assembly plants constructed in the United States in the era of neoliberal globalization. In the next chapter, I will discuss the theoretical underpinnings of this framing and the research that guides it, but first, it is worth specifying the methods of analysis used in this study and the reasoning behind these, before outlining the chapters that follow.

The comparative case study approach to the analysis of policy and industry has a long history in the social sciences (Evans 1995; George and Bennett 2005; Hicks 1999; Perrucci 1994; Rubinson and Sokolovsky 1988; Rueschemeyer, Stephens, and Stephens 1992; *inter alia*). While this legacy strongly informed my choice of research methods, one need only dip their toe into the anfractuous waters of local policy in the United States to begin to see the frustrations that arise with any attempt at systematic comparative analysis at this level of governance. It is worth spending a little time digging into this complexity – if for no other reason than to understand why estimates of incentives' values are often deeply flawed and confusing.

The complexity of the local

Louise Story and her colleagues at the *New York Times* discovered, as did I, that there are several layers of complications in trying to study industrial recruitment efforts at the local level. "A full accounting [of incentives], *The Times* discovered, is not possible because the incentives are granted by thousands of government agencies and officials, and many do not know the value of all their awards...collecting data on property tax abatements is the most difficult because only a handful of states track the amounts given by cities and counties" (Story 2012).

Simply put, the complexity of studying incentives and recruitment derives from the fact that different types of incentives are offered by different agencies at different levels of government with varying degrees of transparency. *These* differences, in turn, vary between states based both on what states *can* offer constitutionally and legislatively and on what state and local agencies and programs exist and participate in recruitment efforts. An example should help illustrate this complexity, or at least demonstrate its confusing-ness. As I discuss in more depth in chapter 4, most states have a basic jobs-based tax incentives program, based on a tiered county-based system in which locating a business in the poorest county will get the largest amount of per-job tax breaks (c.f. Georgia Power 2012). Such incentives are called *as of right* incentives (informally, *off-the-rack* incentives), meaning any company that qualifies and applies can receive them. Yet, on top of this, most states have *enterprise zone* or *opportunity zone* designations that offer enhanced tax breaks – usually higher tax breaks for fewer minimum required jobs created to qualify – which localities (not companies) can specially apply for (nominally intended for the same reason as mentioned earlier – to attract businesses to distressed areas). While most states have some version of both jobs-based and zone-based tax incentive programs, the benefits that accrue in such a zone differ from state to state, or city to city, and the area designated differs from zone to zone. Gaining a clear picture of such zones is impeded by the haphazard way they are designated by the given state authority. For example, according to the Georgia Department of Community Affairs (GDCA) which approves Opportunity Zone designation, whole cities are not awarded OZ status, only sub-sections with particular unemployment or poverty rates are. Hence, even parsing out these off-the-rack forms of development incentives can be a murky undertaking, and the matter becomes even more complicated when we begin to look at the industrial recruitment efforts that target specific private projects for inward investment.

The particular difficulties in obtaining reliable and detailed information about the industrial recruitment processes of particular projects stem from several issues. Targeted industrial recruitment packages are not simply parts of extant legislation, though as mentioned aspects such as specialized zones with particular exemptions (taxes and tariffs) might be. Rather, these packages are usually specially crafted and shaped through the process of competition with other states and in dialogue with the potential firm (McDermott 2011, 2013; Perrucci 1994:32–33; Rubenstein 1992:219–222; Spindler 1994). As such, these packages are special agreements that are not necessarily published in any comprehensive database or systematically recorded. The closest thing to such a system is the requirement by the Government Accounting Standards Bureau (GASB) – which all states and many local governments abide by – that governments (beginning in 2018) release information on revenue lost to tax-based incentives in their Comprehensive Annual Financial Reports (CAFRs). However, my review of these reports shows that even this data is highly irregular:Georgia passed a law making such data private (Skelton 2017:187), Florida devoted five pages to a detailed documentation of abatements (Whitefield and Lieblick 2018:113–119), and South Carolina simply published no information, reporting the amount as negligible (Eckstrom 2018:77).

Some states do publish detailed reports on tax incentive programs, such as Louisiana's Incentive Performance reporting; and other states have so-called sunshine laws and other transparency measures. But these laws tend to apply to specific programs or target specific types of measures, such as assessing the actual jobs that are created by firms given jobs-based tax credits – an assessment process which is itself very opaque. Moreover, what states end up reporting when legally required is not usually commensurable either across states or over time, or even necessarily accurate. Incentive recipients, incentive amounts, local governments involved, the particular type of incentive – data on all of these may vary across different states' reports, reports which again are themselves irregular.

The initially problematic nature of the data on industrial recruitment is compounded by the complexity of different governments and agencies involved in the recruitment process. Recruitment involves development officials from the state, county, and city governments and often private associations such as Chambers of Commerce. For example, in the process of luring

Hyundai to Montgomery, Alabama, the state of Alabama, Butler County, the city of Montgomery, and public-private utilities were all involved in the final package estimated at around $250 million (though my estimates put the number closer to $500 million). In the purchase of the Lincoln, Alabama, site for Honda in 1999, five different county governments were involved (Tomberlin and Pratt 1999). Further complicating the incentives picture, both firms and governments stress the need for confidentiality throughout the process of recruitment and negotiating incentives.[2]

In addition to the clandestine nature of the negotiations themselves, the formal agreements signed by state and local governments and private firms are only one part of a broader array of "good-will" efforts that governments make to show their willingness to be a good partner. For example, in Georgia Governor Nathan Deal signed into law House Bill 259 or the "Georgia Business Act" on May 6, 2015, which exempted Kia (who run the single auto assembly plant in Georgia) from the bidding process used to vet the purchase of vehicles for the state fleet (Reed 2015). A similar measure was attempted by Alabama Governor Jim Folsom when Mercedes-Benz was located in Tuscaloosa in 1993. Public outcry saw the reinstatement of the bidding process after the Governor was seen driving around the state in a new prototype Mercedes model. Thus, while open records requests may be made in order to gain details of an incentives package, requests would need to be submitted to a number of different development agencies (each of which could reject the request) and the official record of the initial agreement may well not contain all of the relevant perks that accrue to the recruited firm.

Finally, it is worth noting that most of the official estimations offered in Table 1.1 are probably low, sometimes very low. This is due both to the problematic and incomplete information, and the fact that estimates offered by state officials rarely include things such as payments of interest on the debt incurred in the provision of incentives (such as bonds purchased), which in themselves can raise overall cost calculations by tens, sometimes hundreds of millions of dollars (Glickman 1989; Mattera and Tarczynska 2013; Perrucci 1994:6–7; Rubenstein 1992:229).[3]

Hence, with data gathered on incentives, there is no way to ensure that statistically significant correlations or trends observed, such as increases in spending over time (or on some types of programs) or changes in types of programs across time or space, are not artifacts resulting from the data gathering process or the primary data sources.[4] Thus, the best way to get a comprehensive and comparative picture of incentives is arguably to focus on recruitment efforts themselves. More importantly, if we are to assess whether there has really been a change in the processes and relations of local governments and businesses, a comparative case study is the most appropriate design.

Table 1.1 AAPs in United States in neoliberal era

Firm	Site location	Year announced	Initial investment (millions)	Reported value of subsidies/ incentives[†] (millions)
Volkswagen	Westmoreland, PA	1978	$250	$63
GM	Hamtramck, MI	1980	$700–800	$350
Honda	Marysville, OH	1980	$750	$21–$27
Nissan	Smyrna, TN	1980	$760	$33–$66
NUMMI*	Freemont, CA	1984	$450	$0?
Mazda-Ford*	Flat Rock, MI	1984	$750	$125
Saturn	Spring Hill, TN	1985	$1,500	$80+
Toyota	Georgetown, KY	1985	$800	$150
Diamond-Star*	Bloomington, IL	1985	$600	$118–274
Subaru-Isuzu	Lafayette, IND	1986	$500	$86–$94
BMW	Spartanburg, SC	1992	$300	$130
Mercedes-Benz	Vance, AL	1993	$300	$250–$300
Honda	Lincoln, AL	1999	$450	$158.4
Nissan	Canton, MS	2000	$900	$295
Hyundai	Montgomery, AL	2002	$1,000	$258
Toyota	San Antonio, TX	2003	$800	$133
Kia	West Point, GA	2006	$1,200	$410
Honda	Greensburg, IND	2006	$550	$141.5
Toyota	Blue Springs, MS	2007	$1,300	$293–$296
Volkswagen	Chattanooga, TN	2008	$1,000	$577
Tesla	Freemont, CA	2010	$115	$20+
Volvo	Charleston, SC	2015	$500m	$210+
Toyota-Mazda*	Huntsville, AL	2018	$1,600	$800+

Notes

* Indicates a joint-venture.

† The reported value of incentives is based on news reports that take into account different factors. Table 4.1 takes a more systematic approach.Sources available on request. NOTE: The Volvo Reporting includes only up-front expenditures and does not detail the value of tax abatements offered, so should be considered quite a low estimate.

- Grey lines indicate brownfield sites

Research design and case selection

Given the messiness of the data on incentives, and the fact that I am primarily interested in the changing *relations between* local governments and private firms, I conducted in-depth case studies on individual recruitment efforts, and compared differences over time and across cases. I first narrowed my case selection to major industrial projects because these take on a particularly competitive tone given the scale of the investments (often between $500 million and $2 billion), the jobs they entail (in the thousands), and the longevity and visibility of the project. Whereas state, city, and county development agencies might pursue different local agendas, large industrial projects require financial and political input from all of these levels and thus act as a centrifugal force binding multiple counties and cities together with the state. The level of analysis here is technically the state level, though this encompasses actors and activities at the county and city level as well. Finally, to ensure cases were properly comparable, I chose to focus on the recruitment of a single industry, for while there are definite generalizations that can be made about the recruitment of large industrial and headquarters projects (as I will discuss in chapter 3), there are strong geographical factors that are industry-specific that limit such comparisons. The choice of the automotive industry was influenced by a number of factors, primarily that automotive production in the United States provides a clear window into the impact that global political-economic forces have had on industry, and there are cases enough to provide material for comparative analysis. Also, as my research will show, the recruitment of automotive plants was crucial to shaping changes in local economic development efforts more generally in the neoliberal era.

Case selection

Ultimately, I focused on the recruitment of consumer automotive *assembly* plants (AAPs), where the final car is put together because the considerations of such a large endeavor are of a different scale than even large automotive equipment suppliers. This led to a total of 23 cases of AAP recruitment since 1978, which were almost entirely non-U.S.-based manufacturers and were primarily located in southern states. For similar reasons as selecting assembly plants, much of my focus will be primarily on greenfield sites (N=19) – as mentioned these are virgin sites that have not been previously developed, as opposed to Brownfield plants that locate in an existing industrial site or structure – because the considerations for choosing such sites are vastly different (e.g., road and utility connections must be established at greenfield sites). Table 1.1 briefly summarizes the cases, and Table A1 in the Appendix to this chapter offers a more detailed summary of recruitment and plant location of greenfield projects.

Secondary research methods

My research on these cases drew on primary documents (when they were publicly available, though few are) such as the Memoranda of Understanding drawn up by localities when an incentives deal is finalized, as well as newspaper reports, local business news, more lengthily accounts by journalists, and professional publications (such as *Area Development* magazine and its sister publication *Site Selection* magazine) (c.f. Lyne 2002; Nelson 2014; Site Selection 1999). I also drew on the extensive secondary research into cases of automotive plant location and economic development in the South more generally. These studies are from various academic fields such as sociological analyses of Japanese and Korean firms in the South (Chung 2009; Hunker 1983; Kim 1995; Perrucci 1994), historical accounts of Southern attitudes toward economic development (Cobb 1993, 2005) and the automotive industry in particular (Hülsemann 2001), geographical analyses of the auto industry (Mair, Florida, and Kenney 1988; Rubenstein 1992), and economic and business studies (McDermott, Luethge, and Byosiere 2011; Woodward 1992; *inter alia*), all of which are tied together by a focus on the cases in question. I also researched numerous newspaper accounts of plant locations and books published by journalists on the cases in question (Gelsanliter 1990; Sherman 1993). All these sources were triangulated with interview data to construct detailed accounts of locational decisions, actors involved, and tables on incentives agreements for each of the cases.

Primary research methods

While the multiple sources mentioned in the previous section offer a great deal of insight into the questions posed here, my specific focus on changes in relations between governments and industry required direct knowledge of the political actors, development professionals, and others involved in the process of local recruitment and development. I thus conducted 18 interviews between July of 2015 and August of 2016 with professionals in economic development and site selection fields, as well as political officials involved in recruitment. These in-depth interviews were restricted to professional accounts and opinions, and expert knowledge. The sampling of respondents followed a purposive or theoretical sampling method, supplemented with snowball sampling techniques (Bryman 2016:410–415; Creswell 2014:178; Warren and Karner 2009:141). Such a strategy seeks respondents only according to the "criteria specified by the research questions" and "purposefully select[s] participants…that will best help the researcher understand the problem" (Creswell 2014:178). There were two primary purposes guiding my sampling, which are discussed as follow:

One primary goal was to conduct general expert knowledge interviews, to gain insight into the general processes, primary actors, and history of industrial recruitment practices. While some such information is derived from secondary sources, I needed to get a clearer picture of what aspects of the recruitment process were standardized, who the key actors were, and how the actual negotiation processes took place. The goal here was to get as comprehensive a view as possible of the activities, strategies, expectations, and limitations of actors involved across different states, in localities of various sizes and wealth, and from within and outside of public office. Thus, eight of the interviews I conducted were with individuals from regional chambers, city and county development authorities, and other development entities that were not directly related to the cases of automotive assembly plant locations. Recruitment of participants was primarily conducted through email correspondence and respondents were selected from professional publications or websites. Diversity was my guiding principle: diversity in the type of locality in terms of size, wealth, and territory (county/city/region), as well as type of entity (public authority or private business alliance or chamber). Almost every development professional I spoke to had worked in multiple agencies and localities, which broadened the professional experiences beyond their immediate occupation. I also interviewed officials from North Carolina purposefully, as the state had been in the running for, and lost, several automotive assembly plants. I ceased conducting these general knowledge interviews once I felt I had reached saturation on general knowledge of economic development and the process of recruitment. I also interviewed three professional site-selection consultants, all of whom had worked on the site selection for a major automotive plant in the United States. These professionals were recruited through snowball sampling and purposive sampling, the latter using *Site Selection* magazine interviews on changes in the field of economic development to discern contacts who had both experience with automotive recruitment and a long history in the professional field.

My second primary research goal was to get further direct knowledge of the cases of automotive assembly plant recruitment and site selection. McDermott (2011, 2012, 2013) has already conducted a number of highly useful interviews with individuals involved, but I wanted to supplement these with interviews that directly addressed my own research questions. Thus, in addition to the three site-selection consultants, I spoke with seven professionals or former politicians who had been directly involved in one of the AAP cases. I targeted recruitment of participants based on my secondary research, again with the goal of the diversity of experience, primarily focused on knowledge of different states but also at different levels of government, as with the general knowledge interviews. A number of these officials had experience with recruiting multiple automotive assembly plants, and some had experience both working as site selection consultants for producers and on recruitment efforts by states. The experience of these professionals covers the entire period of plant locations under analysis, though their experience is more concentrated in the mid-1990s to late 2000s period. All told, respondents collectively had experience in recruiting ten cases of automotive assembly plant locations in Alabama, Tennessee, Georgia, Mississippi, and Kentucky. General experience in economic development, I should note, extends well beyond these five states.

All interviews were semi-structured, with various prompts depending on the specific type of professional and the (non) case-specific nature of the interview. For example, when interviewing an official with a public–private development partnership, I would inquire into how their public–private status made their outlook or interactions different. Where officials had ex-perience with multiple types of agencies or cases, I would include specific prompts in order to get their comparative perspective. Interviews tended to be less structured, and where possible, I let respondents lead the discussion, the goal being to get as close as possible to the professionals' own line of thought. All interviews contained some general prompts, such as how the field of development had changed in that professional's experience. Examples of interview prompts are provided in Appendix 2.

Coding of interviews was guided by my theoretical framework and case analysis, and was both thematic and narrative in nature, the latter narratives primarily establishing conceptions of the historical development of the field of local economic development. As different themes and narratives emerged, new prompts were developed and incorporated into later interviews. Likewise, early interviews were recoded according to themes that emerged from later interviews. Themes and findings that emerged from coding interviews were then triangulated with secondary research materials.

Study outline

The following chapters lay out the findings of this study and the theory and research that help to frame and make sense of those findings. In chapter 2, I gloss the existing research on local economic development strategies, fo-cusing on the United States, before turning to the theory and research of global political economy and critical geography to situate the current mo-ment of what I call neoliberal globalization. We will see that the competitive provision of incentives is part of a broader shift in the global political economy that intensified the interconnection of local governments and global political-economic forces. Within this context, I frame the changing relations between capital and the state exemplified in recruitment efforts as an example of what geographer David Harvey has called a turn at the local level toward "entrepreneurial governance." Arguably, the findings of my research paint a detailed empirical picture of just what this entrepreneurial turn consists of within the particular context of the United States.

In chapter 3, I outline the broader comparative context to help situate local activities within the global relations and patterns of capital accumu-lation that shape those local forces. First, I briefly highlight the particular features of U.S. development and regulation policies and history, and the specific features that characterize state development activities in the South. Then, I highlight the particular opportunities and pressures facing the automotive industries of the various countries involved in locating plants in the United States in the neoliberal era. Drawing on a little industrial location theory, we will see that the inflexibility in production and consumption relations faced by U.S. and West German automakers, combined with new opportunities for rising Japanese and later South Korean firms, shaped the locational decision different firms made. I will also show the central importance of labor concerns in explaining the southern drift of automotive production.

In chapter 4, I turn to recruitment efforts themselves, using a few cases to highlight the typical process of recruiting a major industrial project, elaborating the complex relations between agencies at multiples levels of governance in such an undertaking. Using the theoretical framework of fast-policy regimes (Cleave et al. 2017; Peck and Theodore 2010, 2015), I then map out the ways in which efforts to recruit industry have changed in terms of the process of recruiting, the people involved in that process, and bundles of tax breaks and direct investments offered up. Chapter 5 then digs deeper into the burgeoning field of professional economic developers and site selectors, highlighting key aspects of their worldview and approach to governance, and showing that their partnership perspective marks a troubling shift in public policy, decentering democratic processes.

The last two chapters develop the theoretical and political implications of this study. In chapter 6, I tie the observations and findings from the two previous chapters together with my theoretical discussion of neoliberal globalization. I show that these changes in relations between governments and firms fundamentally affect questions of place, class, and power. In particular, I argue that industrial recruitment is a particular kind of entrepreneurial governance that not only involves increased expenditures and risks absorbed by localities, but also directly affects the fixed-capital investments that connect industries to a particular place. Further, I argue the hegemonic view of governance shared among elites embodies a one-sided view of class relations that heavily diminishes the legitimate political position of labor and local constituencies in local – and global – politics. Indeed, partnership changes the very political articulation of class relations themselves.

In the concluding chapter, I note the limitations and prospects of the partnership approach to entrepreneurial governance discussed in the previous chapters, and argue that while there are limitations built into the notion of partnership, the ultimate fate of these changes in local governance – and that of any challenges to them – is tied to the broader neoliberal globalization project and the dominance of its ideology of market orthodoxy. Yet these terms remain to be defined, which is my task in the following chapter.

Notes

1 Greenfield developments involve constructing a completely new industrial site on relatively virgin land, but there are also so-call brownfield developments, which make use of existing plants, such as Tesla's Gigfactory locating in a previous GM plant.
2 McDermott, for example, attributes Kia's choice of West Point, GA, over a site in Mississippi in part to the latter states' governor betraying at too early a stage their bid for the plant site (McDermott 2012:23).
3 This view was confirmed in a personal correspondence with Dr. J. Craig Jenkins, one of the leading researchers on local economic development strategies. Dr. Jenkins confirmed that "I do agree there is some "race to the bottom" [aspect] but it is very hard to tease out quantitatively and, if that is your aim…you quickly get drawn into the micro details of capturing the various ways to race to the bottom (which are legion and continuously evolving quickly). Plus, that process is so localized that it become[s] very hard to capture…[and] I suspect…data generated by local and state development agencies is exactly what you suspect—basically trash" (Jenkins 2015).
4 The best data available is certainly that is published by the watchdog organization Good Jobs First. Analysts with GJF do conduct regular estimates and comparisons that are very informative, however, the issues with irregularities in reporting across localities still apply here. Probably the best attempt is their analysis of local government school funding lost to incentives, but this again dealt with an incomplete picture due to inconsistencies in publishing (Good Jobs First 2018).

Bibliography

Brenner, Robert. 1977. "The Origins of Capitalist Development: A Critique of Neo-Smithian Marxism." *New Left Review* 104(1):25–92.

Bryman, Alan. 2016. *Social Research Methods*, 5th edition. Oxford; New York: Oxford University Press.

Chase–Dunn, Christopher. 1998. *Global Formation: Structures of the World-Economy*. Updated edition. Lanham: Rowman & Littlefield Publishers.

Chung, Myeong-kee. 2009. "Globalization Strategies of Korean Motor Vehicle Industry: A Case Study of Hyundai." Unpublished Manuscript.

Cleave, Evan, Godwin Arku, Richard Sadler, and Jason Gililand. 2017. "Is It Sound Policy of Fast Policy? Practitioners Perspectives on the Role of Place Branding in Local Economic Development." *Urban Geography* 38(8):1133–1157.

Cobb, James C. 1993. *The Selling of the South: The Southern Crusade for Industrial Development 1936-1990*, 2nd edition. Urbana: University of Illinois Press.

Cobb, James C. 2005. "Beyond the 'Y'all Wall': The American South Goes Global." Pp. 1–18 in *Globalization and the American South*, edited by J. C. Cobb and W. Stueck. Athens, GA: University of Georgia Press.

Cox, Kevin R. 2010. "The Problem of Metropolitan Governance and the Politics of Scale." *Regional Studies* 44(2):215–227. doi: 10.1080/00343400903365128.

Creswell, John W. 2014. *Research Design: Qualitative, Quantitative, and Mixed Methods Approaches*, 4th edition. Thousand Oaks: SAGE Publications.

Eckstrom, Richard. 2018. *State of South Carolina Comprehensive Annual Financial Report Fiscal Year Ended June 30th 2017*. Columbia, SC: Office of Comptroller, State of South Carolina.

Evans, Peter B. 1995. *Embedded Autonomy: States and Industrial Transformation.* Princeton, NJ: Princeton University Press.

Gelsanliter, David. 1990. *Jump Start: Japan Comes to the Heartland.* New York: Farrar Straus Giroux.

George, Alexander L., and Andrew Bennett. 2005. *Case Studies and Theory Development in the Social Sciences.* Cambridge, MA: MIT Press.

Georgia Power. 2012. *Business Incentives.* Atlanta, GA: Georgia Power.

Glickman, Norman J. 1989. *The New Competitors: How Foreign Investors Are Changing the U.S Economy.* New York: Basic Books.

Good Jobs First. 2018. *The New Math on School Finance: Adding Up the First-Ever Disclosure of Corporate Tax Abatements' Cost to Public Education.* Good Jobs First.

Harvey, David. 1989. "From Managerialism to Entrepreneurialism: The Transformation in Urban Governance in Late Capitalism." *Geografiska Annaler. Series B, Human Geography* 71(1):3–17. doi: 10.2307/490503.

Hicks, Alexander M. 1999. *Social Democracy & Welfare Capitalism: A Century of Income Security Politics.* Ithaca: Cornell University Press.

Hülsemann, Karsten. 2001. "Greenfields in the Heart of Dixie: How the American Auto Industry Discovered the South." Pp. 219–254 in *The Second Wave: Southern Industrialization from the 1940s to the 1970s*, edited by P. Scranton. Athens, GA: University of Georgia Press.

Hunker, Jeffrey Allen. 1983. *Structural Change in the U.S. Automobile Industry.* Lexington, Mass: Lexington Books.

Jenkins, J. Craig. 2015. "Economic Development Data." Personal Communication.

Kim, Choong Soon. 1995. *Japanese Industry in the American South.* New York, NY: Routledge.

Lyne, Jack. 2002. "Hyundai's $1B Plant Alabama Bound After 11th-Hour Bargaining." *Site Selection.* Retrieved May 30, 2015 (http://www.siteselection.com/ssinsider/bbdeal/bd020401.htm).

Mair, Andrew, Richard Florida, and Martin Kenney. 1988. "The New Geography of Automobile Production: Japanese Transplants in North America." *Economic Geography* 64(4):352–373. doi: 10.2307/144233.

Marx, Karl. 1976. *Capital: Volume 1: A Critique of Political Economy*, Vol. 1. London: Penguin Books in association with New Left Review.

Mattera, Phillip, and Kasia Tarczynska. 2013. *A Good Deal For Mississippi? A Report on Taxpayer Assistance in Canton, Mississippi.* Good Jobs First.

McDermott, Michael C. 2011. "BMW, Spartanburg, South Carolina: Drivers and Processes in the International Plant Location Decision." *Southern Business & Economic Journal* 34(1/2):73–94.

McDermott, Michael C. 2012. "Hyundai Automotive Group's Investments in the U.S. South: Competition and Decisions." *Southern Business & Economic Journal* 35(1):11–34.

McDermott, Michael C. 2013. "Mercedes-Benz, Tuscaloosa, Alabama: Drivers and Processes in the International Plant Location Decision." *Southern Business & Economic Journal* 36(1):57–73.

McDermott, Michael C., Denise Luethge, and Philippe Byosiere. 2011. "Automotive Investment and Foreign Subsidiary Strategy in the Southern States of the United States." *Southern Business & Economic Journal* 34(3/4):1–30.

Nelson, Gabe. 2014. "Tenn. Politicians Threaten to Kill VW Incentives If UAW Wins Election." *Automotive News*, April 10.

O'Connor, James. 1973. *The Fiscal Crisis of the State*. New York: St. Martin's Press.

Pare, Mike. 2015. "Legislators to Weigh VW Incentives - Approval Not a given in Light of UAW Gains." *Chattanooga Times Free Press (TN)*, January 7.

Pare, Mike, and Andy Sher. 2014. "Tennessee Offered $300 Million to VW as UAW Tried to Organize Chattanooga Plant, Documents Show." *Chattanooga Times Free Press*, April 2.

Peck, Jamie, and Nik Theodore. 2010. "Recombinant Workfare, across the Americas: Transnationalizing 'Fast' Social Policy." *Geoforum* 41(2):195–208.

Peck, Jamie, and Nik Theodore. 2015. *Fast Policy: Experimental Statecraft at the Thresholds of Neoliberalism*. 3rd edition. Minneapolis: University of Minnesota Press.

Peck, Jamie, and Adam Tickell. 1994. "Jungle Law Breaks out: Neoliberalism and Global-Local Disorder." *Area* 26(4):317–326.

Peck, Jamie, and Adam Tickell. 2002. "Neoliberalizing Space." *Antipode* 34(3):380–404. doi: 10.1111/1467-8330.00247.

Perrucci, Robert. 1994. *Japanese Auto Transplants in the Heartland: Corporatism and Community*. New York: Aldine de Gruyter.

Reed, Tesia. 2015. "Governor Signs 'Georgia Business Act.'" Retrieved May 21, 2015 (http://www.myfoxal.com/story/28998713/governor-signs-georgia-business-act).

Rubenstein, James M. 1992. *The Changing Us Auto Industry: A Geographical Analysis*. London England; New York: Routledge.

Rubinson, Richard, and Joan Sokolovsky. 1988. "Patterns of Political Industrial Regulation: Railroads in the World Economy." Pp. 3–20 in *Rethinking the 19th Century*, edited by F. O. Ramirez. California: Greenwood Press.

Rueschemeyer, Dietrich, Evelyne Huber Stephens, and John D. Stephens. 1992. *Capitalist Development and Democracy*. 1st edition. Chicago: University of Chicago Press.

Sherman, Joe. 1993. *In the Rings of Saturn*. 1st edition. New York: Oxford University Press.

Site Selection. 1999. "Incentives Deal of the Month: Alabama's $158 Million for Honda: Initial Embrace Marks Dramatic Shift from 1993s Mercedes Tiff." *Site Selection Magazine*. Retrieved (http://www.siteselection.com/ssinsider/incentive/ti9906.htm).

Skelton, Thomas A. 2017. *State of Georgia: Comprehensive Financial Annual Report: Fiscal Year Ended June 30th 1027. CAFR*. Atlanta, GA: Georgia State Accounting Office.

Spindler, Charles J. 1994. "Winners and Losers in Industrial Recruitment: Mercedes-Benz and Alabama." *State & Local Government Review* 26(3):192–204.

Story, Louise. 2012. "As Companies Seek Tax Deals, Governments Pay High Price." *The New York Times*, December 1.

Tomberlin, Michael, and Ted Pratt. 1999. "State Wins Honda." Birmingham News (AL), May 5.

Wallerstein, Immanuel Maurice. 1974. *The Modern World-System I*. New York: Academic Press.

Warren, Carol A. B., and Tracy Xavia Karner. 2009. *Discovering Qualitative Methods: Field Research, Interviews, and Analysis*. 2nd edition. New York: Oxford University Press.

Whitefield J. R., J. Paul, and Rachael K. G. Lieblick. 2018. *State of Florida Comprehensive Annual Financial Report Fiscal Year Ended June 30th 2017. CAFR.* Florida.

Woodward, Douglas P. 1992. "Locational Determinants of Japanese Manufacturing Start-Ups in the United States." *Southern Economic Journal* 58(3):690–708. doi: 10.2307/1059836.

2 Theorizing local development strategies

In order to research the issue of competitive recruitment of industry by local governments, it is necessary to situate ourselves in terms of what research has already been conducted, and in terms of the theoretical way in which we understand the relationship between the state and industry in the broader context of the current political-economic moment. As discussed in the introduction, the core questions in this research concern the changing relations between local government actors and transnational corporations, and how these have or have not changed over the decades since the 1980s, with a focus on the automotive industry in particular. My perspective on these issues is informed by existing comparative research on comparative economic development, as well as the theory and research in critical geography and political Marxism. What binds these perspectives together is that they understand the separation of the spheres of political and economic activity and power in late capitalism not as an analytical axiom, but rather this separation is itself a form of political power relations, that is historically and locally constituted by- and contingent upon- class struggle (Brenner 1977; Wood 1981).

Types of development strategies

The very language of "development" adopted by local and state governments reflects a broader sociological and political-economic literature that analyzes the mutual constitution of (national) states and capitalist economies and examines the differential development of capitalist economies in various parts of the world (Block and Evans 2005; Evans 1995; Evans and Stephens 1988; Hicks 1999; Moore 1966; Rubinson and Sokolovsky 1988; Rueschemeyer, Stephens, and Stephens 1992). The question of economic development focuses primarily on the role of states in setting economic policy and the reciprocity which is thereby created for relatively stable economic growth. While not quite the same as Marxist literature that examines public or state investment and support of capitalist accumulation (Brenner 1977; O'Connor 1973; Rubinson and Sokolovsky 1988), this development research similarly makes the fundamental assumption that states

DOI: 10.4324/9781003107569-2

play an essential role in the construction and operation of markets and capitalist development more broadly.

Within this broader literature, there is a field of research that focuses on the efforts of sub-national governments to shape local economic development (LED). Since the 1970s sub-national governments have taken on increasingly central roles in development policy formation and fostered policy strategies ostensibly designed to stimulate growth and job-creation in their local or regional economy (Brenner 1999a; Cox 1995; Harvey 1989a). Writing in the 1990s, Leicht and Jenkins noted that "over the past two decades, [US] state governments have become the major setting for innovations in U.S. economic development policy. Ranging from public venture capital firms, technology parks...to industrial revenue bonds, enterprise zones, and right-to-work laws, state governments have adopted an array of new methods for stimulating economic development" (Leicht and Jenkins 1994:256). Jenkins, Leicht, and colleagues (J. Craig Jenkins, Leicht, and Jaynes 2006; J. Craig Jenkins, Leicht, and Wendt 2006; Leicht and Jenkins 1994) argue that there are three broad categories of local development strategies that states and local governments adopt to stimulate growth. "By an *economic development strategy*, we mean a general outlook on the nature of economic growth and the proper role of state [and local] government in encouraging growth" (Leicht and Jenkins 1994:257). They categorize these strategies into *entrepreneurial* (which I will call *high-tech*, for clarity's sake) strategies, *industrial recruitment*, and *deregulation* strategies:[1]

> the [*high-tech*] approach is based on the assumption that economic growth is a qualitative transformation toward higher–value-added production (or "high-technology") and that state government can facilitate this process by assuming entrepreneurial functions...*industrial recruitment* strategy is based on the quantitative increase of existing products by offering incentives for the relocation or expansion of existing enterprises...*deregulation* policies attempt to reduce governmental regulation of private economic activity...the aim is to turn back the welfare state by weakening labor unions, reducing governmental regulation of employer/employee relations and relaxing environmental and similar regulations that directly affect the production process (Leicht and Jenkins 1994:257–258 *emphasis* added)

I will discuss the particular strategies used to promote automotive assembly plant location much more fully in the following chapters, but in general southeastern states have continued a 60-year-old tradition of industrial recruitment and deregulation type policies (Rubenstein 1992; Spindler 1994; Storper and Walker 1989). Leicht and Jenkins argue that industrial recruitment and deregulation strategies follow from (neo)classical locational theory, and focus on minimizing factor costs of inputs and overall "costs of doing business;" I will argue below, however, that such strategies do not simply minimize cost and government regulation, but are deepening the role of government in private enterprise and investment itself.

Approaches to studying development strategies

Within the field of comparative policy research, analysis of development strategies falls under a few general directions. Most studies take up the discussion of whether local development strategies and policies are successful in their ostensible goal of creating jobs and stimulating tax revenues and overall economic development – essentially a *policy-outcome approach* (Jacobs 2012; J. Craig Jenkins et al. 2006; Kebede and Ngandu 1999; Merriman, Skidmore, and Kashian 2011; Weber, Bhatta, and Merriman 2003). Jenkins et al., for example, look at whether programs intended to promote growth in the high-tech sector actually create the high-paying jobs they are designed to (2006), while Kebede and Ngandu (1999) and Bartik et al. (1987) look respectively at the policies designed to lure Mercedes-Benz and Saturn plants to Alabama and Tennessee, and the effect of those plants on the local economies. Florida, a geographer, analyzes which urban policies and strategies are most effective at luring what he terms the creative class to cities. This refers to the young, highly educated intelligentsia and professionals whose work in some way creates new social forms of growth, or is based on creative problem-solving in the contemporary economy (Florida 2003:6–7).

A somewhat more critical vein of this literature focuses on the relative costs and benefits of development strategies for the communities they are intended to benefit. These *critical policy approaches* are still basically a policy-outcome approach to the study of recruitment and development strategies, but with greater emphasis on the costs and debts incurred by local governments (and thus local populations) in the pursuit of businesses. For example, a number of studies have looked at the recruitment of Mercedes-Benz to Alabama (Boudreaux, Coats, and Davis 2012; Spindler 1994) and BMW to South Carolina (McDavid 2010), and questioned whether the incentives offered were excessive given the relative benefits to the communities. Others examine the question of whether development strategies will have long-term impacts on a community or are merely mimetic iterations of "fast policy" intended to generate an immediate and visible return (Cleave et al. 2017; Peck and Theodore 2010, 2015). Thomas takes a more global perspective, examining tax-based incentives and competition across different countries, paying particular attention to the way in which some regions – such as the EU – place regulations on incentives (Thomas 2007, 2011). In general, critical policy outcome approaches echo the themes of Story's article for the *Times*, that localities are caught up in a race-to-the-bottom for highly mobile capital, and in this regard, they tend to reify the distinction between spheres of political and economic activity. Two studies that stand out in this regard are Perrucci's (1994) sociological study of Japanese automotive transplants in the United States in the 1980s, and aspects of Rubenstein's (1992) study of the shifting geography of the U.S. auto industry (also see, Mair, Florida, and Kenney 1988). My theoretical approach, like Perrucci, takes into account the structural forces of global capitalism and the critical geographical literature that examines the contradictory pressures firms face when deciding on a locality. Rubenstein uses a number of different geographical and locational theories to analyze the multiple factors that have shaped the geography of the U.S. automotive industry over its lifetime.

I draw extensively on both authors' research in the following chapters, but this work differs from – and builds upon – this body of research in several ways. First, through a concerted case study of the recruitment of a particular industry, I offer a detailed empirical account of the changing *relations* between localities and global firms through a clear and focused lens. This allows us to situate changing local practices within a broader framework of changing dynamics of the auto industry and the global political economy. Moreover, my approach allows us to go beyond the changes in incentives themselves and look at the entire process of business recruitment and the individuals involved in it as a totality. Examining recruitment efforts themselves also allows us to get beyond the narrow focus of much research on cities (Cleave et al. 2017; Florida 2003), and look at the complex interrelations among cities, states/provinces, and local governments at multiples scales. Second, like Pacewicz (2013, 2016) I frame these changing relations and practices both through external documentation and through the eyes of the elites themselves, which allows us to take head-on the "race to the bottom" narrative because we can see how officials involved in competition understand their situation. Third, I situate my analysis of the recruitment of AAPs within a strong theoretical framework of political Marxism and political geography, which enables me to situate changes in LED within the broader frameworks of patterns of class relations and capital accumulation, while avoiding the assumption of a clear distinction between the political and the economic, state and capital, and thus failing to apprehend that this distinction may be precisely what is in flux.

Theories of capitalist accumulation and change

As briefly discussed in the introduction, the agglomeration of automotive assembly plants in the southeast and the increasing competition to recruit them occurred at a critical and transformative period in the global capitalist economy, which followed from the major structural crisis in the late 1970s. In order to understand why I analyze the development of competitive local industrial recruitment of automotive assembly plants in this light, I must elaborate explicitly on some of the deeper theoretical assumptions and propositions of my position and their connection to the conjunctural crisis of the late 70s.

My approach to the issue of local economic development strategies and industrial recruitment stems from a Marxian political economy orientation informed by critical geography that approaches questions of state policy from the perspective of capital-labor relations. Many sociological approaches to political economy make some basic assumption of a distinction between the economic and political, whether this assumption is one of relatively autonomous spheres of activity and actors (Miliband 1969), or of a more basic economic aspect of society distinct from a political "superstructure" (Poulantzas 1975), or of distinct sources of social power (Mann 1986). The theoretical approach I take begins from the opposite position. This perspective follows Ellen M. Wood, Simon Clarke, Robert Brenner, and other historians and sociologists in the Marxian tradition, in treating the assumption of separate spheres of political and economic activity as an historical, political, and ontological question rather than as a question of abstract (over) "determination" or a *de facto* analytical expedience. My approach asserts and assumes that markets are themselves political formations with historical origins, and that property rights and class relations are politically constituted by the state, and indeed that the state and even locality are essential to the constitution of classes and class relations (Wood 1981).

In this view, relations between capital and labor or "relations of production take the form of particular juridical and political relations – modes of domination and coercion, forms of property and social organization – which are not mere secondary reflexes but a constituent of the productive relations themselves" (Wood 1981:781ali. I discuss the empirical importance of this theorization of the state in capitalist society further in chapter six, but here it should be clear that I see industrial policy, state, and the economy as *internally related* (Gough 2003; Harvey 1982). "The point really is that markets themselves are political institutions, embedded historically in states and the state system at large...commercial bureaucratic states and the capitalist world economy were mutually conditioning" (McMichael 2000:103).[2] Gough – speaking more directly to class relations – points out that this view proposes that "capital's (re)organisation is always formed in relation to labour. This class struggle is played out not just within production but within the state and the heterogeneous forms of the reproduction of labour power" (Gough 2004:189). An analysis of state and state policy therefore must take account of the specific historical formations of the political contradictions inherent in the capitalist mode of production, most importantly the contradictory tension between the necessity for both coercion and cooptation of "free" labor which is definitive of the state-capital-labor relation (Gough 2004; Gramsci 1971; Marx 1976; Wallerstein 1974; Wood 1981).

There are two implications from this deeper theoretical approach to studying local development strategies at the end of the twentieth century. The first is that industrial policy does not, in this view, externally influence class issues but is a constitutive moment in class relations. Indeed, the *absence* of organized labor from the detailed accounts to follow is telling here. The second implication is that studying the specific policy formations in the U.S. South in the last four decades requires taking a theoretical account of this historical period of global capitalism in greater detail.

Theorizing context: projects and relations of production

Most political-economic perspectives agree that the crisis of the 1970s and early 1980s was a major structural crisis that caused convulsions throughout the global capitalist economy and forced expansive efforts at political and economic restructuring (Aglietta 1998; Chase–Dunn 1998; Harvey 1989b; Scholte 2005; Teeple 2000). However, different perspectives have different ways of characterizing the periods around the crisis, and thus the major changes it brought (though most agree that after the crisis the world political economy was more "global" in some sense of that word).[3] Most of these theories hinge on how they characterize period of relatively stable accumulation in the post-World-War-II era, roughly from the mid-1940s until the crises of the late 1960s, and how they differentiate that period from the post-1970s global era.

My theoretical approach takes account of three intertwined factors. The first is the changing geography of capitalist accumulation, which has not only become more global but also more local. Geography is key not only to understand the shifting center of automotive production in the United States, but also why local and state governments have become the site of changing relations between industry and governments in the last 40 years. The second factor to account for is the way in which capital accumulation and class struggle are institutionalized in states and localities, and the way that production and consumption interrelate within and between nations. The third factor to consider is the overall ideology and guiding philosophy that form the principles shaping the actions of governmental and class elites, and serve to establish hegemonic power. Taken together this approach is an amalgamation of a number of different theories I call a *hegemonic class project* approach, with the language of project asserting the importance of classes and elites pursuing interests, while avoiding the overt structuralism and evolutionary terminology that discussion of development often drifts into.

Hegemony here refers to the Gramscian notion of social power in which "the supremacy of a social group manifests itself...[both] as 'domination' and as 'intellectual and moral leadership'" (Gramsci 1971:57). Hegemony is a useful concept because it encapsulates how subordinate classes more or less consent to domination or rule through the acceptance of an ideology and worldview, a worldview which at the same time shapes the role of the state and the process of capital accumulation. A hegemonic *project*, then, is roughly a political and ideological regime that establishes consent through such "political, intellectual, and moral leadership" and achieves hegemony in a given period (or place) (Gramsci 1971:161,170; Jessop 1983:100).

This involves the mobilization of support behind a concrete, national-popular program of action which asserts a general interest in the pursuit of objectives that explicitly or implicitly advance the long-term interests of the hegemonic class (fraction) and which also privileges particular "economic-corporate" interests compatible with this program. Conversely those particular interests which are inconsistent with the project are deemed immoral and/or irrational and, insofar as they are still pursued by groups outside the consensus, they are also liable to sanction. Normally hegemony also involves the sacrifice of certain short-term interests of the hegemonic class (fraction), and a flow of material concessions for other social forces mobilized behind the project. It is thereby conditioned and limited by the accumulation process. (Jessop 1983:100)

McMichael argues that in the postwar period an *inter*national hegemonic project prevailed – the development project. The development project emerged out of the widespread class struggle of the early 1900s and later the decolonization movement, as well as the supposed threat of communism in the postwar era. Both an ideology and policy framework, the development project was hegemonic among nations that viewed state-regulated capitalism as *the* force for creating national economic development and increasing the prosperity of nation-states, and was in this way nation-state *centric* (Aglietta 1998; Kotz 2003; Kotz, McDonough, and Reich 1994; McMichael 2012:14). In fact, the wealth of core nations and the global system which sustained that wealth through accumulation and exploitation were decidedly inter-national, and the development project served the intellectual and moral purpose of justifying that system of exploitation which operated on both national and international scales (for a discussion of the concept of *scale* and notes on terminology see notes to this chapter).[4] This multi-scalar institutional framework for the development project is reflected in the Bretton Woods agreements:

> Under U.S. auspices in 1944, the future members of the United Nations (UN) held a conference at Bretton Woods and established the basis of an international monetary system. The delegates created an exchange-rate mechanism by setting the prices of national currencies against the U.S. dollar; and they established, among others...the International Monetary Fund (IMF) and the World Bank (WB). The IMF was intended regulate international trade balances...the World Bank was designed to manage an international fund for economic development. Alongside these mechanisms, the General Agreement on Tariffs and Trade (GATT)...would provide the institutional means for a negotiated removal of...national barriers to world trade. (Teeple 2000:54)

In this way, the development project was always dual-faceted, oriented toward both national developmentalism and laying the groundwork of global markets. Marxist political economists and geographers characterize the institutionalization of class relations and capital accumulation in this period as "Fordist" (named, appropriately, after the automotive firm) – a period in which mass production was balanced with a new era of mass consumption and the advent of consumerism in Western core economies (Aglietta 1998; Kotz et al. 1994). Fordist production processes are characterized by mass production techniques developed during World War II, with heavy fixed-capital investment in plant and machinery and highly standardized mass products (Harvey 1989b Ch 8; Kwon 2004:37).[5] These production processes were accompanied by social relations of production which also became highly standardized, in which often-large unions negotiated long term contracts across entire industries, typically through tripartite arrangements in which states mediated capital-labor relations in a more or less centralized fashion (national differences will be discussed later) (Harvey 1989b:133–134; Rubenstein 1992:270–271.).[6] The Fordist era was characterized not only by these politicized class relations (which secured for many workers in the West rising wages) but also by the differential spread of Keynsian-ish welfare state policies and more interventionist regulation of industries by nation-states (Harvey 1989b; Hicks 1999). This created conditions for the mass consumption of the prodigious output of Fordist factory systems and contributed to the brief period of consistently rising standards of living in Western nations. Hence, as Harvey puts it, "postwar Fordism has to be seen...less as a mere system of mass production and more as a total way of life. Mass production meant standardization of product as well as mass consumption" (1989:135). Monetary policy in the Fordist regime was tied to the US dollar and based in the Bretton Woods accords among core nations.[7]

Drawing together these two theoretical threads, I characterize the postwar era (roughly the mid-1940s to late-1960s) as the *Fordist-development project*, because this conceptual periodization encompasses both the dominant processes and relations of production and structures of accumulation, as well as the hegemonic project constructed by dominant classes and attendant elites (or the *hegemonic bloc*, led especially by capitalists and elites in the United States) that framed and legitimated (and provided material concessions for) this form of the capitalist world economy.[8] Whatever stability was achieved through this project, however, was confined primarily to the core nations (the West and Japan, and perhaps South Korea) and began to wane into structural crisis no sooner than stability had been achieved.

The globalization project and re-scaling regimes of accumulation

If the Fordist development project began to solidify in the postwar era, it was at the same time laying the basis of its own dissolution and began to unravel as early as the mid-1960s (Teeple 2000:62–71).[9] The problems of the Fordist-development project lay in several places. I have little space here to discuss the anti-colonial movements and the major geo-political factors which led to the fracturing of the hegemonic ideology (but see McMichael 2012; Teeple 2000). Many authors agree that, in conjunction with massive shocks in the global economic system brought on by numerous chronic issues (balance of trade issues, real appreciation of the dollar) (Frieden 2006:342–347; 364–372) that were inflamed by the oil shocks of 1974, the Fordist-development project crumbled beneath the weight of its own *mass-iveness*. David Harvey sums up some of the issues with so-called Fordism:

> These difficulties could best be captured by one word: rigidity. There were problems with the rigidity of long-term and large-scale fixed capital investments in mass-production systems that precluded much flexibility of design and presumed stable growth in invariant consumer markets. There were problems of rigidities in labour markets, labour allocation, and in labour contracts (especially in the so-called 'monopoly' sector.) And any attempt to overcome these rigidities ran into the seemingly immovable force of deeply entrenched working-class power – hence the strike waves and labour disruptions of the period 1968–72. The rigidities of state commitments also became more serious as entitlement programs... grew... the only tool of flexible response lay in monetary policy... and so began the inflationary wave that was eventually to sink the postwar boom. (Harvey 1989b:142)

The declining profitability and rising challenges from newly industrializing countries eroded the material base for the postwar development project. With the onset of major crises in 1974, there began a considerable restructuring of the international economy and a reorientation away from national development towards what I call the *neoliberal globalization project*.[10]

Along with McMichael (McMichael 2000) and Harvey (Harvey 1989b, 2001, 2005), I frame the neoliberal globalization project as a direct confrontation with the nationally centered rigidities of Fordist-developmentalism, particularly the class relations entrenched in national institutions. Following Brenner, I argue we have to understand the neoliberal globalization project as "two dialectically intertwined but analytically distinct moments: the (partial) *destruction* of extant institutional arrangements and political compromises through market-oriented reform initiatives; and the (tendential) *creation* of a new infrastructure for market-oriented economic growth, commodification, and the rule of capital" (2002:362).

On an ideological level, the neoliberal project involves a shift away from state-mediation of capitalist social relations and an attempt to impose market rule and the law of value on firms, labor, and governments. This shift marks a movement *away* from the hegemonic principles of social democracy, citizenship, and collective rights characteristic of the Fordist-development project *towards* different intellectual and moral ideals founded on the centrality of the market and competition in determining social outcomes, and the sacralization of the individual and corporate private property (Boli 2006; Brenner and Theodore 2002; McMichael 2000; Peck and Tickell 2002).[11] What this entails in practices hinges largely on the national context of "inherited regulatory landscapes" (Brenner and Theodore 2002:352), but often entails a relative retreat of the nation-state from extensive mediation of capital-labor relations, the relaxation at the national level of monetary and regulatory barriers to capital flows, and openly coercive state reinforcement of corporate private property and the coterminous expansion of prison systems (Harvey 2005, 2010; McMichael 2000; Scholte 1997; Teeple 2000, 2011). Finally, there has been a marked shift in the discourse, and to a lesser extent the actual structures, of welfare systems towards an ideology of "workfare" and the curtailment or stagnation of state expenditures on social insurance programs (Peck and Theodore 2010).

If neoliberal "globalization, as a political project, concerns the attempt to instiutionalise the neoliberal agenda of market reform by removing public constraints on economies" (McMichael 2000:110), then this project has involved first and foremost the revolutionary restructuring of the Fordist production processes and the simultaneous "upward and downward scalar shifts"(Gough 2004:186) in capital accumulation processes and class relations, circumventing the national scale at which the rigidities of the Fordist class relations were most entrenched (Brenner 1999a).

The response of capitalists within the emergent hegemonic bloc[12] to Fordist rigidities was to revolutionize the means of production and (re)turn to political principles based on the perennial capitalist fiction of the self-regulating market (c.f. Polanyi 1957 Ch. 6). Information and communications technologies (ICTs) removed many spatial and temporal barriers to the flow of money; this allowed not only for the pooling of ever more vast sums of resources, but also for significant increases in the size and pace of commodity flows (Teeple 2000:67; 2011). Beyond the circulation of capital, new technologies facilitated major changes in processes of production and distribution.[13]

So-called "flexible accumulation" marked a shift not only in the production process but also a general shift in the global organization of production, facilitating further development of an international division of labor, and a geographic shift of de-skilled production processes to regions with cheaper labor forces. The mobility of firms and the international division of labor served to discipline labor forces by increasing national – and especially global – competition, subjecting them more extensively to the law of value; this resulted in widespread yet differential enervation of organized labor and a marked decline of unionization in many nations over the ensuing decades (Fröbel, Heinrichs, and Kreye 1980; Harvey 1989b:9; McMichael 2012:3; Scholte 2005:136–140; Teeple 2000:5).

All of these revolutions allowed capital in all its forms – productive, commodity, and finance – to at least partially transcend the territorial framework of the nation-state and reconstitute itself at the global level.[14] In other words, the national state ceased to be *the* primary structure for organizing capitalist production processes, as the enhanced mobility of capital (especially finance) enabled it to scale upwards somewhat, but the inevitable materiality of productive processes meant that at the same time regional and local organizational frameworks became more central. "The post-1970s wave of globalisation has significantly decentered the role of the national scale as a self-enclosed container of socio-economic relations while simultaneously intensifying the importance of both sub- and supranational forms of territorial organization" (Brenner 1999b:435). We can suggest then that capital now *flows* through supra-territorial global structures and institutions, but production and labor relations are primarily or increasingly organized on regional and urban scales. However, this should not be read as suggesting the national state is somehow fading or even necessarily becoming less important as an institutional and regulatory structure:

> Viewing the market as a de-nationalizing movement does not imply a borderless world, rather it implies transformed states. In my view, this transformation involves a shift from states managing national economies, to states managing the global economy – in two senses; facilitating global circuits of money and commodities, and resolving the contradictions of global capitalism...[thus] the globalization project is simultaneously a project of crisis management and a blueprint for continuing development through private means. Like the development project, the globalization project is an attempt to construct a stable hegemonic ordering of the world...[and] a movement to institute market rule by a powerful global managerial class (McMichael 2000:110–113)

Entrepreneurial governance

The neoliberal globalization project has characterized the period since the 1980s in which global automotive firms began locating and agglomerating in the southeast and midwest United States. This larger understanding of the shift toward global flows of capital and the increasing centrality of local governance is important because it highlights why local governments became increasingly *entrepreneurial* in the period in question. On the one hand, increasingly globalized capital not only affected the relations between capital and national-states, but also between nation-states and sub-national government:

> This rescaling of statehood has not only eroded the nationalized formations of urban governance and the redistributive forms of state spatial policy that prevailed during the Fordist-Keynesian period. It has also entailed the consolidation of new interscalar rule-regimes ... that have enhanced fiscal constraints and competitive pressures upon cities

and regions, impelling the regulatory institutions to privilege the goals of local economic development and territorial competitiveness over traditional welfarist, redistributive priorities. (Brenner 2004:176)

Put somewhat more succinctly, Cameron and Palan suggest that, "national economic policies and institutions are increasingly being geared towards promoting internal competition between different industrial regions for investment" (Cameron and Palan 1999:282). On the other hand, local governments facing both declining transfers of funds from the national level and capital flight faced unique difficulties. With capital in some forms now dealing more directly with urban and state governments, competitive pressures on government officials and elites at these scales increased immensely. This is hardly without an element of strategic manipulation – it is precisely *local* governments that are directly responsible to local constituents and their immovable, concrete standards of living (Cox 2010; Storper and Walker 1989). In the context of the neoliberal globalization project, localities adapted their forms of governance to new imperatives. Among local elites there emerged "a strong consensus that urban governments had to be much more innovative and entrepreneurial, willing to explore all kinds of avenues...[to] secure a better future for their populations"(Harvey 1989a:4).[15] As Harvey elaborates:

> The new entrepreneurialism has, as its centerpiece, the notion of a 'public private partnership' in which a tradition of local boosterism is integrated with the use of local governmental powers to try and attract external sources of funding, new direct investment, or new employment sources...the activity of that public-private partnership is entrepreneurial precisely because it is speculative in execution and design...in many instances, this has meant that the public sector assumes the risk and private sector takes the benefits...I suspect this feature of risk-absorption by the local (rather than the national or federal) public sector which distinguishes the present phase of urban entrepreneurialism from earlier phases of civic boosterism in which private capital seemed generally much less risk-averse. (Harvey 1989a:7)

We can now situate the practice of industrial recruitment within the broader frame of the neoliberal globalization project in which localities turned toward an ethos and practice of entrepreneurial governance. This will help to understand the particular pressures faced by both automotive producers and local governments in the historical moment in question, and the patterns of plant location and fixed-capital investment that emerge in the following chapter. In many ways what will emerge from my findings is a detailed account of the entrepreneurial turn in the U.S. context, and we will see precisely how local governments use the hegemonic discourse of *partnerships* to frame the shifting risks and costs that are at the core of industrial recruitment practices. Before we turn to recruitment itself, we must elaborate the comparative context of the industry and U.S. local governments and policies, and analyze the patterns of industry decisions and plant locations. This is the task of the following chapter.

Notes

1 **Clarification of Terminology**: The term "**entrepreneurial governance**" is a general term used to specify the turn in government intervention in economic "development" in the neoliberal era (Harvey 2001; Perrucci 1994; Rubenstein 1992). Jenkins et al. use the term in a more specific sense to try and specify the different types of development strategies. My usage here reflects the more general usage, as the particular usage by Jenkins et al. applies to development strategies that lie outside the scope of this analysis.

2 Hence, for example, Brenner's argument that the rise of capitalist accumulation in Western Europe cannot simply be attributed to unequal exchange for profit, and rather that "'production for profit via exchange' will have the systematic effect of accumulation and the development of the productive forces only when it expresses certain specific social relations of production (Brenner 1977:32).

3 But see Mann (2013).

4 **Two Further Notes on Terminology**: (1) In geographical literature *scale* refers to the particular geographical "level" at which social institutions and actors operate and toward which they are oriented. A typical elaboration of scales in descended order might be: Global, regional, national, provincial, local. The European Union is an example of a regional body, the state of California or the province of British Columbia examples of provincial scales, local governments are often based on cities or counties or both. (**2**) For clarity's sake, and because this study focuses on the United States, I will adopt the U.S. terminology in which the provincial scale is usually seen as the "state" level as opposed to the "federal" or national-state level.

5 It is important to stress that Fordism is an *ideal type* (Clarke 1988), indeed one based on the assembly line production techniques pioneered by the Ford automotive corporation. The degree to which it was characteristic of production outside the Western automotive industry varies substantially.

6 These relations of production were in part a historical outcome of the defeat of revolutionary movements in some European countries in the interwar period (Harvey 1989b:133; Mann 2012:Ch.6), and active class projects in Western nations to both undermine the most radical segments of organized labor while compromising with the least radical segments, compromises encouraged by the looming threat of Soviet state socialism and the brewing cold war.

7 The perspective here is in many ways drawn from regulation theory (Aglietta 1998; Clarke 1988; Jessop 2013), or the similar social structures of accumulation theory (Kotz, McDonough, and Reich 1994). These theories distinguish periods of capitalism as "regimes of accumulation" characterized by institutional arrangements that facilitate relatively stable periods of capital accumulation. It is easy to see how from the account of Fordism how this view has been accused of falling into functionalist explanations and overemphasizing the smoothness of capitalist accumulation (Clarke 1988; Gough 2012; Peck 1996:97–99; Teeple 2011). While I agree with Harvey (1989b:121) that the notion of a regime of accumulation can be useful, I do not use the language here because I reject the notion that the history of capitalism is punctuated by such stable institutional accumulation periods. Indeed, given the many crises of the post-1980s era and the

similarly chaotic prewar and interwar periods, it is difficult to find *any* other solid example of a highly stable period of capitalist accumulation. Moreover, the regime of accumulation perspective deemphasizes actual *actors* such as classes and political elites who shape policies and ideologies, and who struggle and negotiate the regimes of accumulation and modes of social regulation.

8 In this sense, the "mode of social regulation" and the concessions and co-optation which are typically part of a hegemonic project are basically the same thing.

9 This has lead Simon Clarke to challenge "if such a thing as the 'Fordist regime of accumulation' ever existed, [as] it was singularly ineffective at securing the 'stabilization in the allocation of the product between production and consumption over a longish period'" (Clarke 1988:78; *see also* Gough 2012; Peck 1996:97–100). I take this challenge to heart, and it is why I do not include lengthy discussion of regulation theory here.

10 Technically "glocalization" would be a bit more accurate, but I find the word irritating.

11 "Even the published views of representatives of international capital on democracy have been far less sanguine and more realistic than those of social-democratic parties. The Trilateral Commission's analysis of the 'crisis of democracy' concluded in 1975 that there was too much democracy, that curbs on its expansion should be implemented, and that to the degree that democracy 'worked' it was largely because of the political apathy of the working classes" (Teeple 2000:33).

12 Made up of the capitalist and political elites not subsumed in the crisis. See Sklair (Sklair 2000) and Robinson (2005).

13 In the realm of production, the computer transformed the entire labor process... [the application of] computer-aided production and continuous processes... brought into being "lean production," "just in time" assembly, and "flexible manufacturing," developments that immensely facilitated global production in multiple sites and from multiples sources (Teeple 2000:66).

14 Brenner suggests, following Lefebvre (1992), that "the territorial fixity of [nation] state institutions provides a stabilized geographical scaffolding for the circulation of labour-power, commodities and capital on multiple scales"(1999b:434). The nation-state, probably more than any other previous form of organization, "manages space on a grand scale" by "producing large-scale spatial configurations that serve as territorially specific forces of production" (Brenner 1999b:434).

15 "Put simply the 'managerial' approach so typical of the 1960s has steadily given way to initiatory and 'entrepreneurial' forms of action in the 1970s and 1980s" (Harvey 2001:347)

Bibliography

Aglietta, Michel. 1998. " Capitalism at the Turn of the Century: Regulation Theory and the Challenge of Social Change. *New Left Review* I(232):41–90.

Bartik, Timothy J., Charles Becker, Steve Lake, and John Bush. 1987. "Saturn and State Economic Development." *Forum for Applied Research and Public Policy* 2(1 (Spring)):29–40.

Block, Fred, and Peter B. Evans. 2005. "The State and the Economy." Pp. 505–526 in *The Handbook of Economic Sociology*, edited by N. J. Smelser and R. Swedberg. New York: Princeton University Press.

Boli, John. 2006. "The Rationalization of Virtue and Virtuosity in World Society." Pp. 95–118 in *Transnational Governance: Institutional Dynamics of Regulation*, edited by M.-L. Djelic and K. Sahlin-Andersson. Cambridge: Cambridge University Press.

Boudreaux, Christopher, R. Morris Coats, and Earl H. Davis. 2012. "The Dark Side of State Competition for Foreign Direct Investment: That Which Is Seen and That Which Is Not Seen." *Southern Business & Economic Journal* 35(1):35–52.

Brenner, Neil. 1999a. "The Dark Side of State Competition for Foreign Direct Investment: That Which Is Seen and That Which Is Not Seen." *Urban Studies* 36(3):431–451. doi: 10.1080/0042098993466.

Brenner, Neil. 1999b. "Globalisation as Reterritorialisation: The Re-Scaling of Urban Governance in the European Union." *Urban Studies* 36(3):431–451. doi: 10.1080/0042098993466.

Brenner, Neil. 2004. *New State Spaces: Urban Governance and the Rescaling of Statehood.* Oxford: Oxford University Press.

Brenner, Neil, and Nik Theodore. 2002. "Cities and the Geographies of 'Actually Existing Neoliberalism." *Antipode* 34(3):349–379. doi: 10.1111/1467-8330.00246.

Brenner, Robert. 1977. "The Origins of Capitalist Development: A Critique of Neo-Smithian Marxism." *New Left Review* 104(1):25–92.

Cameron, Angus, and Ronen Palan. 1999. "The Imagined Economy: Mapping Transformations in the Contemporary State." *Millennium - Journal of International Studies* 28(2):267–288. doi: 10.1177/03058298990280020801.

Chase-Dunn, C. 1998. *Global Formation: Structures of the World-Economy.* Updated edition. Lanham: Rowman & Littlefield Publishers.

Clarke, Simon. 1988. "Overaccumulation, Class Struggle and the Regulation Approach." *Capital & Class* 12(3):59–92.

Cleave, Evan, Godwin Arku, Richard Sadler, and Jason Gililand. 2017. "Is It Sound Policy of Fast Policy? Practitioners Perspectives on the Role of Place Branding in Local Economic Development." *Urban Geography* 38(8):1133–1157.

Cox, Kevin R. 1995. "Globalisation, Competition and the Politics of Local Economic Development." *Urban Studies (Routledge)* 32(2):213–224.

Cox, Kevin R. 2010. "Globalisation, Competition and the Politics of Local Economic Development." *Regional Studies* 44(2):215–227. doi: 10.1080/00343400903365128.

Evans, Peter B. 1995. *Embedded Autonomy: States and Industrial Transformation.* Princeton, NJ: Princeton University Press.

Evans, Peter B., and John D. Stephens. 1988. "Development and the World Economy." Pp. 739–774 in *Handbook of Sociology*, edited by N. J. Smelser. California: SAGE.

Florida, Richard. 2003. "Cities and the Creative Class." *City & Community* 2(1):1–17.

Florida, Richard. 2014. *The Rise of the Creative Class--Revisited: Revised and Expanded.* 1 edition. New York: Basic Books.

Frieden, Jeffry A. 2006. *Global Capitalism: Its Fall and Rise in the Twentieth Century.* New York, NY: W. W. Norton & Company.

Fröbel, Folker, Jürgen Heinrichs, and Otto Kreye. 1980. *The New International Division of Labour: Structural Unemployment in Industrialised Countries and Industrialisation in Developing Countries.* Cambridge; New York: Cambridge University Press.

Gough, Jamie. 2003. *Work, Locality and the Rhythms of Capital: The Labour Process Reconsidered.* London; New York: Continuum.

Gough, Jamie. 2004. "Changing Scale as Changing Class Relations: Variety and Contradiction in the Politics of Scale." *Political Geography* 23(2):185–211. doi: 10.1016/j.polgeo.2003.11.005.

Gough, Jamie. 2012. "Capital Accumulation in Space, Capital-Labour Relations, and Political Strategy." Pp. 89–112 in *Territory, the State, and Urban Politics*, edited by A. E. G. Jonas and A. Wood. Surrey: Ashgate.

Gramsci, Antonio. 1971. *Selections from the Prison Notebooks*. International Publishers Co.

Harvey, David. 1982. *The Limits to Capital*. Chicago: University of Chicago Press.

Harvey, David. 1989a. "From Managerialism to Entrepreneurialism: The Transformation in Urban Governance in Late Capitalism." *Geografiska Annaler. Series B, Human Geography* 71(1):3–17. doi: 10.2307/490503.

Harvey, David. 1989b. *The Condition of Postmodernity: An Enquiry into the Origins of Cultural Change*. Oxford: Blackwell.

Harvey, David. 2001. "From Managerialism to Entrepreneurialism: The Transformation of Urban Governance in Late Capitalism." Pp. 345–368 in *Spaces of Capital: Towards a Critical Geography*. New York: Routledge.

Harvey, David. 2005. *A Brief History of Neoliberalism*. Oxford: Oxford University Press.

Harvey, David. 2010. *The Enigma of Capital: And the Crises of Capitalism*. New York: Oxford University Press.

Hicks, Alexander M. 1999. *Social Democracy & Welfare Capitalism: A Century of Income Security Politics*. Ithaca: Cornell University Press.

Jacobs, A. J. 2012. "Collaborative Regionalism and Foreign Direct Investment The Case of the Southeast Automotive Core and the 'New Domestics.'." *Economic Development Quarterly* 26(3):199–219.

Jenkins, J. Craig, Kevin T. Leicht, and Arthur Jaynes. 2006. "Do High Technology Policies Work? High Technology Industry Employment Growth in U.S. Metropolitan Areas, 1988–1998." *Social Forces* 85(1):267–296.

Jenkins, J. Craig, Kevin T. Leicht, and Heather Wendt. 2006. "Class Forces, Political Institutions, and State Intervention: Subnational Economic Development Policy in the United States, 1971–1990." *American Journal of Sociology* 111(4):1122–1180. doi: 10.1086/ajs.2006.111.issue-4.

Jessop, Bob. 1983. "Accumulation Strategies, State Forms, and Hegemonic Projects." *Kapitalistate* 10:89–111.

Jessop, Bob. 2013. "Revisiting the Regulation Approach: Critical Reflections on the Contradictions, Dilemmas, Fixes and Crisis Dynamics of Growth Regimes." *Capital & Class* 37(1):5–24.

Kebede, Allene, and Sylvain Ngandu. 1999. "Neoliberalism and the US Economic Expansion of the 1990s." *Journal of Agricultural and Applied Economics* 31(2):371–382.

Kotz, D. M. 2003. "03.al of Agricultural and Applied Economics Reflections o *Monthly Review* 54(11):15–33.

Kotz, David M., Terrence McDonough, and Michael Reich. 1994. *Social Structures of Accumulation: The Political Economy of Growth and Crisis*. Cambridge England; New York: Cambridge University Press.

Kwon, Hyeong-ki. 2004. *Fairness and Division of Labor in Market Societies: A Comparison of the U.S. and German Automotive Industries*. New York: Berghahn Books.

Lefebvre, Henri. 1992. *The Production of Space*. 1st edition. Malden MA: Wiley-Blackwell.

Leicht, Kevin T., and J. Craig Jenkins. 1994. "Three Strategies of State Economic Development: Entrepreneurial, Industrial Recruitment, and Deregulation Policies in the American States." *Economic Development Quarterly* 8(3):256–269.

Mair, Andrew, Richard Florida, and Martin Kenney. 1988. "The New Geography of Automobile Production: Japanese Transplants in North America." *Economic Geography* 64(4):352–373. doi: 10.2307/144233.

Mann, Michael. 1986. *The Sources of Social Power. Volume 1, a History of Power from the Beginning to A.d. 1760*. Cambridge: Cambridge University Press.

Mann, Michael. 2012. *The Sources of Social Power. Volume 3, Global Empires and Revolution, 1890-1945*. New York: Cambridge University Press.

Mann, Michael. 2013. *The Sources of Social Power. Volume 4, Globalizations, 1945-2011*. Cambridge: Cambridge University Press.

Marx, Karl. 1976. *Capital: Volume 1: A Critique of Political Economy*, Vol. 1. London: Penguin Books in association with New Left Review.

McDavid, Kathleen E. 2010. "Giving State Tax Incentives to Corporations: How Much Is Too Much." *South Carolina Journal of International Law and Business* 7:257.

McMichael, Philip. 2000. "Globalisation: Trend or Project?" Pp. 100–113 in *Global Political Economy: Contemporary Theories*, edited by R. Palan. London: Routledge.

McMichael, Philip. 2012. *Development and Social Change: A Global Perspective*. 5th edition. California: Pine Forge Press.

Merriman, David F., Mark L. Skidmore, and Russ D. Kashian. 2011. "Do Tax Increment Finance Districts Stimulate Growth in Real Estate Values?" *Real Estate Economics* 39(2):221–250.

Miliband, Ralph. 1969. *The State in Capitalist Society*. New York: Basic Books.

Moore, Barrington. 1966. *Social Origins of Dictatorship and Democracy: Lord and Peasant in the Making of the Modern World*. Boston: Beacon Press.

O'Connor, James. 1973. *The Fiscal Crisis of the State*. New York: St. Martin Crisis.

Pacewicz, Josh. 2013. "Tax Increment Financing, Economic Development Professionals and the Financialization of Urban Politics." *Socio-Economic Review* 11(3):413–440.

Pacewicz, Josh. 2016. *Partisans and Partners: The Politics of the Post-Keynesian Society*. University of Chicago Press.

Peck, Jamie. 1996. *Work-Place: The Social Regulation of Labor Markets*. New York: Guilford Press.

Peck, Jamie, and Nik Theodore. 2010. "Recombinant Workfare, across the Americas: Transnationalizing 'Fast' Social Policy." *Geoforum* 41(2):195–208.

Peck, Jamie, and Nik Theodore. 2015. *Fast Policy*. 3rd edition. Minneapolis: University of Minnesota Press.

Peck, Jamie, and Adam Tickell. 2002. "Neoliberalizing Space." *Antipode* 34(3):380–404. doi: 10.1111/1467-8330.00247.

Perrucci, Robert. 1994. *Japanese Auto Transplants in the Heartland: Corporatism and Community*. New York: Aldine de Gruyter.

Polanyi, Karl. 1957. *The Great Transformation*. Boston: Beacon Press.

Poulantzas, Nicos. 1975. *Classes in Contemporary Capitalism*. 2nd Edition. London: NLB.

Robinson, William I. 2005. "Gramsci and Globalisation: From Nation-State to Transnational Hegemony." *Critical Review of International Social & Political Philosophy* 8(4):559–574.

Rubenstein, James M. 1992. *The Changing Us Auto Industry: A Geographical Analysis*. London England; New York: Routledge.

Rubinson, Richard, and Joan Sokolovsky. 1988. "Patterns of Political Industrial Regulation: Railroads in the World Economy." Pp. 3–20 in *Rethinking the 19th Century*, edited by F. O. Ramirez. California: Greenwood Press.

Rueschemeyer, Dietrich, Evelyne Huber Stephens, and John D. Stephens. 1992. *Capitalist Development and Democracy*, 1st edition. Chicago: University Of Chicago Press.

Scholte, Jan Aart. 1997. "Global Capitalism and the State." *International Affairs* 73(3):427–452.

Scholte, Jan Aart. 2005. *Globalization: A Critical Introduction*, 2nd Edition. New York: Palgrave Macmillan.

Sklair, Leslie. 2000. *The Transnational Capitalist Class*. New York: Wiley.

Spindler, Charles J. 1994. "Winners and Losers in Industrial Recruitment: Mercedes-Benz and Alabama." *State & Local Government Review* 26(3):192–204.

Storper, Michael, and Richard Walker. 1989. *The Capitalist Imperative: Territory, Technology, and Industrial Growth*. New York: Basil Blackwell.

Teeple, Gary. 2000. *Globalization and the Decline of Social Reform: Into the Twenty-First Century*. 2nd edition. Ontario: Garamond Press.

Teeple, Gary. 2011. "Notes on the Continuing Crisis." Pp. 227–257 in *Relations of Global Power: Neoliberal Order and Disorder*, edited by S. McBride and G. Teeple. Toronto: University of Toronto Press.

Thomas, Kenneth. 2007. *Investment Incentives: Growing Use, Uncertain Benefits, Uneven Controls*. Geneva, Switzerland: Global Subsidies Initiative.

Thomas, Kenneth. 2011. *Investment Incentives and the Global Competition for Capital*. London: Palgrave Macmillan.

Wallerstein, Immanuel Maurice. 1974. *The Modern World-System I*. New York: Academic Press.

Weber, Rachel, Saurav Dev Bhatta, and David Merriman. 2003. "Does Tax Increment Financing Raise Urban Industrial Property Values?." *Urban Studies* 40(10):2001–2021.

Wood, Ellen Meiksins. 1981. "The Separation of the Economic and the Political in Capitalism." *New Left Review* (I/127):66–95.

3 Patterns in the industry – patterns in location

Entrepreneurial governance appears to emerge as a set of practices and re-lations between localities and industries that were both facing the dis-ciplining forces of neoliberal hegemony and the exigencies of a global economic crisis. However, we will see that it was actually protectionist U.S. policies that kicked off major changes in the global automotive industry, as well as the particular opportunities and pressures faced by firms dealing with very different institutional and class dynamics. In the next three chapters, we will explore the emergence local entrepreneurialism through the lens of transforming automotive production in the United States during neoliberal globalization. I do this through three different lenses, first by examining the institutional, class, and market forces that shaped firms' considerations and plant construction decisions. Then, in the next chapter, I explore the process of recruitment and changes within it, then finally examine the hegemonic views of elites. But first, we need to take a step back to understand the comparative context of U.S. automotive production, and industrial and class relations more broadly. The goal of this chapter is twofold: first, to explain the changes in U.S. automotive production in the neoliberal era, which saw new plants built almost exclusively by foreign-owned companies, and generally built in the southeast – away from the older center of car manufacturing. Second, to explain this southern drift and the particular locational decisions firms made, and show that class relations were central in this process. This will allow us tease apart the ways in which the vicissitudes of neoliberal globalization impacted global auto firms situated in very dif-ferent institutional contexts. After a brief introduction to geographical lo-cation theory and some discussion of the unique feature of the South, we can grasp the locational choices of primarily foreign-owned firms in their full breadth, and locate the role of class antagonism in the industry patterns.

U.S. industrial policy (such as it is)

The discussion in the previous chapter of the major crises of the 1970s and the shift away from Fordist developmentalism towards neoliberal globalism needs greater contextual detail in order to understand the way automotive

DOI: 10.4324/9781003107569-3

manufacturers in different nations responded to new dynamics and pressures and produce the geographical picture we see today in the United States. While all nation-states were affected by the rescaling of neoliberal globalization, national institutional contexts still strongly shape the effects of the globalization project (Huber and Stephens 2005). As we shall see, despite very different industrial histories and industrial relations/policy frameworks, the crisis in the global auto industry produced similar pressures on both the German and U.S. automotive industries.[1]

The germane point for the following analysis is the relatively unique form that industrial relations and regulation have taken in the United States, especially compared with the late industrializing nations that have located automotive assembly plants there – Japan, Germany, Korea, and China (or Sweden, depending on how one locates the ownership of Volvo) (Evans 1995; Hicks and Kenworthy 1998:1633). In most comparative work on capitalist development and institutions – whether of the varieties of capitalism genre or the corporatist/neo-corporatists vein (which essentially look at many of the same questions) – the United States and Britain tend to stand out historically as very liberal in their policy orientation (Hall and Soskice 2001; Hancké, Rhodes, and Thatcher 2007; Thelen 2012; but see Wuthnow 1985). What this generally means is that in both nation-states, but most pronouncedly in the United States, the state takes a very hands-off approach to regulation and policy – a sort of "let markets and competition do their work" approach to economic development, and a "wait until after an unmitigated disaster" approach to industrial regulation (Dobbin 1994; Rubinson and Sokolovsky 1988).[2] This differs strongly from postwar Japan, West Germany, and South Korea in which the state has typically taken a much more active role in economic development and industrial regulation, helping to foster industries and their development and usually taking a more proactive approach to the regulation of industrial activity and labor relations (Evans 1995; Hicks and Kenworthy 1998:1649; Kwon 2004).

The United States also differs from these other countries in that its industrial policy approach has been highly localized in two senses of the word. First, industrial policy has been historically very de-centered – or engineered at the state as opposed to the federal level of government. Even Germany, which also has a history of de-centralized provincial governance (Heaton 1948; Mann 1993:673; Milward and Saul 1973; Rueschemeyer, Stephens, and Stephens 1992) has not had the sort of industrial policy seen in the United States. As Lancaster and Hicks note, one "argument is that federalism…institutionalizes a greater degree of political and policy competition and *laissez-faire* economics than unitary systems" (2000:229), and indeed there is literature studying the "market-preserving" or competitive effects of federalism on developmental outcomes (Cai and Treisman 2006; Sail 2001; Weinsgast 1995). This is critical for understanding why entrepreneurial governance emerged so strongly in the U.S. institutional context.

The second sense in which U.S. industrial policy and labor relations are localized is by industry; Rubinson and Sokolovsky's (1988) analysis of railroad development and Luger's (2000) analysis of the U.S. automotive industry both show that the U.S. state is highly permeable to capitalist interests. Put succinctly, industries and segments of capital in the United States can gain a fair amount of control over the regulation of their own industry, especially if their interests in controlling that regulation are more persistent and not spasmodic reactions to cycles of accumulation. This was the case with railroad corporations, with large segments of the cattle and beef industry, pharmaceuticals (Light, Lexchin, and Darrow 2013), and of the automotive industry. Thus, where the federal industrial policy does emerge in the United States, it is heavily controlled by the very industry it is meant to regulate.

There are two important implications of this uniquely segmental form of industrial policy. The first is that, by insinuating themselves narrowly in the regulation of their own industry, segments of capital do not mitigate issues of market forces and competition more broadly, meaning that even where industrial capitalists gain influence over the regulation of their industry they are still subject to pressures of markets and competition between different segments of capital (Dobbin 1994; Rubinson and Sokolovsky 1988). Crucially, this kind of competitive monopolization broke down with the globalization of markets and competition. At the same time, as industries become more powerful and exercise greater control over the regulatory and political apparatus, there is a class polarization effect that tends to occur as the workers in that growing industry organize around their interests. Given the monopoly position of the industry, capitalists faced with such polarization are able to relatively privilege the segment of labor with which they deal, forming a sort of mini-corporatist relation (Burawoy 1985:66–67). "Where unionization is consolidated after the transition from competitive to monopoly capitalism, it generally takes root most firmly in the monopoly sector, as in…the United States. Concessions made to labour in that sector can be pushed onto the consumer – and onto the weaker competitive capitalists" (Burawoy 1985:67).

Changes in the industry

Both of these forms of localization of industrial policy and relations are critical for understanding the situation various global automakers faced as the forces of competition were unleashed at the neoliberal turn. As many nation-states turned toward the project of managing the vicissitudes of volatile and liberalized global capital accumulation, global leaders from politics and business set about the construction of more *flexible* relations of production and capital accumulation. A major goal of this research is to elaborate how that globalization project has affected the relations between local government and capital. But in order to do this, it is important to elaborate on the effect of the crisis of the 1970s on the auto industry, particularly the competitive and political pressures it created. David Harvey nicely sums up some of the most important impacts of the crisis of Fordism:

> [by the mid-1960s] the West European and Japanese recoveries [from WWII] were complete, their internal market saturated, and the drive to create export markets for their surplus output had to begin. And this occurred at the very moment when the success of Fordist rationalization meant the relative displacement of more and more workers from manufacturing...declining corporate productivity and profitability after 1966...meant the beginnings of a fiscal problem in the United States that would not go away except at the price of an acceleration of inflation, which began to undermine the role of the dollar as a stable international reserve currency...It was at about this time too that import substitution policies in many Third World countries... coupled with the first big push by multinationals into offshore manufacturing... brought a wave of competitive Fordist industrialization to entirely new environments, where the social contract with labor was either weakly enforced or non-existent. International competition thereafter intensified as Western Europe and Japan, joined by a whole host of newly industrializing countries, challenged United States hegemony within Fordism to the point where the Bretton Woods agreement cracked and the dollar was devalued. Floating and often highly volatile exchange rates thereafter replaced the fixed exchange rates of the postwar boom. (Harvey 1989:141)

Improvements in communications and transportation technologies that led to intensified global and international flows of commodity and money capital meant that automotive firms in the United States were now in more direct competition with Japanese and West European producers who sought to export as much as possible to the world's largest consumer market. This increasing competition was only exacerbated by the crises of the 70s and the oil shocks that drove up the prices of gas, further eating away at demand in the automotive sector. It was in this environment that Japanese automakers began to dominate global automotive markets.

The rise of Japanese competition

The auto industry was the paradigmatic case for the shift from Fordist to flexible production processes, which in turn reflected broader socioeconomic shifts across the world economy. Ford and other Western automakers (including the then West-German firms) in the 1960s and 1970s tended to have long-run production platforms that allowed for little variability in design or response to consumer demands. Variability in platforms and production technology was further limited by highly entrenched labor relations, in which workers resisted major changes in manufacturing processes (Rubenstein 1992:275–280). "Fordist methods of production…[are] characterized by the deployment of machinery dedicated to single tasks, strict job demarcations with multiple skill classifications for the workforce, and clear divisions between employees responsible for mental and manual labor" (Mair, Florida, and Kenney 1988:353). This rigidity was further exacerbated by the high degree of vertical integration of supplier firms within U.S. auto industries (and to a lesser degree the European auto industry) that lessened competition among supplier firms and is generally seen as lowering the quality of U.S. automobiles at the time (Hunker 1983:80–81; Rubenstein 1992:166–170).

It is in this context that Japanese automakers began to gain a dominant position in the global economy and international markets, particularly in the largest global consumer market at the time, the United States (Hunker 1983:65–70; Kwon 2004:40–41; Perrucci 1994:2;23; Rubenstein 1992:154–155;166–167; Yang 1995:99). This was due to the fact that Japanese producers had developed what came to be called "lean" production techniques and relations that, in contrast to Fordist-style mass production, are

> "lean" because [they use] less of everything compared with mass production—half the human effort in the factory, half the manufacturing space, half the investment in tools, half the engineering hours to develop a new product in half the time. Also, it requires keeping far less than half the needed inventory on site, results in many fewer defects, and produces a greater and ever growing variety of products. (Womack, Jones, and Roos 1990:13)

The lean-ness of these production techniques also extends to the firm organization and inter-firm relationships. Japanese automakers were much less vertically integrated than were their U.S. competitors, tending to farm out parts manufacturing to different tiers of suppliers, among whom the top tier would have access to tightly controlled technological and design information (Rubenstein 1992:170–171). This horizontal integration is argued to create higher quality through competition for contracts (Hunker 1983:80–81; Rubenstein 1992:169–170),[3] and allows for the "just in time" (JIT) system of delivering parts on a short-term, needs basis,[4] though it also requires the development of strong relations of trust between manufacturers and suppliers (Yang 1995 Ch.3).

All of these factors, combined with lower labor costs meant that Japanese producers tended to create cheaper, higher-quality cars than their Western European and U.S. competitors. With the increasing global flows of capital and increasing competition among automotive manufacturers, Japanese companies became a dominant player in the global automotive market by the early 1980s. "Japanese production and customer-supplier relations were regarded as the "best practice" in comparison with American and European suppliers" (Kwon 2004:41). Saturated domestic markets had begun pushing

West European and Japanese firms to export to the United States in the 1960s, and by the 1980s the Japanese vehicles' cost and performance superiority gave their manufacturers a strong edge over their Western competitors and an increasingly dominant position in the U.S. market. In response to this competition, "early in 1980 the leadership of the Big Three auto firms and the United Auto Workers (UAW) began a systematic two pronged campaign pressing for restrictions on imports of foreign-made cars and urging the Japanese to open auto plants in the United States" (Perrucci 1994:2–3).[5] The newly elected Reagan administration had made campaign promises to this effect and followed through by applying intense pressure on the Japanese government, which responded

> by adopting voluntary restrictions in 1981 on the number of automobiles which could be imported to the United States. The limits were originally set at 1.68 million vehicles, or 22% of the US market, and raised to 1.85 million vehicles in 1983...the Japanese Ministry of International Trade and Industry told each automaker how many vehicles could be imported to the United States...this allocation system favored Toyota, Nissan, and Honda...the purpose of the quotas was to allow US carmakers time to retool to produce cars that could compete in price, quality, and fuel efficiency with the Japanese imports. (Rubenstein 1992:162–163)

One of the immediate effects of these protectionist measures was actually swelling profits for Japanese automakers, who took advantage of high demand to import their more expensive models and mark up prices (Rubenstein 1992:163). In the long term, however, these policies raised fears that import limitations would restrict sales, and were one of the major factors in compelling Japanese firms to locate transplants in the United States, which was contrary to their more centrist, export-oriented international strategy (Hunker 1983:73–78; McDermott 2012; McDermott, Luethge, and Byosiere 2011; Perrucci 1994:3; Yang 1995:96–99). These fears compounded with the negative impacts on profitability and price competitiveness of Japanese cars incurred by the weakened dollar and volatile exchange rates (McDermott 2012:17; Perrucci 1994; Spindler 1994:197). The protectionist policies in the United States clearly were a trigger for Japanese firms warily considering plant locations outside of Japan, but to fully understand why the Japanese automakers decided to cross the Pacific we need a bit of locational theory and economic geography to tie the threads of global crisis, rhythms of capital accumulation, and firm locational decisions together.

Locational theories: open windows on the South

There are a number of different theories on why firms choose particular sites for fixed capital investment and development, which I will not review in detail here as these are not the primary focus of this study (but see Rubenstein (1992:10–19)).[6] Storper and Walker (1989) offer the most detailed structural analysis of the factors that affect and limit firms' locational decisions in the broader context of the capitalist mode of production, and the particular way that capitalist industry produces spaces (see also Harvey 1982 Ch. 12). The authors are highly critical of neoclassical (as known as "Weberian" – though not for the sociologist Max Weber) locational theory that sees firms as tightly constrained by existing infrastructure and resources. Two interrelated factors are seen in neoclassical theory as constraining plant-choice,

> [an industry or plant has certain] **"locational specifications"** comprised of the kinds of input-output relations that are the focus of conventional approaches. These include, first of all ... labor, natural resources, and consumers ... these are non-ubiquitous and spatially-differentiated needs that vary in availability and cost at different sites ... Locational specification becomes a more general and more difficult problem ... when it is recognized that most commodity inputs and outputs pass between firms in an extensive division of labor within and between industries..."**Locational capabilities"** on the other hand, refers to the capacity of a plant, firm or industry to secure what it needs – labor, suppliers, buyers – at a given location. (Storper and Walker 1989:73, emhasis added)

From the neoclassical perspective, for major industrial projects such as an automotive assembly plant, the primary locational specifications aside from the land itself are (1) a large labor supply, (2) proximity to transportation infrastructure (highways and rail and, if export-oriented, ports and airports) with access to consumer markets, and (3) and networks of parts producers and suppliers (Klier and Rubenstein 2010; Mair et al. 1988; McDermott et al. 2011; Rubenstein 1992). As one site selection professional I spoke to elaborated these specifications:

> There's three areas of consideration – the way we approach things – for location. Physical factors, which are primarily site infrastructure. Operating factors, which include recovering costs, labor dominating that category but [also] utilities, taxes. And then living factors, quality of life factors. So every project has criteria in all three of those areas... for automotive the physical site and infrastructure demands are so intense that...our approach to siting automotive is, there's no point in looking at a place that has good quality of life, or apparently a lot of available labor, if they don't have the property and infrastructure...so do you say that is *the* most important thing? ...Depending on who you talk to...labor is the most important thing, because labor is ultimately critical. (SEL02 2016)

From the neoclassical approach, the degree to which these factors limit the locational choices of a firm often depends on the maturity of an industry and the extent to which production is agglomerated in a particular region. That is, the degree to which suppliers and relationships between firms and governments build up in place, such as the concentration of U.S. auto producers in the Rust Belt. The problem with limiting ourselves to such input-output analyses is that it ignores the dynamism of capitalist industry and the *rhythms* of capitalist accumulation, as different and unequally developed regions are shaped through the processes of accumulation and growth, crisis and recession, and restructuring (Gough 2003; Harvey 1982). An industry, or a part thereof, has different locational options at different points in its development, and rapidly growing industries (as well, we shall see, as radically restructuring ones) have the capacity to produce their own locational specification because their growth gives them new locational capabilities:

> Fast-growing industries achieve locational freedom by locational specifications and dynamic locational capabilities. To begin with, fast-rising industries enjoy enhanced locational capabilities due to above normal profits...as important, however, is the way a dynamic sector generates its own inputs over time rather than simply competing for a stable quantity of goods and labor-power...in other words, there is ample reason to believe that leading firms in a rising industry do not face severe locational specification constraints...because innovation necessarily means solving technical problems presented by new ways of producing, [and] organizing...inputs, and labor problems...these moments of enhanced locational freedom may be called **windows of locational opportunity**. (Storper and Walker 1989:74–75 emphasis original)

Such locational windows also present themselves to industries that are mature but face radical restructuring due to declining profitability and competitiveness, precisely because their extant forms and relations of production become unprofitable or stagnant (Storper and Walker 1989:91; Mair et al. 1988).

The crisis of the 1970s is so important because it forced a critical juncture in the restructuring of the global automotive industry (among many other effects), forcing struggling U.S. and German automakers to look outside their countries to reorganize production and discipline entrenched unions in their home countries in order to compete with Japanese production. At the same time, the Japanese (and later South Korean) automakers were quickly growing which endowed them with a degree of locational freedom, and the capacity for creating their own locational capabilities. Thus, their rise within the global automotive industry gave Japanese automakers the *capacity* to locate plants within the United States – outside of the existing producer-supplier networks – but it was political restrictions on exports to their major consumer market there which pressured Japanese firms to make the trans-national leap, with Honda leading the way in 1980 in Ohio, followed by Nissan in Tennessee that same year.

U.S. transplant locational decisions part I: *new domestics of the 1980s*

The 1980s saw four Japanese auto manufacturers locate assembly plants in the United States: two in the Midwest (Indiana and Ohio) and two in the South (Tennessee and Kentucky). In addition to these, G.M. chose Tennessee for the location of its new Saturn line and plant in 1985. For the moment, we will leave to the side the question of local and state incentives offered to firms to develop in their locality, and focus on the more gen-eralized locational specifications Japanese firms considered in their initial plant location decisions (I will address actual *processes* of locational deci-sions in more detail in the next chapter). Two locational specifications be-yond transportation and infrastructure requirements and labor supply that are routinely raised in accounts of locational decisions are *supplier bases* and *labor control*. As discussed earlier, Japanese firms had developed flexible JIT production methods that require (a) a reasonable proximity to supplier bases and (b) a malleable labor force willing and able to embrace changes and adaptations in the production process (Klier and Rubenstein 2010; Rubenstein 1992:171–181). The imperative of indigenous supplier networks for the initial AAPs was initially a focal consideration, but this quickly declined in importance as quality and relationship issues with the first round of Japanese transplants led to the pursuit of alternative strategies. First of all, it should be reiterated that not all parts suppliers are treated equally in the just-in-time system; rather, parts suppliers are organized in a tiered hierarchy, with top tier or first-tier suppliers producing major components such as seats, suspensions systems, and occasionally even engines at separate plant sites and shipping to the final assembly plant as needed (Rubenstein 1992:170–171; Kwon 2004). First-tier suppliers also have closer relationships to major auto manufacturers because they require occasional access to re-stricted knowledge; such suppliers also "opt for locations near their customers—the assembly plants—to minimize aggregate transportations costs" a distance of about 100 miles or less, while "lower]-tier suppliers may not be operating on just-in-time delivery, as is the case for most first-tier suppliers" (Rubenstein 1992:171).

Japanese firms concluded that the importation of parts from Japan would undermine the timing and quality-control aspects of the JIT system (Mair et al. 1988:365). Hence, Honda's decision in 1979 to locate in Ohio was in fact

> precisely in order to establish JIT linkages with Midwestern supplier firms. Most indigenous suppliers, however, were largely unfamiliar with

JIT quality and delivery requirements. While Honda's expectations were not very high, quality turned out to be much worse than expected...even obtaining basic items such as glass and steel proved quite problematic... as a result assembly firms have encouraged many of their Japanese suppliers to construct transplants in North America. (Mair et al. 1988:365)

A number of major auto manufacturers from Japan essentially held their first-tier supplier firms captive in relocating along with them, threatening not to continue buying from them in Japan if they did not also transplant to the United States (Rubenstein 1992:171–172).[7] Thus, the existing supplier base should not be considered a significant locational specification, and so the major locational consideration is therefore the question of labor.

The question of labor in the South

The question of the importance of labor forces for firm locational considerations is a strong thread winding through critical geography and locational theory since the 1980s (Cox 1995; Gough 2012; Peck 1996). Many within the field emphasize the spatially fixing power of labor force specifications – such as skills and capacities – can have on a firm (Cox 1995, 2010; Jonas 1996, 2009) as these particular qualities of labor forces are typically developed *in situ*. The role of labor in Japanese and other foreign automakers' plant decisions point to some of the limitations of the so-called regulation school of thought in critical geography. This is in part because such theories do not take enough account of the temporally and geographically uneven and unstable processes of industrial development and accumulation that were the impetus for locational decisions of Japanese automakers in the first place. Because they were operating within a window of locational opportunity, Japanese firms intended from the outset to cultivate their own labor forces, and as such the skill capacity of the workforce was not a major concern. Indeed, "like other Japanese firms before and after, Nissan preferred to hire people without automotive, often without any industrial background" (Hülsemann 2001:228).

Rather than skill, one of the main concerns for transplant locations for Japanese firms was then the avoidance of organized labor. Multiple accounts of the locational decision process (Hülsemann 2001:228–232; McDermott et al. 2011; Rubenstein 1992:209–212) and comparative analyses of such decisions (Jacobs 2012; Miller 1997; Spindler 1994) reiterate the importance ascribed by foreign firms (not just the Japanese) of the avoidance of militant workforces. It is worth noting that unionization and industrial relations in Japan were at the time quite different than in the United States or other Western countries. Due in part to scarcity within labor markets, firms tended to promise what was basically employment for life, and had a system of advancement and promotion based on length-of-service

(Kim 1995:103–132). These relations tended to produce what Kim calls "enterprise unions" or unions within the firm – in part because worker organization across different enterprises would bring no additional benefits to the worker due to coordination among employers (Kim 1995:115; Burawoy 1985:66).[8] Such relations generated a certain reciprocity between worker and firm that in part accounts for the flexibility of Japanese workers and their willingness to re-skill and re-learn in adaption to changes in the production process. Kim suggests that such an employment model is clearly incompatible in the United States (and indeed has declined in Japan sharply since the 1990s when the author conducted his ethnography), and most incoming firms in the 1980s generally wanted to avoid the confrontational style of labor relations the UAW had normalized. This notion is supported by Mair et al.'s research which suggests that "Nissan considered sites in Illinois and Ohio, in the heart of … automobile supplier infrastructure. But it eventually selected Tennessee … to minimize likelihood of worker representation…while Honda chose…Ohio, it's site is in a rural area distant from any large cities" (1988:366) and unionized workforces. Thus, in addition to requiring a significant supply of labor, incoming automotive firms required what they referred to as a "quality" workforce. One site selection consultant I interviewed clarified what qualities, in particular, were important: "good work ethic, adaptable to manufacturing, work[ing] in a team setting, willing to take on new skills. That's for the so-called unskilled workers, and then you need to have a compliment of skilled work force, electricians, mill wrights that type of thing" (SEL01 2016). Given that UAW was formed in part to gain greater control over the changes in the production process described by this professional, the avoidance of unions was clearly imperative from the perspective of incoming firms. This led to a pattern in which almost all of the transplant firms from the 80s on chose a relatively *rural-ish* location, small towns outside of "union country" that were nonetheless relatively close to major highways and a major metropolitan areas (Hülsemann 2001:233; Mair et al. 1988:361). "Rural workers were also viewed as having low levels of occupational and geographical mobility, thus reducing the likelihood that highly trained production workers would quit" (Mair et al. 1988:366). Thus, labor control was a central locational specification for transplanting auto firms, which made the South and its labor regime an attractive location.

The South

Understanding the core concerns of incoming firms helps to explain the southern drift of new automotive production, because the South had a number of unique characteristics that were a draw to many manufacturers. While industrial policy in the United States does not adhere to any coherent pattern at the nation-state level, shared aspects of the political-economic history in the South have given those states relatively homologous approaches to class relations and the institutionalization of market forces and capital accumulation. For the purposes of this study, I limit my definition of "the South" to the 13 confederate states of the South (stretching roughly from Virginia to Texas), and I do so precisely because of the elements of their shared history (Hülsemann 2001).

The states of the American South are bound together by their political-economic past basis in a plantation-based agricultural economy, in which landlords primarily relied on slave labor and indentured servitude. While this shared past continues to have myriad impacts on contemporary life in the South, for the purposes of this research the most important factor is the negative effect this form of production had on the process of industrialization, and what Jonas has called the *local labor control regime* (Jonas 1996; Peck 1996). A local labor control regime (local LCR) then refers "to an historically contingent and territorially embedded set of mechanisms which co-ordinate the time-space reciprocities between production, work, consumption and labour reproduction within a local labour market" (Jonas 1996:325).

The local labor control regime of the American South is intrinsically tied to its industrial history. The South lagged well behind northern states in terms of their industrialization until well after the American Civil War, in many ways directly due to the labor repressive conservatism attached to large landowners engaged in agricultural production (Cobb 1993:1–3; Rueschemeyer et al. 1992:121). Even through the second World War, the South was seen as an "economic embarrassment" by some federal politicians (Cobb 1993:1). The lingering legacy of labor-repressive government, and the relative poverty that accompanied the industrial stultification in the South (Jacobs 2012:201–202) mean that the region is characterized in part by an outright antipathy toward organized labor (among business, workers, and government) and a cheaper environment in which to do business due to a relative lack of development. The LCR in the South is not just a legacy of labor-repressive practices in the pre-Civil War era either; these policies were actively pursued by local government officials well after Reconstruction. In 1947 when the Taft-Hartley Act was passed, allowing local governments to ban shops requiring union dues (or "closed" shops) "seven southern states enacted open–shop legislation in the form of so-called right-to-work laws" (Hülsemann 2001:224) by the end of that year. Attempts to unionize in the South throughout the postwar years met with repeated failure, and "by the end of the 1970s anti-unionism had practically replaced racism as the South's signature prejudice" (Cobb 1993:259) indicating an aversion to organized labor not only among businesses and government officials but also to some degree within the workforce.

Such activist pursuit of labor control policies by government officials is not unique to the area of industry-labor relations. Precisely because their states had languished in industrial production, many local and state officials in the South pursued economic and industrial development more directly and actively than in other states. Southern leaders developed a "philosophy of industrial development...that remained socially conservative but nonetheless recognized the importance of an expanded government role in promoting economic development" (Cobb 1993:4). Hülsemann agrees, "the dominant recipe for industrial growth in the South remained to lure industry from the North by the promise of cheap land and labor" (Hülsemann 2001:223) among other factors (McDermott 2011:80).

The largest industry that was first lured from the Northern states was textiles and apparel manufacturing, which between the 1920s and 1940s shifted from being heavily concentrated in New England to being primarily centered in the Carolinas (Storper and Walker 1989:92). Textiles and furniture manufacturing, both of which are relatively low-skill sectors, dominated in the South through the 1990s (Jacobs 2012:202–203, 206); Cobb notes that the labor environment, and the lack of unions in particular, was a key factor in those industries migrating south (1993:214–215). Precisely because these industries were low-skill, widespread capital flight crippled southern states in the 1980s and 1990s and intensified industrial recruitment efforts by officials. All of these factors created a strong lure for incoming automakers to the region, which can be seen in the map in Figure 3.1, where production moves south steadily after the 1980s. With this regional context in hand, we can consider some of the cases of locational decisions in more in depth.

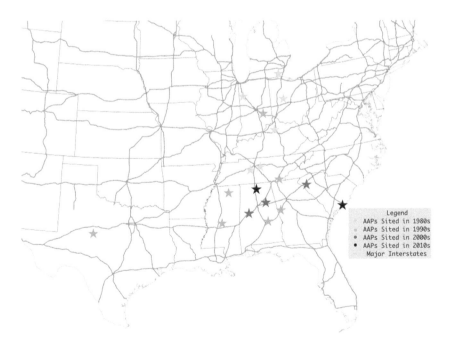

Figure 3.1 Map of Greenfield Plant Locations.

Honda, Marysville, OH, 1980

The first greenfield transplant decision, Honda's choice of Maryville, Ohio, is exemplary of the rural-ish approach to plant location. Honda was one of the later developing auto manufacturers in Japan and never captured a large share of the Japanese market, "because Toyota and Nissan [had] a monopoly on most car dealerships" (Gelsanliter 1990:142). Rubenstein argues that "as a result, Honda from its inception was highly dependent on overseas sales. At the same time, Honda's Japanese plants were operating at full capacity in the late 1970s, while Toyota and Nissan could expand production" (1992:210). As the trailblazer, Honda tested the waters in Ohio in late 1970s by first constructing a motorcycle plant there, as "motorcycle production would test the ground for the possible manufacture of automobiles, an experiment deemed necessary because internal feasibility studies had predicted financial losses from transplant…production. Soon after the plant opened in 1979, however, Honda announced construction of a \$250 million automotive assembly plant adjacent to the Marysville facility" (Mair et al. 1988:356).

Honda chose an Ohio location because had initially intended to use indigenous parts suppliers, and Marysville was located relatively close to the Detroit 3 manufacturers (Ford, Chrysler, and GM). As already mentioned, Honda and other Japanese producers ultimately had major quality control issues with suppliers, and "some indigenous supplier firms…resit[ed] adopting JIT. Even by 1988, Mazda [in it's joint venture with Ford]…reported that its biggest single problem remained obtaining materials of adequate quality… supplier firms preferred not to do business with Mazda rather than alter their manufacturing practices" (Mair et al. 1988:365). Given these issues, this consideration was not significant for later transplants.

Another draw in Ohio was that the site itself was actually somewhat pre-developed through a stalled initiative of then Governor James Rhodes, who had intended to establish an automotive research hub called the Transportation Research Center (Gelsanliter 1990:22–25). Another attraction was that several major Japanese parts manufacturers, such as Mitsubishi Electric Automotive America, had also already established a presence in Ohio and nearby states, with the intention of serving the Detroit Big 3 assembly plants that were increasingly outsourcing parts production. Yet the Midwest location was still some distance from northern automotive production centers, as "Honda and Nissan were particularly concerned about the quality of North American workers […]. In order to avoid areas with traditions of labor union organization they sought rural greenfield sites" (Mair et al. 1988:366). Hence, the site filled the parameters of supplier proximity and union-distance, fitting the rural-ish pattern of later plant locations of being in a rural area that is relatively near to a major city (Columbus and Dayton) as well as two interstates and an airport. Honda was thus both a follower and a leader in automotive assembly transplants.

Nissan, Smyrna, TN, 1980

Nissan's site consideration was somewhat different than Honda. "More strongly than Honda, Nissan sought a location distant enough from the established centers of American auto production (and the UAW) to allow it to create its own company-specific production system and workforce environment" (Hülsemann 2001:228). Indeed, Nissan by most accounts had a very strong anti-union attitude, even preferring non-union construction workers to build the plant. Thus, the South was the primary region Nissan investigated for a plant, both because the local LCR was strongly anti-union and because, as Hülsemann notes, "as recently as the 1970s there had been little change [...in the] relative absence of [auto] manufacturing centers in the southeast" (2001:219). Automotive manufacturing had not been *wholly* absent from the South: G.M. and Ford both located branch plants and parts production in southern cities around the turn of the century, and some locations were refurbished (or torn down and rebuilt) after WWII. G.M. located in "Georgia, Alabama, Mississippi, and Louisiana, ... chiefly made electrical components, requiring rather low-skilled labor" (Hülsemann 2001:226; see also Rubenstein 1992:125). The Detroit 3 assembly plants located in the South (and other regions outside of the Northern central manufacturing belt) were what are known as *knock-down* plants which are "assembly platforms at the lower end of a product cycle, whose employees do little more than build knocked-down kits of components" (Mair et al. 1988:359). The development of these plants was primarily intended to mitigate shipping costs of fully constructed products (Rubenstein 1992). Thus, these domestic plant locations never developed into automotive manufacturing centers that the foreign plants and Saturn ultimately did (Hülsemann 2001:219; Mair et al. 1988:359–360), and what pockets of unionization did exist were primarily seen as places to *avoid* when foreign automakers were choosing locations (Hülsemann 2001; McDermott 2011, 2012).

Labor control, then, was a key factor in Nissan's choice of Smyrna, Tennessee in 1980 over contending sites in Georgia, reflecting the fact that "no *large* auto industry employer operated in the state. Thus the UAW... had no sizeable local organizations in Tennessee (as it did in Georgia with the Ford and G.M. plants)" (Hülsemann 2001:229).[9] At the same time, like Honda, Nissan did initially intend to build using some American suppliers and encountered similar issues, as American parts were "rejected at least twice as often as Japanese companies'" (Gelsanliter 1990:57). There are other interesting parallels with Honda here too, including the fact that "Honda and Nissan...long had been faced with very difficult competition in a Japanese market dominated by Toyota. The eventual establishment of North American production facilities represented a competitive strategy designed to circumvent Toyota and take advantage of the relative stagnation of the North American Fordist production system" (Mair et al. 1988:355).

The plant was also exploratory, "like Honda's motorcycle plant, the Smyrna plant was viewed as experimental, with the initial products to be pick-up trucks...[which] was seen as less risky" (Mair et al. 1988:356).

It's worth noting that in the early 1980s there was little competitive recruitment of Japanese auto firms, as "in the late 1970s and early 1980s, Japanese companies had not yet adjusted to American-style press conferences and were still not sure that building plants in the United States was a good idea" (Rubenstein 1992:210). At this earlier point, the rabid competition for automotive FDI had not kicked into high gear and the process of location consideration was not highly publicized; hence the subsidies to recruit Honda and Nissan were relatively small relative to both the size of the overall investment by the firms themselves and to the ever-increasing incentive packages offered after the recruitment Saturn and Toyota in 1985. The comparison to Toyota is interesting because Honda and Nissan arguably give us an (albeit brief) glimpse of the locational specifications that were decisive *before* companies began exploiting their own recruitment by opening up the incentive bidding process kicked off in 1985 (Rubenstein 1992:228–229). And it is clear from this comparison that aside from transportation considerations (proximity to rail and interstate systems), and a small consideration of existing supplier bases, distance from the U.S. auto core – and its highly militant unions – was a decisive factor for firms who wished to establish their own local labor control regimes and production bases in the United States. In other words, industrial recruitment packages are not the primary specification in locational considerations, rather industrial histories and class relations are crucial.

Saturn, Spring Hill, TN, 1985

The next plant sited and built in the United States came in early 1985, when GM decided to build its new Saturn plant in Spring Hill, Tennessee. Saturn is the only non-foreign owned automotive greenfield plant located in the United States by the Detroit 3 after 1980 (Hülsemann 2001; Klier and Rubenstein 2010; Rubenstein 1992). The Saturn company was formed by General Motors, "and was to be America's answer to Japanese imports...[and] aimed at beating Japanese cost and quality" (Gelsanliter 1990:77). The choice of location in the South had to do with a number of factors. When "GM formed the Saturn Corporation and officially sought a US location for a new production facility [in January of 1985]...38 states made direct appeals to GM, making Saturn one of the most sought after investments in industrial history" (Milward and Newman 1989:214–216). While Nissan had also made a public announcement, the Saturn plant location was much more publicized and openly competitive than previous plant locations. While part of Saturn's decision involved consideration of the recruitment efforts of the final two states competing for the plant, Kentucky and Tennessee, there was a broader strategy involved for the firm. On the one hand, in an attempt to approximate

Japanese style labor relations, the plant was unionized through an agreement with the UAW that stipulated that "first preference in hiring would go to UAW members laid off elsewhere. The UAW, in return, had agreed to eliminate most job classifications and work rules" (Gelsanliter 1990:77). Given the anti-union sentiment in Tennessee, the company ended up bringing most employees from outside the state through this arrangement (Hülsemann 2001:230). Moreover, the UAW "urged Saturn to source parts from existing GM-owned, UAW-organized suppliers. While Saturn could have relied more easily on a local supplier based that had grown because of business from Nissan...in many cases it ended up contracting with suppliers from GM's parts plants network. Thus, Saturn's supply lines are much longer than those of Nissan, with many of its supplier partners...located in the Midwest and Great Lakes area" (Hülsemann 2001:232). The attempt to compete with the JIT system meant the Saturn plant in Tennessee had to develop an extremely sophisticated parts and supplier management system. Also, unlike earlier knock-down plants located in the South, the Saturn facility was a very highly integrated one with many parts manufactured on site.

The location was also strategic in another sense, as the company "located 30 miles Southwest of Smyrna, in part so that Nissan would be less able to resist union organizing pressures" (Gelsanliter 1990:77). Hülsemann suggests that GM saw "Tennessee [as a] 'level playing field' [as it was pitched by then governor Lamar Alexander] which would allow GM's Saturn to go head to head with the largest Japanese-owned plant. Competing directly with the Japanese exactly matched GM's conception of Saturn" (2001:230). Thus, the choice of Tennessee was part of GM's overall attempt to restructure and force American unionization on Japanese plants. The effort met with limited success for the company, "almost as soon as GM announced its [Saturn] plans, it began to scale back" (Gelsanliter 1990:77) and the planned expansion of that plant never materialized, nor did Nissan acquiesced to unionization pressures.[10] Given that neither GM nor any other of the Detroit 3 constructed a major assembly plant in the United States after Saturn, the Tennessee plant is best seen as a last-ditch effort to restructure within the United States before pursuing other locational strategies such as Maquiladoras just across the Mexican border.

I address the Toyota (1985) case more later in this chapter and the next, but put simply they followed the lead of both Nissan and Saturn, following Nissan into the southern labor climate and exploiting the new competitive landscape opened up by Saturn. Indeed, the competition for Toyota is a critical case, which is why it reserved for the discussion in the next chapter which focuses on recruitment efforts themselves.

U.S. transplant locational decisions part II: Das Auto Y'all

The 1990s saw three major foreign-owned consumer auto assembly plants built in the United States – all in the South. Indeed, the southern drift of auto manufacturing agglomeration after the 1980s is quite distinct, as can be seen in Figure 3.1 (see also Hülsemann 2001; Klier and Rubenstein 2010; McDermott 2012; McDermott et al. 2011). Of these plants, German firms built two (Mercedes-Benz and BMW) and Japanese built one (Honda).

The German automakers faced very different structural pressures coming out of the late 1970s recession than did the Japanese (McDermott 2012:16). While not as Fordist as Ford and the Detroit 3, West German automakers suffered many of the same rigidities as the U.S. manufacturers in their production processes and production relations (Kwon 2004:40–41). Hence, with the crisis of the 1970s, the German automakers suffered a major decline in their U.S. sales (Beaver 1992; McDermott 2011, 2013), as their price competitiveness declined relative to Japanese competition. "European producers could not compete with lean systems pioneered by Toyota and suffered an efficiency deficit of 30 percent compared to their Japanese rivals...German auto workers were the highest paid and enjoyed the shortest working week...given Germany's domestic labor relations environment it was not feasible to introduce radical changes in manufacturing processes at plants in Germany" (McDermott 2011:78). I already mentioned in passing that (West) German industrial relations were organized in a much more corporatist or "neocorporatist" fashion (Gough 2014:199; Hicks and Kenworthy 1998). This meant that negotiations between capital and labor typically took place through peak associations (business and union organizations)[11] usually with the government coordinating these relations (c.f. table 3 in Hicks and Kenworthy 1998). In some instances, this high degree of institutionalization or "politicization" of class conflict can have the effect of mitigating or smoothing over what might otherwise be contentious and disruptive class conflicts. However, in the case of an automotive industry that needed to radically restructure its production processes and relations (both within and between [supplier] firms) to remain competitive, these organizational structures limited the ability of German firms to respond to market pressures and the crisis of 1970s–1980s (much the same problem arose in the United States). German firms that transplanted in the 1990s also shared with the Japanese concerns over currency exchange fluctuations following the abandonment of Bretton Woods. "The sharp depreciation of the U.S. dollar against the Deutschmark took its toll on German Exporters...BMW's US sales plummeted...in the mid-1980s" (McDermott 2011:77). Thus, for the German firms it was not their fast-rising status that opened locational opportunities for them, but rather the need to radically restructure due to market *loss* to Japanese competition.

BMW, Anderson, SC, 1992

When BMW chose to locate its plant in Anderson, South Carolina, in 1992 it was the first non-Japanese auto firm to locate in the southeast besides Saturn and at the time the South Carolina location it chose was far-removed from other automakers who had plants in the region. As discussed, the decision to locate in South Carolina (and to produce outside of Germany) was influenced by the desire to restructure as a way to circumvent labor: "By late 1991, BMW decided that a radical change was required...it recognized that success required a radical departure from BMW's traditions. It had to forge a new culture, a new mentality" (McDermott 2011:78–79). Part of this desire to restructure and become more competitive meant a "preference" for non-union labor was a distinct concern (McDermott 2011:85). Another goal was to gain greater propinquity to their American market, though at the time BMW was not sure what role the plant would play in its overall global strategy – that is, whether it would be primarily geared toward domestic U.S. production or a broader global strategy. BMW approached the Chicago-based firm PHH Fantus as its primary site consultant on the project, and the firm initially presented them with 215 possible sites. By early 1992, this had been narrowed to four potential sites in the United States: Anderson, South Carolina; Omaha, Nebraska; Phoenix, Arizona, and Tulsa, Oklahoma (McDermott 2011:84–85; Monk 1992). While McDermott suggests that BMW was "discrete about its site selection process...[and] did not encourage competitive bidding" (2011:89–90) the site search had leaked out in the media and encouraged a good amount of speculation. By this point in the selection process, executives had already decided they wanted the U.S. plant to be a globally oriented export platform. "As soon as BMW was clear on its preference in terms of the plants' [export platform] role, South Carolina was the preferred location. However, as long as Nebraska was regarded as a viable contender, it increased BMW's bargaining position with South Carolina" (McDermott 2011:86). This last point is an important distinction between the initial orientation of Japanese and German auto firms, given that the former intended their plants to produce primarily for the American consumer market, while the latter intended for their plants to produce for markets beyond the United States. For BMW, proximity to coastal ports was a key locational specification, and an expansion of the Spartanburg airport an important inclusion in the incentives offered by the state.

The choice of South Carolina for BMW was also informed by the attraction of agglomeration and clustering of West German investment there, which resulted from South Carolina's success in recruiting major textile firms from Northern states who had multiple West German suppliers. "By the mid-seventies...no southern state proved more successful at attracting foreign plants than South Carolina...state promoters...were proud of the fact that there was more West German industrial capital in their state than anywhere else in the world except West Germany" (Cobb 1993:189). As McDermott elaborates, this concentration of West German investment only continued through the 1980s, and "by 1989 there were 86 German plants in South Carolina, and 39 of these were in Spartanburg County...thus there was a concentration of German investments or agglomeration in

Spartanburg which had the highest per capita concentration of inward investment of any county in the United States" (McDermott 2011:81). As the first major automaker from Germany to establish a plant in the United States, the West German cultural and economic concentration in South Carolina was perceived as a potentially supportive network. Local firms' knowledge of the business environment and labor control regime could quite possibly have been major factors; when BMW executives first visited potential sites in South Carolina "they spent more time talking with other German firms than with state and local officials" (Monk 1992).[12] So, like Honda in 1980, BMW was both a follower and trailblazer, choosing proximity to extant German parts manufactures as a sort of locational safety net.

Mercedes-Benz, Vance, AL, 1993

Less than a year after BMW decided on South Carolina, Daimler AG announced its intentions to locate a plant to manufacture a new Mercedes-Benz SUV in the United States in April 1993. Mercedes-Benz faced similar broad-based pressures to restructure their production processes and labor relations, and these were key strategic goals in addition to a greater desire for U.S. market proximity (McDermott 2013:59–62). "After Germany, The United States was by far its largest market and it faced a growing threat from recent new entrants…such as the Japanese. Building in the United States afforded…[an opportunity] to introduce a cultural revolution within the company. The South offered locational advantages for competitively serving the domestic [US] and international markets." (McDermott 2013:71). From the outset, "Mercedes wanted the ability to export to Europe…[so] it needed ready access, at low cost, to eastern ports. Proximity to the east coast was 'very, very important'" (McDermott 2013:63). Mercedes hired the consulting firm Global Location Services and despite a clear East Coast locational preference, the firm began with 150 potential locations (Boudreaux et al., 2012:39) which were then reduced to 19 states who were sent lengthily questionnaires and asked to submit suitable potential sites. Rather quickly, the potential sites were narrowed to locations in Alabama, Georgia, Nebraska, North Carolina, South Carolina, and Tennessee; then the competition narrowed to Merbane, North Carolina; Summerville, South Carolina, and Vance, Alabama (near Tuscaloosa). While I discuss the details of the recruitment itself in the following chapter, one new consideration for Mercedes-Benz was the proximity to its West German competitor. One site selection professional I spoke to told me "I worked very close [*sic*] to the consultants who were with Mercedes and in the end, one of the most important final decisions for Mercedes was – what we had suspected in South Carolina at the beginning – [...] they did not want to follow BMW and they didn't want the world to see them following BMW… in the end that was a major part of the decision" (SEL02 2016). Ultimately,

Mercedes decided on a site near Tuscaloosa, Alabama that provided the desired proximity to the East coast as well as the distance from a perceived rival in BMW (McDermott 2013:63–64); "unlike BMW, agglomeration was not an important factor in the Mercedes decision" (McDermott 2013:57). The large incentives package offered by the state of Alabama was an added benefit, and the labor control regime was a necessity for their plans to restructure.

Into the 2000s: Korean manufacturers and agglomeration effects

After Mercedes-Benz opened its plant in Alabama in the early 90s there were no new consumer AAPs opened in the southeast (or anywhere else) in the United States until 1999. Much of the Western world and Japan were in recession (the 1990s is often referred to as the "lost decade" in Japan, despite the surge in excellent films being produced at the time). At the same time, economies in a number of smaller East-Asian countries began to thrive, including that of South Korea (Evans 1995); these so-called "Asian Tiger" economies briefly challenged the neoliberal orthodoxy in economic theory before they too fell into recession in 1997, with South Korea hit the hardest.[13] The 1990s also intensified capital flight from many southern states, particularly in the textile and furniture industries previously dominant there, industries whose low-skill labor requirements could be more profitably taken advantage of in China and other semiperipheral countries (Jacobs 2012:201–205).

The next round of automotive FDI in the South begin in 1999 when Honda announced it was going to invest $450 million to open an assembly plant in the small town of Lincoln, Alabama. Between 1999 and 2008 five more foreign-owned automotive assembly plants would be announced in the South, and one in the Midwest. These third round of assembly plants were primarily Japanese producers already in the country, again seeking to meet growing domestic demand, with two South Korean firms (actually a joint-owned company) and a new German firm (Volkswagen) opening plants as well. The longest gap between the announcement of plant locations after 1999 was four years. As Japanese production was largely following the agglomeration of plants and suppliers already located in the South, I spend more time considering these last three cases.

Hyundai, Montgomery, AL (2002) and Kia, West Point, GA (2006)

The South Korean firms had many of the same goals and faced similar pressures as Japanese firms in locating plants in the United States, but faced a different set of difficulties. In fact, Hyundai, Kia, and the German Volkswagen all located plants in the United States in part to circumvent ever-fluctuating exchange rates, and all three corporations were, like the

Japanese, intending to produce primarily for the U.S. or North American market (McDermott 2012; Seetharaman 2011). Also, like both German and Japanese automakers (respectively) "South Korean plants saw their competitiveness erode due to rising labor costs, and the appreciation of the Won" (McDermott 2012:14). The Korean automakers also had their own distinct challenges in the global automotive market; they were not nearly as large or as old as the more mature German and Japanese automotive industries – indeed, Hyundai and Kia between them make up the bulk of South Korean automotive production. The firms also struggled with quality perception issues, especially in the United States (McDermott 2012:14–15).

McDermott (2012:14–15) and Chung (2009:5) both suggest that quality and productivity issues were what doomed Hyundai's first attempt at locating a plant in North America, which was built in Bromont, Quebec in Canada in 1989. There are some interesting parallels here with Volkswagen, who had also opened a plant in the late 1970s in Pennsylvania, and that plant also closed due to competitiveness and quality issues. In both cases, low productivity still produced excess capacity as quality (and design for VW) issues stultified demand (Beaver 1992; McDermott 2012). The Bromont plant closed just four years after it opened in 1993, while the VW plant lasted longer, closing in 1987. I discuss the failed VW plant in more detail later.

Global economic changes pushed Hyundai to again look to American production. As McDermott elaborates "a sharp depreciation of the Won in 1997 due to the Asian economic crisis restored cost competitiveness of Korean auto exports...however, the company's brand image [of poor quality] remained a major barrier...in 1998 exports to the United States amounted to just 90,217." Hyundai still managed to acquire Kia that year, and as the century turned over they managed to turn around their quality/ image issues such that by 2001 exports to the United States had risen to 350,000 (McDermott 2012:15). Interestingly, at this point in the early 2000s, the U.S. government began to express similar concerns over trade deficits with Korea as they did with Japan 20 years earlier. Such export limitation pressures had a similar effect on the Koreans, and Hyundai chose to build a plant in Montgomery, Alabama in 2002, with its sister company Kia following up with a plant just across the Georgia border in 2006.

In the decade of the 2000s, a clear pattern of agglomeration of automotive manufacturing took place in the South, a pattern solidified by the further location of three Japanese companies who already had assembly plants and supplier networks in the region as well as the new South Korean manufacturers. While Kia and Hyundai were fast-rising within the auto industry, the failure of Hyundai's 1989 plant in Canada and the postponement of their next plant until 2002 is indicative of the fact that they did not have the same size and strength as Japanese and German firms. Hence, in addition to the locational windows opened by their rapid growth, the Korean firms were also drawn to the South in part by the advantages gained from extant networks of suppliers and, more importantly, the learned knowledges and relationships that come with experience and history with an industry. The smaller Korean firms had more to gain from technology and process-knowledge spillovers from their rivals, hence when Hyundai located in Alabama in 2002 it chose a state that already had two foreign-owned AAPs up and running, and Kia located very close to the Alabama border, drawing on the established Korean supplier network (Jacobs 2012:212; McDermott 2012:18–19, 25). Kia, like Mercedes-Benz, also did not want to be seen as following its predecessor. As one official who worked on recruiting Kia told me, "they wanted that site because it was on the edge of Alabama but it wasn't *in* Alabama…they wanted Hyundai to have the Alabama identification, but they wanted one of the surrounding states… but they also wanted to be close to where there were existing suppliers" (EDP03 2015).

There is less extensive research on the plants established throughout the mid to late 2000s, likely because except for Volkswagen all were new plants constructed by manufacturers already in the South or Midwest, and thus much of the same regional considerations and locational specifications apply. McDermott et al. (2011) suggest that these plants were also intended to target primarily the American market. Volkswagen was likely concerned with keeping pace in the American market with its German competitors, and according to one official who recruited the carmaker to Tennessee, well before the official search economic development officials "kept hearing that Volkswagen was thinking about a US manufacturing site, a greenfield US manufacturing site" (EDP06 2016). I discuss the recruitment of Volkswagen in greater detail in the following chapter, but it is fair to say that by the late 2000s agglomeration effects constituted the strongest locational consideration for incoming firms, in addition to the locational specifications (especially labor control) that were important in the detailed cases discussed above, and recruitment efforts detailed in the next chapter.

Peripheral cases: brownfields, joint-ventures, and a curious failure

Volkswagen missteps, and a GM windfall

For the myriad reasons (discussed in chapter 1) concerning locational factors I largely exclude brownfield – or existing industrial sites – and joint ventures from my analysis because they exceed comparative parameters, but I will briefly discuss them here. If one were to refer back to Table 1.1 in the first chapter, they might note that Honda was not the first foreign automaker to attempt a transplant in the United States. That distinction lies with Volkswagen, who crossed the Atlantic in 1978 and located a new plant in Westmoreland, Pennsylvania, in an "unfinished Chrysler plant 35 miles south of Pittsburgh" (Beaver 1992:21). The plant was beset with problems from the start and ultimately closed just as the Japanese boom of the 1980s was in full swing in 1987, but the process of siting and recruiting the plant is strikingly similar to the pattern of the 1980s. Pressures on the company were similar to other German and Japanese manufactures: there was "fear of a wave of protectionist legislation," issues with currency fluctuation, and "the rise of the deutsche mark, along with the higher costs of production in Germany, made Volkswagens increasingly expensive in the United States," and as with American and other German manufacturers "Japanese were beginning to offer cars that were judged to be higher quality...and at a lower price" (Beaver 1992:19). Upon the announcement in 1976, "a bidding war began in which incentive packages were offered by different states with hopes of landing the assembly plant. The *Wall Street Journal* called it 'the greatest industrial courtship of all time'" (Beaver 1992:21). The WSJ superlatives, one might note, are strikingly similar to what was said of GM's Saturn a decade later. And like later recruitment and site selection efforts, the company examined five sites, and narrowed it ultimately to Westmoreland, and was offered $63 million dollars in incentives.

Other aspects of the VW case are quite distinct. VW did not attempt to alter labor relations, as one official noted "our philosophy is to bend and adjust to the American system" (*quoted in* Beaver 1992:21). Quality issues and labor disputes were common in Westmoreland, with one worker (ironically perhaps?) quoted as saying of the moderately lower wages VW offered "if VW thought they could pay slave wages they should have gone south" (*quoted in* Beaver 1992:22). What is interesting is that there is very little mentioned of the plant in the development or business literature (academic or professional publications), or geographical analyses concerning the geographical impact or effects on economic development. As we will see, this absence is not so much a failure of collective memory, but reflective of the fact that the field of professionals who would refer to the case was germinal – but auto manufacturers certainly took note. Gelsanliter observes that Japanese firms were alarmed at the failure, as "Volkswagen was much admired by Japanese...the fact...that Volkswagen...could establish a major American manufacturing presence, build cars here for nine years...and then fail had given the Japanese much cause for concern" (1990:141). The tentative nature of the Japanese expansion into the United States – through the experimental plants mentioned earlier and joint-ventures with U.S. manufacturers in the mid-1980s – was in part influenced by reflection on the VW misstep. It may also have pushed Japanese and German manufacturers to have an even stronger anti-union attitude, given that some of the problems of the Westmoreland plant were chalked up to difficulties with labor, along with quality and design issues (Beaver 1992). The ultimate failure of the plant itself, arguably, arose from the fact that the firm was *not* adapting to competitive pressures of the neoliberal age, and established a Fordist plant at the crux of Fordism's decline.

Another important brownfield plant location is that of the GM Hamtramck, MI, plant in 1980. This plant was sited in an old dodge plant in a suburb of Detroit, and the time of its construction came at a time when the

Detroit metro area lost nearly 50,000 jobs to structural crisis (Luger 2000:109; Rubenstein 1992:204). Due to these conditions, city officials went to extraordinary lengths to incentivize GM to choose the Hamtramck site – which was too small for their plans – including massive incentives, site purchase, and most importantly the forcible eviction of many residents of the Poletown neighborhood. Rubenstein elaborates, "in order to present GM with a cleared parcel of land, complete with utilities, roads, and rail sidings, the two cities [of Detroit and Hamtramck] had to acquire 1,675 structures and relocate 150 business and 1,500 households" (1992:205). The uprooted residents would take the city to court to fight their eviction, ultimately losing in the state Supreme Court.

It is not surprising that the location of the GM plan near Detroit does not fit the geographical pattern of the foreign manufacturers, as the incentives to remain were large and the factors keeping the company in the rust belt are the same ones, which drove foreign auto firms south. What is of interest is the extraordinary lengths the locality went through to secure the sight, and the case as an early example of local development goals manifestly conflicting with the interests of local constituents, both topics I explore in later chapters (4 and 6, respectively).

Joint ventures

The three joint venture plants established in the mid-1980s follow a very different pattern than single-ownership plants. Unlike the rural-ish pattern of locations for single-ownership plants, the joint ventures "have located plants in metropolitan areas with strong traditions of labor union activism" (Mair et al. 1988:367) and Mair et al. suggest that the U.S. partners pushed for the use of union labor. Finally, all joint venture plants located in areas that had previous production facilities located by the Detroit Big 3, which is unsurprising given the joint nature of the enterprises. While the spree joint venture assembly plants established in the mid-1980s fall well outside the southeastern trend of later decades, the plants did play an important role in those later decisions. Of particular importance is the New United Motors Manufacturing Incorporated (NUMMI) joint venture announced in 1984 between Toyota, the largest of the Japanese manufacturers, and General Motors. For Toyota, NUMMI was an exploratory venture, taken to ensure that they could successfully establish Japanese work relations and to test the waters with indigenous suppliers and JIT methods (Gelsanliter 1990; Mair et al. 1988). The plant itself was completely refurbished to resemble Toyota's Takata plant and was by most accounts quite successful, only shuttering in 2010. At that time, the emergent electronic automotive company Tesla bought the plant for $40 million, making it also a brownfield location. That company has a number of different specifications given the novel nature of its technology and production techniques, so it too exceeds the parameters of this analysis – though the ever-present struggle with labor has reared its head there, too.

All of the joint ventures were eventually unionized by the UAW, but Japanese firms usually controlled factory management and blended U.S.- and Japanese-style labor relations. Yet it is also telling that Toyota built three more plants in the United States and all were located in the southeast, indicating that locating *outside* the South was largely a result of the joint-venture status of the NUMMI plant and GM's influence. The other joint ventures, Mazda-Ford and Mitsubishi-Chrysler (Diamond-Star Motors) followed from the smaller size of the Japanese firms who had "trouble projecting the...annual sales needed in North America to justify construction of an assembly plant" (Rubenstein 1992:164). Mazda "openly, if apprehensively, welcomed UAW organizing...[though] the firm was apparently pressured to recognize the UAW by Ford...to 'level the competitive playing field'" (Mair et al. 1988:367). Ford owned a 25% stake in Mazda, and the site ultimately chosen was a former Ford plant, and the two firms shared production knowledge in their venture. Diamond-Star follows a similar pattern, where the U.S. partner-owned 25% of Mitsubishi, though unlike the Mazda joint venture Diamond-Star was more of a tentative stepping stone for Mitsubishi, which took full stakes in the plant in 1991.

The Fuji–Isuzu plant announced in Indiana in 1986 was also a joint venture, though between two Japanese manufacturers (Pastor 1986). There is very little research into the location process of this plant, though like previous Japanese transplants the two firms were looking to expand their position in the American market (Milward and Newman 1989:218), but it is unclear if there was similar pressure to unionize the plant (almost 40% of Isuzu stock was owned by GM) or if the plant is unionized. Certainly, Indiana was an aggressive recruiter which may have been a deciding factor, as I discuss in the following chapter.

Texas trucks

The Texas pickup truck factory Toyota established near San Antonio in 2003, while falling within all of the parameters of the comparative criteria for this study, is tied more directly to Toyota's contingent of parts-suppliers in Mexico and the large consumer base for pickup trucks in the Texas region. Thus, while technically within the former confederate South, agglomeration effects in the southeastern automotive core are not as critical as the Texas market and proximity to agglomeration in Mexico (Lyne 2003).

A few generalizations

The major shifts that began in the global economy after World War II led to a major restructuring of the global automotive industry in the late 1970s and early 1980s, in which carmakers in Japan began to overshadow Western automakers. This competition opened up windows of locational opportunities for car manufacturers in Japan and Western Germany, the former due to their rapid industrial growth, for the latter due to the need for radical restructuring. While German firms began locating some of their plants in Mexico and the United States, the Big 3 automakers in the United States closed myriad plants and opened no new solo ventures in America, including the closures of plants in Georgia in Atlanta (2006) and Doraville (2008) (Jacobs 2012; Klier and Rubenstein 2010).

The plants built in the 1990s by Mercedes-Benz and BMW were from their outset intended to service both the U.S. and global markets, and today Mercedes exports around 60% of its total product, BMW around 70% (McDermott 2011, 2013). The different strategic role of the plants for these firms stems from the constellation of forces that informed their decisions to produce in the United States. In other words, locations in the United States (and elsewhere) were as much about getting *out* of Germany and re-structuring their organizations, as they were about getting closer to the U.S. market (Miller notes that the German firms did not face the same export limitations that Asian firms did (1997:47)). For Volkswagen, in 2008, the goal seems to have been primarily to locate closer to the U.S. market and to cut labor costs (Ramsey 2011; Seetharaman 2011). The Japanese expansions through the 2000s all were directed toward meeting the demand of the North American market (primarily the United States), though Toyota has begun to shift some of its production towards exports (McDermott et al. 2011). Volvo's recent selection of the port city of Charleston, SC, in 2015 suggests an export orientation, but may also reflect a desire to import parts. Indeed, some authors have speculated that the comparatively low investment in the Volvo plant (around $250 million) suggests it will be a knock-down plant.

In this chapter, I have focused primarily on the locational considerations of particular firms in the context of the pressures they faced due to national origin, size, and competitiveness within national and global markets. One clear theme that is consistent across most cases is the centrality of class conflict, though at times it is submerged beneath the instrumental language of business and quality labor inputs. For all the firms, even when locating outside the South, labor and labor control are crucial concerns in locational decisions.

I have deliberately avoided in-depth discussion of the recruitment process itself or incentives because I wanted to clarify that incentives, while part of the focus of this study, are not the crucial factors leading to locational considerations. As should be clear from the earlier-mentioned accounts, there are numerous factors beyond recruitment that led companies to locate where they chose to in the United States. This makes the competitive es-calation of recruitment efforts all the more problematic given the refrain of capital mobility offered by development officials. In the next chapter, I cover the process of recruiting automotive firms and constructing incentives agreements in detail and discuss how they have changed since Honda started building motorcycles in Ohio in 1978. This will show the other side of this location process, the highly competitive recruitment efforts among localities for automotive assembly plants. And as we will see, along with the various strategies of automotive producers, localities themselves are key actors in the growth of competitive efforts.

Notes

1 Arguably this is because the penetration of the Auto industry into U.S. government and policy formation, and the relative privileging of auto-workers which derives therefrom (Luger 2000; Rubinson and Sokolovsky 1988) created something similar to the corporatist arrangements in Germany, albeit in a more concentrated fashion.

2 The fiasco in the United States over e-cigarettes and vaping technology is emblematic here: major producers of these technology became billion-dollar companies before vaping-related illness and deaths stoked efforts to regulate.

3 While the quality of a commodity is difficult to analyze systematically, there was a general consensus in the early 1980s that Japanese cars were among the best made (Hunker 1983:80–81; Rubenstein 1992:165–170) while some U.S. cars, such as the Buick Lesabre, were rated among the worst (at least in the U.S. consumer markets) (Rubenstein 1992:165).

4 The development of "just-in-time" delivery was also a product of revolutions in the means of production that emerged from the 1970s crisis, particularly the new reliance upon microprocessors. The development of computers and information and communications more broadly were critical for the just-in-time system to work (Teeple 2000:65–71). Even producers who had long supplier chains, such as Saturn, could only do so because of computer coordination.

5 This two-pronged campaign is a perfect example U.S. industrial relations described in the previous chapter. That is, a segment of capital and the segment of labor form a kind of mini-corporatist relationship and attempt to influence the state thusly. It is also indicative of how this industry was not, thereby, shielded from the competitive pressures of the market.

6 Rubenstein (1992) has unquestionably provided the most systematic geographical overview of the geography and locations of the U.S. automotive industry.

7 For Nissan, in the 1980, proximity to extant supplier bases was not a major locational specification but rather "regarded having regionally near suppliers as advantageous should it begin looking for more US content" (Hülsemann 2001:228).

8 In the comparative development literature this sort of employment organization, characterized by "coordination among groups of companies across industries [typical] in Japan and Korea…[is categorized as] group-coordinated market economies" (Huber and Stephens 2005:612).

9 A later attempt by UAW to organize the plant in 1989 was "bitterly defeated" and marked the end of attempts to organize workers in the South until the Volkswagen plant in 2013 (Hülsemann 2001:229).

10 Bartik et al.'s research suggest that the "unique work environment" of Tennessee may have been important here – suggesting perhaps that the southern labor control regime had an effect on the UAW workers imported to Spring Hill (1987:32–33).

11 *Peak associations* essentially refers to large conglomerations of business or labor actors. So, business associations like ALEC or large union conglomerates like IG Metall in Germany would be examples of peak associations.

12 Several major German auto parts manufacturers had already located in South Carolina, such as "Michelin Tire Corporation [which] chose Greenville, South Carolina as the site for its first American plant because, with only 2 percent of its

work force organized, the South Carolina Piedmont seemed the safest possible refuge from the United Rubber Workers [union]" (Cobb 1993:191)

13 Orthodox economists proclaimed the successes of the Asian Tigers until the 1997 crisis. It seems such economists have an existential incapacity to perceive the cyclical nature of capitalist accumulation. Nonetheless, state involvement in the South Korean economy remains comparatively high to this day.

Bibliography

Bartik, Timothy J., Charles Becker, Steve Lake, and John Bush. 1987. "Saturn and State Economic Development." *Forum for Applied Research and Public Policy* 2(1 (Spring)):29–40.

Beaver, William. 1992. "Volkswagen's American Assembly Plant: Fahrvergnugen Was Not Enough." *Business Horizons* 35(6):19–26. doi: 10.1016/0007-6813(92)90096-R.

Boudreaux, Christopher, R. Morris Coats, and Earl H. Davis. 2012. "The Dark Side of State Competition for Foreign Direct Investment: That Which Is Seen and That Which Is Not Seen." *Southern Business & Economic Journal* 35(1):35–52.

Burawoy, Michael. 1985. *The Politics of Production: Factory Regimes Under Capitalism and Socialism.* London: Verso.

Cai, Hongbin, and Daniel Treisman. 2006. "Did Government Decentralization Cause China's Economic Miracle?" *World Politics* 58(04):505–535.

Chung, Myeong-Kee. 2009. "Globalization Strategies of Korean Motor Vehicle Industry: A Case Study of Hyundai."

Cobb, James C. 1993. *The Selling of the South: The Southern Crusade for Industrial Development 1936-1990*, 2nd edition. Urbana: University of Illinois Press.

Cox, Kevin R. 1995. "Globalisation, Competition and the Politics of Local Economic Development." *Urban Studies (Routledge)* 32(2):213–224.

Cox, Kevin R. 2010. "The Problem of Metropolitan Governance and the Politics of Scale." *Regional Studies* 44(2):215–227. doi: 10.1080/00343400903365128.

Dobbin, Frank. 1994. *Forging Industrial Policy: The United States, Britain, and France in the Railway Age.* Cambridge England; New York, NY, USA: Cambridge University Press.

EDP03. 2015. "Economic Development Professional 03."

EDP06. 2016. "Economic Development Professional 06."

Evans, Peter B. 1995. *Embedded Autonomy: States and Industrial Transformation.* Princeton, NJ: Princeton University Press.

Gelsanliter, David. 1990. *Jump Start: Japan Comes to the Heartland.* New York: Farrar Straus Giroux.

Gough, Jamie. 2003. *Work, Locality and the Rhythms of Capital: The Labour Process Reconsidered.* London; New York: Continuum.

Gough, Jamie. 2012. "Capital Accumulation in Space, Capital-Labour Relations, and Political Strategy." Pp. 89–112 in *Territory, the State, and Urban Politics*, edited by A. E. G. Jonas and A. Wood. Surrey: Ashgate.

Gough, Jamie. 2014. "The Difference between Local and National Capitalism, and Why Local Capitalisms Differ from One Another: A Marxist Approach." *Capital & Class* 38(1):197–210. doi: 10.1177/0309816813514211.

Hall, Peter A., and David W. Soskice. 2001. *Varieties of Capitalism: The Institutional Foundations of Comparative Advantage.* Oxford England; New York: Oxford University Press.

Hancké, Bob, Martin Rhodes, and Mark Thatcher. 2007. *Beyond Varieties of Capitalism: Conflict, Contradiction, and Complementarities in the European Economy*. Oxford; New York: Oxford University Press.

Harvey, David. 1982. *The Limits to Capital*. Chicago: University of Chicago Press.

Harvey, David. 1989. *The Condition of Postmodernity: An Enquiry into the Origins of Cultural Change*. Oxford: Blackwell.

Heaton, Herbert. 1948. *Economic History of Europe*. Rev. ed. New York: Harper.

Hicks, Alexander, and Lane Kenworthy. 1998. "Cooperation and Political Economic Performance in Affluent Democratic Capitalism." *American Journal of Sociology* 103(6):1631–1672. doi: 10.1086/231403.

Huber, Evelyne, and John D. Stephens. 2005. "State Economic and Social Policy in Global Capitalism." Pp. 607–629 in *The Handbook of Political Sociology: States, Civil Societies, and Globlization*, edited by T. Janoski, R. Alford, A. M. Hicks, and M. A. Schwartz. Cambridge: Cambridge University Press.

Hülsemann, Karsten. 2001. "Greenfields in the Heart of Dixie: How the American Auto Industry Discovered the South." Pp. 219–254 in *The Second Wave: Southern Industrialization from the 1940s to the 1970s*, edited by P. Scranton. Athens, GA: University of Gerogia Press.

Hunker, Jeffrey Allen. 1983. *Structural Change in the U.S. Automobile Industry*. Lexington, Mass: Lexington Books.

Jacobs, A. J. 2012. "Collaborative Regionalism and Foreign Direct Investment The Case of the Southeast Automotive Core and the 'New Domestics.'" *Economic Development Quarterly* 26(3):199–219.

Jonas, Andrew E. G. 1996. "Local Labour Control Regimes: Uneven Development and the Social Regulation of Production." *Regional Studies* 30(4):323–338. doi: 10.1080/00343409612331349688.

Jonas, Andrew E. G. 2009. "Labor Control Regime." Pp. 59–65 in *International Encyclopedia of Human Geography,*, Vol. 6, edited by R. Kitchin and N. Thrift. Oxford: Elsevier.

Kim, Choong Soon. 1995. *Japanese Industry in the American South*. New York, NY: Routledge.

Klier, Thomas H., and James M. Rubenstein. 2010. "The Changing Geography of North American Motor Vehicle Production." *Cambridge Journal of Regions, Economy and Society* 3:335–347. doi: 10.1093/cjres/rsq024.

Kwon, Hyeong-ki. 2004. *Fairness and Division of Labor in Market Societies: A Comparison of the U.S. and German Automotive Industries*. New York: Berghahn Books.

Lancaster, T., and Alexander M. Hicks. 2000. "The Impact of Federalism and Neo-Corporatism on Economic Performance." Pp. 228–242 in *Federalism and Political Performance*, Vol. 16, edited by U. Wachendorfer-Schmidt. New York; London: Routledge.

Light, Donald W., Joel Lexchin, and Jonathan J. Darrow. 2013. "Institutional Corruption of Pharmaceuticals and the Myth of Safe and Effective Drugs." *The Journal of Law, Medicine & Ethics* 41(3):590–600.

Luger, Stan. 2000. *Corporate Power, American Democracy, and the Automobile Industry*. Cambridge, UK; New York: Cambridge University Press.

Lyne, Jack. 2003. "Toyota Picks Texas for 2,000-Employee, $800M Assembly Plant." *Site Selection*, February 10.

Mair, Andrew, Richard Florida, and Martin Kenney. 1988. "The New Geography of Automobile Production: Japanese Transplants in North America." *Economic Geography* 64(4):352–373. doi: 10.2307/144233.

Mann, Michael. 1993. *The Sources of Social Power. Volume 2, The Rise of Classes and Nation States*, Vol. 2. Cambridge [U.A.]: Cambridge University Press.

McDermott, Michael C. 2011. "BMW, Spartanburg, South Carolina: Drivers and Processes in the International Plant Location Decision." *Southern Business & Economic Journal* 34(1/2):73–94.

McDermott, Michael C. 2012. "Hyundai Automotive Group's Investments in the U.S. South: Competition and Decisions." *Southern Business & Economic Journal* 35(1):11–34.

McDermott, Michael C. 2013. "Mercedes-Benz, Tuscaloosa, Alabama: Drivers and Processes in the International Plant Location Decision." *Southern Business & Economic Journal* 36(1):57–73.

McDermott, Michael C., Denise Luethge, and Philippe Byosiere. 2011. "Automotive Investment and Foreign Subsidiary Strategy in the Southern States of the United States." *Southern Business & Economic Journal* 34(3/4):1–30.

Miller, J. 1997. "The German Transplants: An Economic Comparison of Site Selections for Foreign Automakers." Honors Thesis, Emory University, Department of Economics, Atlanta, GA.

Milward, Alan S., and S. B. Saul. 1973. *The Economic Development of Continental Europe, 1780-1870*. Totowa, NJ: Rowman and Littlefield.

Milward, H. Brinton, and Heidi Hosbach Newman. 1989. "State Incentive Packages and the Industrial Location Decision." *Economic Development Quarterly* 3(3):203–222.

Monk, Fred. 1992. "BMW Courtship Long and Rocky." *The State*, June 24.

Pastor, Susan. 1986. "Fuji, Isuzu Plan U.S. Auto Plant." *New York Times, Late Edition (East Coast); New York, N.Y.*, December 3, D.1.

Peck, Jamie. 1996. *Work-Place: The Social Regulation of Labor Markets*. New York: Guilford Press.

Perrucci, Robert. 1994. *Japanese Auto Transplants in the Heartland: Corporatism and Community*. New York: Aldine de Gruyter.

Ramsey, Mike. 2011. "VW Chops Labor Costs in U.S." *Wall Street Journal*, May 23.

Rubenstein, James M. 1992. *The Changing Us Auto Industry: A Geographical Analysis*. London England; New York: Routledge.

Rubinson, Richard, and Joan Sokolovsky. 1988. "Patterns of Political Industrial Regulation: Railroads in the World Economy." Pp. 3–20 in *Rethinking the 19th Century*, edited by F. O. Ramirez. California: Greenwood Press.

Rueschemeyer, Dietrich, Evelyne Huber Stephens, and John D. Stephens. 1992. *Capitalist Development and Democracy*, 1st edition. Chicago: University Of Chicago Press.

Sail, Martin. 2001. "Politics and Economic Development: Why Governments Adopt Different Strategies to Induce Economic Growth." *Policy Studies Journal* 29(2):203–214. doi: 10.1111/j.1541-0072.2001.tb02086.x.

Seetharaman, Deepa. 2011. "Volkswagen Sees U.S. Plant as Key to Topping Toyota." *Reuters*, May 24.

SEL01. 2016. "Site Selection Professional."

SEL02. 2016. "Site Selection Professional."

Spindler, Charles J. 1994. "Winners and Losers in Industrial Recruitment: Mercedes-Benz and Alabama." *State & Local Government Review* 26(3):192–204.

Storper, Michael, and Richard Walker. 1989. *The Capitalist Imperative: Territory, Technology, and Industrial Growth*. New York: Basil Blackwell.

Teeple, Gary. 2000. *Globalization and the Decline of Social Reform: Into the Twenty-First Century*, 2nd edition. Ontario: Garamond Press.

Thelen, Kathleen. 2012. "Varieties of Capitalism: Trajectories of Liberalization and the New Politics of Social Solidarity." *Annual Review of Political Science* 15(1):137–159. doi: 10.1146/annurev-polisci-070110-122959.

Weinsgast, Barry. 1995. "The Economic Role of Political Institutions: Markett Preserving Federalism and Economic Growth." *Journal of Law, Economics, and Organization* 11:1–31.

Womack, James P., Daniel T. Jones, and Daniel Roos. 1990. *The Machine That Changed the World: Based on the Massachusetts Institute of Technology 5-Million Dollar 5-Year Study on the Future of the Automobile*. New York: Rawson Associates.

Wuthnow, Robert. 1985. "State Structures and Ideological Outcomes." *American Sociological Review* 50(6):799–821. doi: 10.2307/2095505.

Yang, Xiaohua. 1995. *Globalization of the Automobile Industry: The United States, Japan, and the People's Republic of China*. Westport, Conn: Praeger.

4 The Industrial recruitment of automotive assembly plants in the South

As we turn to examine the processes in which local governments try to attract private investment and promote growth through recruitment efforts and incentives, there are two guiding questions that will direct our efforts. First, are recruitment and incentives anything new? Particularly in the United States, there is a history of states trying to lure and entice industry; Mississippi, for example, used tax plans and regulatory streamlining in their attempts to "balance agriculture with industry" in the mid-1930s (Cobb 1993:6–12; Hülsemann 2001:223–224). Hence, as journalists periodically raise the alarm about a "race to the bottom" among states competing for investment, professionals in the field of economic development say this is just business as usual and what has really changed is the overall structure of the global economy. Second, if recent industrial recruitment efforts are indeed different from previous governmental activity, what is it that has changed?

In this chapter, I present a close analysis of the core elements of the process of industrial recruitment, painting a picture of the complex efforts through which localities find and recruit inward investment. The unit of analysis here is the recruitment process itself, for when large projects with a high number of potential jobs come into a locality, this acts as a centrifuge, drawing in governments and private interests at multiple scales, and resources from all these sources are negotiated in a complex – but increasingly scripted – competitive process. I then show how the process of industrial recruitment has changed in the era of neoliberal globalization, arguing that these changes are neither reducible to quantitative extensions of earlier historical efforts to recruit industry nor are they a race to the bottom in zero-sum game of competition. Rather, the relative growth and routinization of recruitment efforts represent the institutionalization fast-policy processes and rules that are characteristic of local policy in the Neoliberal era, and political elites are central to – rather than victims of – this process. In the next chapter, I shift focus to elaborate the ideological tenets of this practice in the familiar language of partnerships, before turning to the implications for class struggles in chapter 6, tying the findings of my research together with theoretical and historical framework laid out in the preceding chapters.

DOI: 10.4324/9781003107569-4

Who recruits? Key entities involved

In order to get a general sense of how industrial recruitment efforts have changed in the last 40 years, a good starting point will be to systematically work through what industrial recruitment looks like today, beginning with who are the key *players* in recruitment efforts? What makes up incentive *packages*? And, what does the recruitment *process* look like more generally? However, I should note at the outset that the only pure generalization that one can make about the process of industrial recruitment in the United States is that it is a highly decentralized process whose shape is contingent upon both cases – and locality-specific factors. Hence, one refrain oft recited by development professionals was that "every deal is different" (EDP01 2015). Thus, the generalizations that follow should be taken with the appropriate circumspection.

Players: public agencies and authorities

State development authorities

State development authorities are typically the central point of contact for major projects looking to locate a new facility or expansion within a state. State development authorities are the largest publicly funded organizations that will engage in business recruitment activities and differ widely in their size, complexity, and character. Development authorities (such as the Georgia Department of Economic Development (GDEcD) or the Alabama Department of Commerce) are established through state legislation and have leadership appointed by the Governor of the state, and their ultimate authority typically rests with the governor herself. These authorities will engage in a wide variety of activities designed to increase economic activity within a state, of which business recruitment is one subset. Such activities include helping local communities enhance their development efforts, working to develop and market the state workforce (through university systems, for example), providing funding and grants to businesses and communities, coordinating economic incentives, and other activities broadly designed to be a marketing and sales effort for the state.[1]

In almost all major location projects – such as an automotive plant or business headquarters – the state development authority (specifically its lead recruiter or executive) is the lead, or the primary point of contact and communication between governments involved and the corporation looking to site a project. The reasons for this are fairly straightforward. First, major corporate investments typically pit states against each other in competition, and it is more expedient to deal directly with state rather than local level officials. As one city development official put it "usually...the bigger guys... will come through the state...every [company] is different but, typically we're competing for [the larger projects] with other states, and so, since the company doesn't want to have to deal with all the little guys, or the individual cities, they'll just deal with the state" (EDP02 2015). Another state development official echoed this reasoning, and elaborated that "because a lot of these large companies...want to look at multiple sites in a state they will come through the state agency to begin the process" (EDP08 2016). The second reason the state typically leads a major recruitment is simply that the state has a much broader array of resources and incentives, can float larger bonds, etc. While all major projects will involve incentives from different levels of government and different entities, states are typically the only level of government with a tax base and credit rating that can support the large incentives packages required to win hundred million-dollar investments. Lastly, state authorities organize and structure sub-state players involved in the recruitment process, coordinating various financial inputs for the final package.

Beyond these broad generalizations, state development authorities differ widely in their scope and organization, reflecting the idiosyncrasies of state legislation and regulations. In Georgia, for example, some community development activities are housed in the Georgia Department of Community Affairs (DCA), which also plays a role in providing funds for some incentives negotiations such as what are known as "deal-closing funds" or grants. Some states may also split their recruitment activities off into a public–private partnership (PPP), which I will discuss in the following sections.

County governments and development authorities

County governments and development authorities often play a critical role in recruiting businesses, in part because county governments typically administer school districts as well as property taxes, making them central to the provision of tax-based incentives. The scope and scale of efforts that county development agencies undertake is again locality-specific, and often dependent upon what they are enabled to do through state-based legislation. In Mississippi, for example, Pontotoc, Union, and Lee counties formed the PUL Alliance to develop a site specifically to lure automotive production, while in Georgia, the Development Authority of Fulton County, which includes Atlanta, only offers a standardized bond-financing package and Payment In Lieu of Taxes (PILOT) agreements.

County Governments and development authorities follow the direction of state-level officials negotiating the site selection. Typically, this will happen after the site-selection process has been narrowed to a few particular sites within different states, at which point local governments must be involved in order to secure ownership of the land options. As one county development official in Georgia put it, "we don't get involved...sometimes early on, but we're more on the back end" (EDP01 2015) of the recruitment process. Note, however, as sites are increasingly optioned and prepared prior to firms announcing a project (discussed later) the timing of locality involvement shifts when county/local governments are the key investors in such certified sites.

Local (city and community) development authorities

Today, most cities and local communities will also have at least one official who works on local economic development, though not every locality will actively work to recruit businesses. Major global cities like Atlanta, GA, or Chattanooga, TN, have large, well-funded, and staffed development authorities such as Invest Atlanta (formerly Atlanta Development Authority), while smaller towns such as Huntsville, Alabama, or Blue Ridge, Georgia, may have only one official who works on development. Smaller and more rural towns may also rely on county development authorities that possess broader tax bases and can commit more manpower and money toward development efforts. Both city and county development authorities typically have a governing board made up of elected officials – mayors, county commissioners, and local elected officials – who appoint the executive leadership of the authority. The key difference from county offices is that city development authorities will limit their activities to the city limits and citizens thereof; as one city development officer told me emphatically, "we typically do not offer...we, not typically, we *never* offer our incentives outside of the city boundaries" (EDP02 2015).

As with counties, the scope and power that local development authorities possess in terms of incentives vary widely and are dependent upon the wealth of the locality and the laws that constitute it. Cities can also control a number of locally specific taxes and ordinances that make them crucial to the recruitment process and the provision of tax and property-related incentives. As one development official summed up "The city and the county on big projects have to participate both because of the resources necessary and because of the need to negotiate PILOT agreements and other things" (EDP06 2016).

Players: private and other actors involved in recruitment

Public–private partnerships

A number of states such as Indiana (Indiana Economic Development Corporation), Missouri (Missouri Partnership), North Carolina (Economic Development Partnership of North Carolina), and Florida (Enterprise Florida) have split off their recruitment activities into public–private partnerships (PPPs). I will discuss the impetus behind forming a PPP in-depth in the following section on changes in industrial recruitment as well as in the following chapter, but speaking very generally, a public–private partnership can potentially increase the operational flexibility of recruitment efforts, as

PPPs operate with a different set of restrictions and parameters than do purely public authorities. Said a former Commerce Secretary of North Carolina, who helped develop their PPP, "it simply allows that entity to move a bit more quickly...have some flexibility in terms of travel and all those kinds of things that's so tightly regulated by the state" (EDP04 2015).

Utility providers

Utility providers, particularly gas and electrical corporations, are major pseudo-private corporations involved in economic development and especially industrial recruitment efforts. Most major utility providers are state-regulated corporations – though the southeast is also home to the Tennessee Valley Authority, a federally owned corporation that services areas of multiple southeastern states. The role played by these utility providers varies for each state, and they can offer financial incentives or discounted rates – a major cost consideration for large industrial projects. Georgia Power, for example, runs the Georgia Resource Center, which collects data relevant to site selection projects; the publicly owned Santee Cooper in South Carolina simply offered up about $50 million in financial incentives to Volvo (Cope 2015). Some also play the role today of certifying major sites for industrial or other projects, which I address in the next section.

Chambers of commerce, and local and regional business alliances

Local businesses also stand to benefit from a major industrial project raising the profile and consumer and spending base in their region, and private business development organizations usually play an important role in the recruitment of industry. The role played by chambers of commerce and regional or city-wide business alliances does, of course, vary for each case. In some cases, chambers of commerce play the role of "convene-ers – convening...the business center and industry, convening them with the local government to talk about issues" (BDP02 2016). When Honda came to Alabama in 1999, the firm's initial contact was a regional business association – the Metropolitan Development Board (MDB). One official who worked with that business association at the time noted, "I won't say it's unusual [to be the initial contact]. It's not the norm – it's not rare. Because locals like MDB, which is one of the larger local organizations at the time, they're out recruiting, and they're out making contacts" (EDP08 2016).

Both utility providers and private business organizations can provide an important bridge when the prospect of a change in government leadership at the state level creates uncertainty in the recruitment process. As one official at the TVA put it "one of the advantages of TVA is we're probably the only consistent economic development agency out there. I don't mean that critically. What I mean is, when we have a new governor, we don't leave, we're still here. Typically, when a state hires a new governor, well guess what? He hires a new economic development commissioner, they typically hire their new staff. Right? They have a lot of turnover, we don't have the turnover." (BDP01 2016).

Any major recruitment project will involve an admixture of the agencies, associations, and actors outlined earlier, whose importance for a given project is case-specific – though the state development agency will always close the deal. One important point to note is that cooperation among local businesses – and between them and the government – is an important signal for potential projects, which serves to show that the locality is eager for the project, and that the overall business climate in the area is welcoming.

Site selection firms

Besides the corporations themselves searching for a new site, the most important actor on behalf of the corporation is a firm that specializes in locating a site for their project, or has a specialized branch for this work. The growth of the field of site selection firms is itself of importance, but for the moment it will suffice to say that on major projects (at least in the tens of millions of dollars) companies hire these site selection firms (such as Fantus, Jones, Lang, Lassalle [JLL], Deloyte, and MaCallum-Sweeny [now defunct]) to guide them through the process of finding a location, and the site selectors are the primary contact for governments and localities involved in the selection process (Thomas 2011:9).

The incentives packages: what do they get?

Incentives packages are a mix of tax breaks, cash offerings, and various perks that local coalitions put together ostensibly to make locating in their locality more alluring, primarily by impacting the overall cost of the project. Incentives are a very important part of site selection and recruitment, but they are far from the only consideration a business and site consultant analyze. Rather, incentives become more important at the end of the site selection process, when businesses have several strong but relatively similar candidates. One site selection consultant I spoke to reviewed the other considerations industrial projects need to take into account:

> How I view it is, the number one factor, 85% of the time is going to be human capital – the quality and cost of that human capital in a marketplace. And then taxes, real estate, those types of issues. And when we get down to say the final three locations that are under consideration, then yes that's when the discussion starts about incentives. Because…those three finalist locations are all going to look fairly similar from a cost and quality standpoint – so the incentives then can be the tipping point, right at the end, where if a location can be a little

more aggressive or they can be more flexible in how the incentives are structured to offset project and operating costs – that's when it really makes a difference. (SEL03 2016)

Another site selection professional said much the same thing, that "all the incentives in the world can't make a bad location good…now that's not to say incentives aren't important, it's just when in the process they become important…by the end of the project everybody cares about it, and we tend to spend a lot of time on it…[so] incentives become more important as you move through the project, they become critically important in the final phases of the project" (SEL02 2016). In the previous chapter, I outlined the unique industrial relations and labor regime of the South, and the locational capabilities that were critical to automotive firms coming into the region, factors which are most important in the early phases of the site selection.

In the following section, I detail what incentives packages look like, specifying which are offered by different levels of governments in a typical recruitment today, and then discuss what the process of recruitment itself looks like. In each section, I denote tax-focused incentives and those focused on up-front costs of an industrial project.

Federal government incentives and recruitment

The only involvement from the federal government in automotive plant location and recruitment is the designation of a plant area as a "foreign trade zone" (or FTZ) or subzone status that designates particular areas as being outside the territory of U.S. customs and as such exempting goods in the FTZ from tariffs. This is not properly considered an "incentive" in the sense that local government has no direct control over FTZ designation, it rather depends on the automaker applying to the federal government. Such zones were originally intended to apply to ports and airports (and surrounding areas) to stimulate international trade, but starting with the ill-fated VW Westmoreland plant, foreign plants began applying for – and being approved as – foreign trade zones/subzones. "Japanese-owned and joint venture assembly plants subsequently built in the United States routinely asked for foreign trade subzone designation during construction… US-owned producers realized…[FTZ designation] could benefit them as well…a flood of applications hit from the Big Three producers between 1983 and 1985" (Rubenstein 1992:217). As is typical of the neoliberal policy landscape, the federal government is most conspicuous in its absence.

State development authorities' incentives

State development authorities can offer a broad array of incentives to businesses looking to locate in their state – though the particular scale and scope of these incentives are again dependent upon state-specific legislation and case-specific factors. Note that *all* tax incentives may be as-of-right (apply to a company simply based on meeting specific criteria) or specifically tailored to major projects.

Tax-based incentives: As is perhaps obvious, state-based tax incentives refer to state levied taxes, and typical tax incentives are as follows:

• County-specific jobs-based tax credit

    Most states rank each county based on income and employment in a tiered system, and offer tax credits based on the tier of the county in which a company is investing and hiring. For example, if Toyota Motors Manufacturing locates in a "Tier 3" County – that has low mean income or high unemployment – they qualify for a higher tax credit per-job created.

• Job-based tax credits (usually applied against corporate income taxes)

    States typically have several levels of jobs-based tax credits offered to employers depending on the number of jobs they create. For example, Tennessee offers a "Super Jobs Tax Credit" of $5,000/job for companies creating at least 100 jobs and investing $100 million.

• Industry- or activity-focused tax credits

    Many states offer industry- or activity-specific tax credits. Indiana and Georgia offer Research and Development based tax credits, many states offer "skill-enhancing" or retraining tax credits. The specific form these credits take (e.g., sales tax credit, transferable tax credit) depends upon the state.

• Sales and use tax exemptions

    Full or partial exemptions from the sale and use of particular types of machinery involved in industrial production are a typical feature of packages.

• Port or freeport tax exemptions on inventory stocks

    Full or partial tax exemptions are often offered at ports and airports, and relieve taxes on inventory and storage of materials involved in production and commerce.

Cash incentives: state government and agencies also typically take on a large share of the up-front costs of potential projects in incentives packages, which typically target infrastructure: roads, utilities, and sewer connections, the actual site, and its development. These incentives also cover the costs of training workers. Typical incentives offered by the state:

- Training expenses

  Every automotive project sited since the 1980s has included state funds for worker training of some kind. The extent and nature of this training vary – in some cases, it involves trips to Japan or Germany so workers get a sense of how work is done in the home country.

- Training center

  Many projects include the cost of constructing a training center, which will have classrooms and mock assembly lines for training workers.

- Site purchase and preparation

  In all cases since the mid-1980s, the state or local governments have purchased the actual land and site, and pass it on to the manufacturer at nominal or no cost. The site is also usually prepared for the plant by state or local governments, meaning the site is cleared and graded and ready for construction. This may now happen before any project even is suggesting interest through the creation of "certified" sites.

- Road improvements and connections

  In all cases since the 1980s, states have paid for the enhancement of roads near the site, in order to take the increase in traffic, especially trucks that have industrial loads. States also pay for connecting roads to major interstates and highways – though federal money from the Department of Transportation may be used here.

- Rail connection

  As with roads, states also pay for rail spurs – or connections to local freight lines. Rail is the major mode auto manufacturers use to transport materials and products to and from the site.

- Utility and sewer connection

  States also typically pay for utility-based infrastructure, including the costs of water, power, gas, and sewer lines. The extent of these expenses is dependent upon the site, and the environmental factors and impacts. These costs may be included in cite pre-certification.

- Various financial and nonfinancial incentives (the perks)

States and local governments will typically offer special incentives that are relative to the specific project – which can include advertising revenue, welcome centers, naming rights to stadiums or local attractions, etc. Sometimes, the state simply offers money in the form of "deal-closing funds." One critically important incentive typical of packages is agreements to streamline regulation and permitting. These agreements stipulate timelines (e.g., 30 days) for the issuing of permits, and agreement by parties indicated in the contract to expedite the permitting and regulatory process.

Local government recruiting incentives

Tax incentives: as with state-level government, county, and city governments will usually offer tax incentives relative to the particular taxes they levy:

- Property tax abatement, exemption, or PILOT agreements

In every project, the local governments have agreed to modify the property tax arrangements for a given period (10–25 years), either through a reduction of the tax rate, a full or partial exemption from property taxes, or a Payment In Lieu of Taxes or PILOT arrangement. Full property tax exemption is not very common. NOTE: Local governments typically levy taxes for school districts – in most cases, these taxes are supposedly not included in the tax reduction agreements. However, see the report by Good Jobs First on the direct impact of incentives deals on school funding (Good Jobs First 2018).

Cash incentives: Local governments also offer incentives against the up-front costs of the industrial site – and will usually contribute to those incentives outlined above that the state will cover. The particular role of local governments is project dependent, but can include:

- Full or partial site purchase
- Site preparation
- Training funds
- Miscellaneous financial incentives

Nongovernment actors

Nongovernmental actors such as utility corporations and business associations can also offer incentives, and can play an important role in recruiting a large project. Major incentives can include:

- Reduction of rail rates by railroad companies
- Allowing nonexclusive access to rail lines
- Reduction of utility rates
- Cash incentives by business associations or by local/regional chambers of commerce
- Contribution to site/utility preparation
- Training by local/regional chambers of commerce

In every project, a mix of state, local, and private entities offer incentives to corporations, the trends and breakdowns of which are summarized in Table 4.1, and elaborated in detail in Table 1A in the Appendix to chapter 1. While Table 1A offers an overview of the incentives packages offered to automotive manufacturers in as much detail as possible, it will help to review a few particular cases to see how different levels of government incentives are entwined in a particular deal, the kinds of perks that are often thrown in, and the complexities of accurately estimating the total value of the package. Given that extensive research has been conducted into the recruitment of – and incentives given to – BMW and Mercedes-Benz, these cases, as well as others, will be used for elaboration throughout this chapter, as the data and accounts are the most reliable.

BMW

The deal between BMW and South Carolina was struck on June 24, 1992. The final reported incentive package totaled $130 million dollars (not counting the interest payments incurred by new state debt). The Port Authority of South Carolina acquired the site for a reported $36.6 million dollars (the state contributing the bulk at $31.6 million, with the county contributing about $5 million), which does not include the unspecified expense of removing the 250 homeowners. The state then leased the site to BMW for $1 a year for 30 years with an option to renew, effectively giving them the site for free, a maneuver typical of states that have laws against the government making outright gifts to private corporations. Site prep was undertaken by state and local governments, including the provision and improvement of infrastructure such as water and sewer lines, highway connections and improvements, and expansion of airport runways (for which unspecified amounts of federal Department of Transportation [DOT] funding was secured). Employee training was also covered by the state, including both pre-employment training and on-the-job training, both of which were overseen by BMW and included the costs of flying engineers to Germany for training there. Goode reports that these infrastructural and training incentives added up to around $22.5 million (1992). Further incentives involved the construction of a multi-county industrial park at the site, which was specially designated as solely part of Union County so that BMW could receive the largest per-job tax credit available in the state,

Table 4.1 Greenfield plant – up-front/cash incentives

Year	Company	Plant$†	Incent$†	Train	Road	Rail	Utility	Site	Megasite
1980	HONDA	$750	$27	X	X				
1980	NISSAN	$750	$66	X	X				
1985	SATURN	$1,500	$80+	X*	X				
1985	TOYOTA	$800	$147	X	X				
1986	ISUZU	$500	$260	X	X		X	X	
1992	BMW	$300	$129.2	X*	X		X	X	
1993	MBZ	$300	$496	X	X	?	X	X	
1999	HONDA	$450	$248	X*	X	X	X	X	
2000	NISSAN	$900	$1,162	X*	X		X	X	X
2002	HYUNDAI	$1,000	$358	X*	X	X	X	X	
2006	KIA	$1,200	$404.7	X	X	X	X	X	
2007	TOYOTA	$1,000	$450+	X*	X			X	X
2008	VLKSWG	$1,000	$557.5+	X	X	X		X	X
2015	VOLVO	$500	$210+	X	X		X	X	
2018	TY-MZDA	$1,600	$800	X	X	X	X	X	X

Notes
† In Millions.
* Indicates coverage of training and training center.

which amounted to a $1,500/job credit. The state also passed a bill allowing the firm to pay a "fee in lieu of tax" (or payment in lieu of tax or PILOT) of 6% as opposed to the 10.5% charged most companies (Monk 1992), and gave the firm an exemption on sales and use tax of heavy equipment and production machinery, and industrial electricity. These tax-based incentives reportedly add up to roughly $70.7 million, rounding the initial package out at $129.7 million, though given that the complexity of the deal included things such as discounts for employees at the local YMCA, it is clear if this is not the complete figure.

The plant came online in 1994, ahead of schedule, initially producing the X5 sport-utility. It has since expanded a total of six times: in 1998, the company invested $600 million dollars in an expansion for a new SUV model, and while details are sketchy, a new incentives package was negotiated with per-job tax credits extended to new employees and a further $6–$9 million offered by the state for training (Meadows 1998). In 2000, and again in 2002, the plant expanded to meet increased demand, for a total of $800 million in new investment and an unclear amount of incentives (DuPlessis 2002). Further expansions costing $500 million and $750 million were undertaken in 2008 and 2012, though again incentives by state or local governments are unclear (DuPlessis 2008; Schaffer 2012). The point of elaborating these later developments is that, with each expansion, the original set of tax abatements is re-negotiated and extended such that, in addition to new incentives, supposed sunset clauses (expiry dates) attached to some tax incentives become effectively meaningless.

Mercedes-Benz

The incentives deal reached between Mercedes-Benz and Alabama in 1993 was quite similar to that of the BMW deal a year earlier. The overall investment by Mercedes was initially about $300 million; the reported incentives from Alabama and local governments were incorrectly reported to be around $250–$300 million, much larger than the package reported for BMW. This is perhaps why there has been a great deal of research on the Mercedes-Benz recruitment and whether Alabama got a "good deal," given the state invested as much as or more than the firm itself (Boudreaux, Coats, and Davis 2012; Jacobs 2012; Kebede and Ngandu 1999; McDermott 2013; Spindler 1994).

The city of Tuscaloosa, Jefferson county, and nearby Birmingham city all contributed to the purchase of the 1,000 acre site for $30–$35 million and its leveling and development, and the site was later transferred to Mercedes-Benz for the nominal fee of $100 dollars (Cooper and Ruggenbach 1993; Spindler 1994:198). The state also contributed by constructing a worker training facility (estimated at $35 million) and paid not only for the cost of providing training to workers, but also paid the workers' salaries during training for an estimated $45 million. The state also spent $5 million constructing a new Welcome Center, and the state-owned Alabama Power contributed another $11 million (in addition to reducing utility taxes by an unspecified amount); these up-front costs alone amount to $126 million – or near to the total value of the BMW Spartanburg package.

While initial reports suggested that the total package was worth around $300 million, more careful analysis reveals that the tax breaks alone are worth around that much (Cooper and Ruggenbach 1993; Spindler 1994:198). Alabama extended a 25-year corporate income tax holiday and added a unique caveat to that proposal; incorporated into the "so-called Mercedes-Benz bill passed by the Alabama legislature... companies which invest at least $5 Million and create at least 50 jobs that pay a minimum of $8 an hour are allowed to use their state income tax to pay off debt. In addition, they can use the state income tax deducted from their employee wages to pay for land, equipment, and their new plant" (Spindler 1994:198; Patterson 1993). This tax incentive, which essentially allows Mercedes (and all companies after it who fit the bill) to tax their own employees to pay off fixed capital costs, amounted to an expected value of $280 million in itself (Mattera et al. 2012). In addition to this break, the city government agreed to an exemption of property taxes amounting to an estimated $9 million per year (Spindler 1994:198); if we assume the property tax agreement is extended for a minimum of 10 years (the lowest year limit of any tax-based agreement I have researched) this would amount to $90 million dollars, not accounting for increases in the value of the land after development. If the property tax agreement were part of the overall 25-year deal (as Spindler suggests it may be) this would amount to around $225 million in local tax breaks alone.

Given the figures mentioned earlier, we can offer a low estimate of the value of the initial package offered to Mercedes-Benz at around $496 million dollars.[2] It is worth keeping in mind that there were aspects of the deal that were not quantified here: the University of Alabama agreed to offer German cultural and language courses; there were likely sales and use tax exemptions most machinery; there is no estimation on the costs of borrowing on bonds. The governor also tacitly included an agreement to change the fleet of state SUVs to the new Mercedes model being produced over a five-year period – amounting to 100 vehicles per year at an estimated $30,000 dollars each (Patterson 1993), which would amount to a further $15 million expenditure. This last agreement created public outrage, and the Governor had to walk back this part of the agreement, asserting that Mercedes would have to bid for the contract like any other company.

These accounts offer insight into the complexity of the final incentives packages created by the state, county, and city/town governments, and how each package is both similar to others but has distinct elements – something that is typical of fast policy processes, as I discuss later. Having built an understanding of the entities involved in recruitment and which actors provide different incentives in a package, it will be useful to review what a typical recruitment and site selection process might look like today. Doing so will allow us to clarify how industrial recruitment and incentives today have changed in a number of significant ways from the beginning of the southern drift of automotive production in the 1980s.

The process of industrial recruitment

Once a business decides, it needs a new location for any of the reasons outlined in previous chapters, the first step in the process for larger firms and projects is to hire a professional site selection consultant to direct and manage the process and negotiate the incentives deal. Once that firm is chosen, the first part of the process involves determining the needs of the particular project, including physical requirements, functional inputs, and business goals, as discussed in the previous chapter. As one site selection professional told me, "we have some basic automotive criteria, but every company will be a little different. So the final criteria that goes out with the project is ultimately reflective of *that* company's particular needs" (SEL02 2016). The specific needs of the project are used as inputs into a computer-based or "desktop" analysis, and typically hundreds of locations are con-sidered – and many state and local development agencies advertise sites and their capacities precisely for these searches. As McDermott summarizes, "normally the process begins by identifying a very large number of possible locations in the United States (e.g. more than 200 sites) and this is quickly (i.e. within six months) reduced to perhaps 20 sites…this process of elim-ination is conducted by the appointed site selection consultants, and is a highly analytical and rational process." (2012:15–6). Today, desktop ana-lyses will usually take place with little actual contact with localities or states and, indeed, that is often the point of bringing in professional site selectors:

> [Site Selectors used to] come in and look at 50 sites…well now they can do desktop analysis, eliminate forty of those and only come in and look at 10. (BDP01 2016)

> That's why companies use consultants because our job is to immediately screen out – first of all establish the minimum criteria and what and when, and if they [the locality] can't demonstrate they meet it then they don't even get a visit. (SEL02 2016)

The active recruitment begins in the second phase of the site selection when the firms looking to site their project contact state or local officials at the 10–20 localities on the shortlist, often going directly to the Governor of the state. "[Automotive assembly plant] projects are big enough that they're usually starting off at the state level. Probably their first phone call is to the capital, the Governor's office, because they're such high stakes opportunities… they're not bashful about reaching to the very top state executive with kind of an invitation to bid" (EDP05 2015).

This initial contact, or lead, might come through other channels such as a state chamber of commerce or the top state development official, often depending on whether there are extant business connections. "Leads come in from... the state, from the [power company], from the chamber, they'll come in sometimes through lawyers...through other contacts that we've known, so they'll come in through word-of-mouth. Now what's interesting is that usually the big ones that I've seen have come through the state...the chamber [of commerce] does both really" (EDP02 2015). One former lead recruiter of an automotive plant – at the time head of the economic development agency – described how the lead came into his office: "I get a call in my office, early in the evening, from someone – I don't know how he got my number but – you know, with a voice that I neither knew nor recognized... and basically he said 'would the state of Georgia be interested in a billion and half dollar investment?'" (EDP03 2015).

This exchange also illustrates the confidentiality that characterizes the early phases of negotiations between states and firms siting projects. "What happens is, at some point the consultant will pick up the phone, and they'll *typically* call the state. And say 'hey, I have a corporate headquarters deal' – and when they talk to the state it's very confidentially, and they won't tell them the name of the company, but they'll give them the parameters. And so the state person will say 'based on these criteria these are probably some of the general locations'" (EDP01 2015). Businesses demand confidentiality in negotiations with public development agencies and governments in the same way they might in the negotiation of private business transactions, and these demands stem from factors that are both exogenous and endogenous to the competition to close the deal. Given that siting a project can be a maneuver intended to impose market discipline on class relations, as well as a major fixed capital investment, confidentiality is critical to limiting workforce knowledge and concerns among employees, and containing rampant speculative activity in prospective communities.[3] Competition with competitors is predictably also a major reason why policy elites cite the necessity of confidentiality, as one site selector noted "when something has been leaked out when [a] company is looking to do something in a geographic area...one of their largest competitors may try and beat them to that marketplace...and given the nature of competition in different industry sectors that can be problematic" (SEL03 2016). Given the size of industrial projects, however, and the limitations placed on firms siting by the rhythms of capital accumulation, the idea of a competitor leapfrogging a hopeful firm is relatively nil. Of more import is for the local leaders to demonstrate their ability to behave in the manner of a private business, as I discuss in the next chapter.

In this second phase of the site selection and recruitment process, the state typically takes on the role of project manager and organizes the complex process of crafting a recruitment pitch to the interested corporation. At some point, the county and city governments where the physical site is located are brought into the picture, as the state attempts to secure land options and craft the final incentives package with the inputs of those governments. When exactly local governments are brought in and precisely who speaks to whom is case-specific, but then, at the local level, usually only top development officials and government leaders are involved, in part to ensure the maintenance of secrecy. One of the state leads on the Kia project in Georgia describes this phase:

> The first phase of the negotiation was finding the site...once that was done it was 'alright, how do we engage the right people?' So, the city of West Point, the city of LaGrange, Troup County...so at the same time you're negotiating with Kia, on the property – and moving forward, you're beginning to have some discussion with some local entities. And having the discussion with local entities is about, first and foremost, confidentiality. And they – the economic development professionals get that...but...you're dealing with elected officials, with *appointees* of elected officials. (EDP03 2015)

One of the important changes I will discuss in the next section is that today most local governments or development authorities have already purchase potential sites for major projects, and have performed due diligence prior to any contact for a specific project. For example, the aforementioned alliance in Mississippi of the Pontotoc, Union, and Lee counties was undertaken precisely to lure in an automotive manufacturer; in that instance, according to one local official involved, "we actually got Toyota to visit before the state knew anything about it, when it was still 27, 28 states in the hunt" (EDP07 2016). Many utility providers and development offices have programs specifically to evaluate and certify sites that will meet the needs of major industrial projects (the largest designated *Megasites*) – a designation sought and won by the PUL alliance from the Tennessee Valley Authority. Volkswagen also located at an official Megasite, and as the lead recruiter on that project clarified "the local community, who owned the site, had pursued the Megasite designation" (EDP06 2016). For the moment, it will suffice to say that securing the options to the site and gaining official designation serves to take some of the guesswork out of the process of recruitment and site selection, and also helps to maintain confidentiality as the land already has due diligence performed and there is less need to involve local authorities earlier in the process of recruitment.

In the last phase of the site selection and recruitment, the candidate sites are narrowed to two or three locations and the competition breaks wide open, anonymity and confidentiality fall by the wayside as finalists aggressively recruit the project, and the firm and its consultant play finalists off each other to ratchet up incentives packages. The dynamics of this stage of the process are, again, case-specific, but a lead recruiter that brought

Volkswagen to Chattanooga, Tennessee, offers a fairly typical account of how it played out in the mid-2000s:

> So when we were notified that they had a project and were going to make a visit, they had self-selected down to eight sites that the team was going to visit. They considered many more sites, and had gone through...their desktop analysis and narrowed it down to seven...so in March, they visited [those seven sites], they ultimately narrowed that seven down to three, and they returned for additional visits in April or May, and then narrowed it down to two sites and we had meetings in Washington with the VW team in June.

> And it was extremely competitive, in the end it became between us and Alabama...that meeting that took place in Washington...we were the second group to meet with them...and the Alabama team came out [of the meeting room]. They were very excited...you could tell they felt celebratory...usually they would put the other group in a room so you didn't interact with each other but they had not done that here. We went in and it was a very cool reception. And ultimately, I – as the one leading the state's efforts – asked the VW team "what's more important to you? Is it dollars at the bottom line, or is it zeroes in your cost model? Because depending on which is more important to you depends on how you address how we're capable of addressing your needs."

> And there was a gentlemen who was from Germany who was on the finance side, who said "it's the zeroes in our cost model"... and we started talking individually about how our program could do certain things, or we couldn't do something. Because Alabama had offered pretty much a blank check, and Tennessee can't do that...And that discussion lasted well over two hours. And at the end of it, they asked if we could have that written up and submitted to them by five o'clock the next afternoon...so we got on the state plane, went back to Chattanooga, dropped off the two mayors and the gentlemen from the chamber, and...when we were in Chattanooga, I called the [state] troopers for the Governor and said "I'm going to need to have the Governor available as soon as we land. And [the commissioner of finance] and I...called the governor and explained what we had done, because it was significantly different fromm what we had been discussing...the governor said... "I support y'all." We went and had it written up soon after. (EDP06 2016)

This account is indicative of many of the typical elements that characterize the final aspects of the negotiation process that Tennessee ultimately won. First, as the competition increases with the elimination of candidates, the incentives package takes on a more central role in recruitment and selection.

The Governor of the state will almost always be closely involved throughout the entire process and is the person who ultimately has to sign off on the final deal offered by the state, but in the final phases, local leaders and chambers of commerce must also be closely involved as their contributions make up large parts of the final package. The comment about Alabama offering a blank check is also indicative of the fact that states competing for these projects have to do so while navigating the peculiarities of state laws that govern spending. Tennessee, for example, cannot simply offer public monies to private corporations, while Alabama and Georgia can; thus, in this instance, Tennessee had to use infrastructure and other programs to craft a competitive incentives package. The intense competition also is typical of very large projects. In these final phases, confidentiality is dropped and the last contenders will have a back and forth process with the firm and its consultants, as the firm tests the limits of what localities and states will offer – within reasonable limits (e.g., specific to the needs of the project).

In another example in the case of BMW, when they reached the final stages of recruitment, executives began negotiating intensely with South Carolina (primarily with then-Governor Carroll), using the supposedly open site selection process as a negotiation lever. Executives decided the sites offered were not sufficient to meet their desire for airport and interstate proximity and the high visibility afforded by both. BMW executives were persuaded to consider a 1,200 acre site near Spartanburg, SC – and even as the firm was still negotiating, the state began buying options on the site and had to relocate more than 250 homes located there. In his report on the location decision in *The State* newspaper, Monk notes that several times throughout the negotiations officials with the firm said outright that "South Carolina's incentive package was inadequate" – and used these claims to add to the package details like expansions of the Greenville–Spartanburg airport to handle their large 747 cargo jets. Even smaller minute details such as the cost of power supplied to the plant were negotiated, which was one aspect where South Carolina could not be competitive because the electric company was not state-owned but investor-owned; one executive told reporters "they made it quite clear that we had to be very competitive with Nebraska" (the other main contender) (Monk 1992). From the numerous accounts given there was clear and calculated use of the competitive process by BMW to shape the incentives package to meet their needs and desires – particularly considering the Nebraska site did not meet some of the basic locational specifications the company wanted, and was thus not viable. While several authors note that BMW did not go with the largest incentives offered (Nebraska reportedly came back with an offer amounting to $180 million) – given their desire for proximity to ports on the East Coast, it is fair to say that the firm got the largest package they could at a site they desired, and clearly manipulated the competitive process to that end.

As the site selection consultant quoted earlier in this chapter noted, the final sites are relatively equivalent in the cost and quality – so the last phase of the competition is where firms can get a sense of how much a location wants them, and offers localities an opportunity to show the firms they will be willing and active partners. Incentives play a major part in this, but it also involves a more nebulous sense of the feeling corporation gets for the place and the atmosphere. This was briefly described by one site selector, "you met with [local officials], ask questions. You know, you just get a feel" (SEL01 2016). While this last phase is fairly predictable in many respects, it remains the least rationalized part of the site selection process. Another former development professional, who at the time operated his own site consulting firm, tried to put this aspect into words: "there's something more than what's on paper. And it is about – I use the word 'atmospheric' effect… it's really about comfort level. You know… 'do I like this?'…Now, that's not the *core* of it, but that's the piece that tends to close things" (EDP03 2015). Once the final incentives package is agreed upon, the state and the firm will sign a Memorandum of Understanding that details all of the incentives and agreements made between the various parties involved. Once passed through the legislature and signed, a public announcement is made – with much fanfare – and the details of the recruitment are typically covered in journalistic accounts in an exciting and triumphalist manner.

Changes and developments in industrial recruitment: fast-policy in Southern climes

Having clarified the key actors, elements, and incentives that go into recruitment, and given an account of what the process looks like today, we can return to the question of whether this process looks qualitatively different than it did in 1980. I argue that there are important differences in the process today that reflect a deeper shift in industrial relations at the local level. The best way to frame these changes is in terms of what Peck and Theodore have described as "an ascendant regime of transnational 'fast-policy'" among local governments that has become globally predominant in the neoliberal era (Peck 2002; Peck and Theodore 2010:195; Peck and Theodore 2015). They summarize these kinds of policy processes:

> In fast-policy systems—which have arisen to prominence in tandem with the neoliberal emphasis on technocratically essentialized, "best-practice" policy development—jurisdictions engage in increasingly energetic forms of rapid appraisal, extra-local "lesson-drawing," technocratic modeling, and accelerated reform, actively enabled by a sprawling network of policy intermediaries and entrepreneurs. (Peck and Theodore 2010:195–196)

Fast-policy emerged from the glocal conjunctures of the neoliberal policy landscape, as translocal (indeed, transnational) corporations (TNCs) and class elites attempted to bend disparate subnational policy structures outward towards their more global ends. TNCs do this by leveraging their supposed mobility which gives them the

> ability to shape **extralocal rule regimes** that constrain and channel the strategic option and tactical behavior of local actors. Many of the activities of entrepreneurial cities, for example, are strongly conditioned by such rule regimes, whether they are the formalized bidding systems and funding programs of national and transnational states... orchestrated competitions for inward investment (public or private), or the pressure to make a distinctive mark in international "image markets."Ironically, entrepreneurial cities' strategies are typically hailed by neoliberal ideologues as example par excellence of local agency, in general, and elite vision, in particular. (Peck 2002:338, emphasis added)

These extra-local rule regimes are both formal and informal (e.g., comprise both legislation and implicit norms/expectations), and are institutionalized more or less organically through the interactions of elites engaged in global-local activities. If we trace the history of changing recruitment efforts of automotive assembly plants in the neoliberal era, the outline which emerges is precisely one of transnational actors shaping an incipient rule regime to cultivate fast-policy systems that facilitate and subsidize capital-intensive investments through incentives. We can outline this process in four rough phases, which will also help us see how recruitment has changed – and why it has changed in the *way* it has – during the neoliberal globalization project: **(1)** in the 1980s automotive firms gradually shape an extralocal rule regime around recruitment, which **(2)** through mid-1980s leads to new, contested rules around incentives. **(3)** By the 1990s, this rule regime has given rise to a field of local development technocrats "that is populated by a mobile class of policy gurus, entrepreneurs, consultants, bloggers, evaluator-advocates, and model-peddlers" (Peck and Theodore 2015:xv), **(4)** finally shaping an era of recruitment fast-policy diffusion and policy modeling among states and localities. I will cover each period and the changes in turn.

1. *The early-mid 1980s: Incohate Extralocal Recruitment Rule Regime*
    Cases: VW (1978), GM (1980), Honda, and Nissan (1980)

The organized process of recruiting a major firm in the fashion described earlier simply did not happen in the early 1980s – the policy, people, and processes were not in place. While today one can go to any small town and likely have someone familiar with the policy of economic development and recruitment, this was not the case in the 1980s. As one business development professional noted, "in the last 20 years, there was really no pervasive knowledge of economic development... just the understanding of the term, and [the] more general concept of that has led to more people entering the field, which raises the game for being more professional. Some very rural locations, a decade ago, literally it could have been a secretary at a desk, and that was the 'economic development' person" (BDP03 2016). A site selector on the other side of the process of recruitment, echoed this observation: "communities are much more knowledgeable... more prepared when they go in and... generally speaking, particularly when it comes to automotive, the locations are more knowledgeable, more professional, and more prepared than they were 15 years ago" (SEL02 2016). Because there existed no network of development professionals, the process of recruitment was much more ad-hoc in the 1980s, as there were no best practices or expectations for how the process of recruitment would unfold. "When I started in the late 90s, you would hear people talk about how deals used to be consummated between state and companies, and it was a lot less formalized of a process. I mean it really was... I don't want to simplify it to the point of saying it was a handshake...on the golf course, but there was a lot less discipline to the way in which companies conducted that [process]" (EDP05 2015). In response to a question on the professionalization of the process since the 1980s, another economic development official observed "there's no question that [in 1980 in Tennessee] the state was almost exclusively [*sic*] – and governor [Lamar] Alexander was...the key negotiator, and Tennessee the state almost drove the deal...it has become more professional...and in the earlier projects the state had pretty much packaged it together" (EDP09 2016).

As these development professionals had yet to hear their calling, in the late 1970s through early 1980s, there were no clear channels of communication to disseminate knowledge and practices around recruitment and development. This explains why early cases with larger and more extensive public investments, Volkswagen in Pennsylvania (1978) and GM in Michigan (1980), did not necessarily influence the actions of later policymakers trying to lure automakers through the mid-1980s: the conditions for fast-policy diffusion were not in place. Indeed, despite an enormous public expenditure of $350 million in Hamtramck, MI, in 1980 – one which resembled later incentives packages in many ways, including the purchase and removal of residents from the site there – local officials in Tennessee could not justify the public expenditure on the land for their site in 1980 for Nissan (nor in 1985 for Saturn), even though Michigan has just made exactly this expenditure. When I asked an official who worked on both of those recruitments whether they had considered the 1980 deal with GM in Hamtramck, he told me "I don't think so...are you talking about the Hamtramck project?...No, I don't think we gave [it] too much [thought]...I don't remember that being any kind of discussion" (EDP09 2016).

There are important two points I would make here. First, it is worth pointing out that GM was the parent company of Saturn, the competition for which began to mark out the rule regime for such activity. The second is that the removal of residents by the Detroit government was bitterly resisted by those residents, and "while General Motors could not compel people to sell their property, the local governments could, under eminent domain, as long as...compulsory purchases were shown to be for a legitimate public purpose" (Rubenstein 1992:205). The residents of the Poletown neighborhood who were to be evicted brought the site acquisition into the national spotlight as they battled to save their neighborhood, a mix of well-maintained homes and condemned shells.[4] The neighborhood council sought a court injunction, and in 1980, a Circuit Court ruled that "the uncertain promise that the plant would employ 6,000 people" (Luger 2000:109) and enhance the tax base was a legitimate "public purpose." Both of these are key moments in forming the rule regime that would structure later recruitment policy, as GM understood that governments desperate for jobs would fight for projects that brought them, and that the courts would back such expenditures as public goods (I return to this legal reasoning and its broader importance in chapter 6).

These early moments of structuration had little effect on the two Greenfield plants sited in 1980, Honda in Marysville, OH, and Nissan in Smyrna, TN, where the consideration of actually purchasing the site itself was not considered legal state activity. Ohio Governor James Rhodes had actually purchased and developed the site ultimately chosen by Honda in his first term, in a move somewhat similar to contemporary site pre-development, and ultimately the state sold the site (termed the Transportation Research Center) to Honda for $30 million (Gelsanliter 1990:33–35). In the case of the Nissan plant, then-Governor Lamar Alexander put a team together to pursue the project, and specifically directed legal advisors to find "how can I justify spending money on this" land for the plant site – but ultimately they decided they could not justify purchasing the site to taxpayers (Gelsanliter 1990:49). Alexander did decide that the government could extend utilities to the plant, but only up to the property line of the eventual site. Nissan began to push rules around competition for industry in 1980 when it publicly announced its intentions to build a plant in the United States with the intention of creating a "big splash" – and creating intense competition among finalists for the site (Perrucci 1994:54). Thus, the late 70s and 80s saw transnational auto companies beginning to push at old ideas and rules around industrial relations and development, though localities themselves were not yet catching on. By all accounts, it was the competition for Saturn in 1985 which was a spectacular break from precedent.

2 Mid-late 1980s: structuration of extralocal recruitment rule regimes (inundated with Hams)

The seriatim recruitment of Saturn and Toyota in 1985 shifted the policy landscape significantly and in lasting ways. The competition for Saturn reshaped rules and norms around the competitive recruitment process itself, and the competition for Toyota shifted the boundaries of incentives packages used to recruit. "If Nissan's arrival generated fanfares, that furor was nothing in comparison to Saturn. GM's nationwide search for a plant, conducted in spring and summer of 1985, prompted 'the largest site selection bidding war of all time.' 'Saturn Mania' swept the country, and thirty-eight states and dozens of communities expressed their interest in hosting the plant"(Hülsemann 2001:229–230). Rubenstein continues this account,

> instead of discretely planning for the new product, GM chairman Roger Smith chose to shower lavish publicity on Saturn at a preliminary stage... by announcing that Saturn would be built... at a new plant, Smith unleashed a fierce battle among localities to attract the facility. Smith may have deliberately encouraged the competition in order to secure higher concessions, but it was probably unwittingly [was it, though?]. (Rubenstein 1992:208)

The professional I spoke to that worked with Tennessee in recruiting Nissan, Saturn, and Toyota to the state (the latter project they did not win), suggested that while both Saturn and Toyota were quite public – and generated intense competition – it was Saturn that shifted the norm on competition:

> It was a *different world*. Obviously [Saturn] was an American and the other was a Japanese company. The Saturn folks came out and announced directly – the Chairman Smith of GM – came on television [and said] "well, we're going to build a new car and it's going to be super gas efficient...named Saturn" and then the bidding wars were just wide open...I mean it was just amazing, it was very competitive. I would go to Detroit I...remember the Akron High School Band marched down the street in front of General Motors and had them deliver a petition with 50,000 signatures... [GM] said they were inundated with hams. It was a different world. Saturn was unlike anything we'd ever seen, because most folks like to keep what they're going to do, and how they're going to do it, quite confidential. (EDP09 2016)

As Peck notes, this competition should not simply be seen as something imposed on governments, but a process of mutually shaping the terrain of policy and action. Therein, local government elites are part and parcel of a process which "should be seen as one of scalar-structuration, in which the competitive (local) behavior of urban elites both reflects and reproduces the extralocal rule regimes that subsequently canalize and circumscribe local action" (Peck 2002:338). If Saturn and the many local governments shipping hams were producing a rule regime for competition, the company coterminously shaped rules around the need for state leadership on recruitment efforts, and the kind of dedicated development officials we see today:

> [there were some recruitment efforts which] certainly began prior to the Saturn competition, but awareness of the need for industrial

development policies was less widespread and recruitment...highly dependent on the behavior of local officials... The Saturn site selection process demonstrated that leadership in attracting and retaining large projects, such as automobile plants, must reside at the level of the governments of the fifty states. Overwhelmed by requests from hundreds of communities, General Motors turned to states to bring order to the selection process. States were asked to coordinate the flow of material from individual communities to GM. (Rubenstein 1992:208–212).

It was the competition for Toyota later that same year that rewrote the rules on incentives themselves in an important way. When Honda sited its $750 million plant in Marysville, Ohio, in 1980, the state and local governments combined paid only about $22 million dollars "in new highways, site improvements, and tax abatements, a commitment considered by many at the time as excessive" (Rubenstein 1992:209). Incentives for Saturn, and Nissan five years prior, were larger than Honda – at around $80 million dollars – but all were limited to road connections and improvements, training funds, and tax abatements (Gilbert 1994; Milward and Newman 1989). At first, Toyota mimicked the site selection process of Nissan and Honda, quietly "generat[ing] a short list of sites, including Kansas City, Kansas and Lebanon, Tennessee, a northern suburb of Nashville" (Rubenstein 1992:228), localities whom they had been in contact with since their early 80s research into possible plant locations. But in the summer of 1985, after the highly publicized recruitment of GM's Saturn plant in January of that year, "Toyota backed off from Kansas City and Nashville and decided to throw open the choice to the highest bidder...thirty communities responded" (Rubenstein 1992:229). I note here the inter-local comparative learning model typical of fast-policy processes.

The proximity of Saturn and Toyota competitions is critical, as the Tennessee recruiter who worked on Nissan, Saturn, and Toyota confirmed:

> [With Toyota] the world changed dramatically in terms of support – incentives –because Governor Collins, Martha Layne Collins, was the Governor of Kentucky and no question, she and her administration really stepped up...when Governor Collins stepped up, their total package was one hundred and thirty, forty million dollars. So Nissan [in Tennessee] was forty million dollars, most all of that was training. Then, the bidding wars went crazy for the big plants, but the one that really did break it was Toyota. No question. (EDP09 2016)

The Toyota package was not only the largest to date, valued at $147 million (not including unspecified tax abatements), it also was the first case to include site purchase, preparation, and utility provision by the state, the cost of training *and* a training center, as well as perks tailored to the company, such as money set aside for the education of Japanese families who would transplant to Georgetown (Gelsanliter 1990:87; Perrucci 1994:7). State Governor and the transnational auto company were mutually shaping a regime of recruitment fast-policy rules by pushing the envelope on incentives. Governor Richard Celeste of Ohio suggested Toyota essentially demanded blank check, and "I had already offered $105 million. It was as high as I could go, perhaps already higher than I should have gone. To have offered more couldn't have been justified to a comparable American company" (*quoted in* Gelsanliter 1990:79). There is a striking echo here of Lamar Alexander, five years earlier, struggling to justify the purchase of the Nissan site and failing to do so – and this echo is indicative of the rule regimes governors faced in that time period.

Interestingly, Toyota and Kentucky were challenged in their mutual effort to rewrite the rules around incentives. Amidst negative press coverage and public unpopularity of the incentives package, activist Ralph Nader took the Collins administration to court, challenging the constitutionality of direct state expenditures on the Toyota incentive. The case went to the state Supreme Court, and "in June [1986] the Kentucky Supreme Court ruled 4-3 that the Collins incentive package was constitutional. At issue had been whether the state had the power to raise and spend money for the benefit of a private business. Proponents argued that the purchase and transfer of 1,600 acres, along with the other inducements, were not a gift... Kentucky would eventually receive fair market value through new tax revenue... [and] the potential benefits to be derived were so great that the constitution must be judicially amended" (Gelsanliter 1990:128; Perrucci 1994). In December of that year, Fuji-Isuzu would announce a $500 million plant to locate in Lafayette, Indiana, and receive incentives valued between $260 million and $346 million, including the purchase of land and its development, and funds set aside for Japanese families' transitions.[5] Simply put, transnational auto firms were forming extralocal rule regimes around incentives to extend public coverage to the costs and risks of fixed-capital investments, a pattern seen clearly in Table 4.1.

The Saturn and Toyota site selections also reshaped the best practices of recruitment: "local government officials learned from the Saturn [and Toyota] experience that aggressive marketing practices to attract or retain industries were not only acceptable behavior, they had become expected. Overseas trips by politicians, once considered thinly veiled holiday junkets, became a necessary undertaking to attracting investors... secret deals were replaced by highly publicized signing ceremonies" (Rubenstein 1992:208–209). Many accounts suggest that Governor Collins was instrumental in pushing the incentives package into new territory. As the development official who worked for Tennessee observed "when [Nissan] selected Tennessee, I think Martha Layne got pretty red-faced, and anyhow she said 'we won't let that happen again'" (EDP09 2016). Gelsanliter also suggests that Collins felt she had "lost" Saturn and feared losing the Toyota project to Indiana; "Kentucky won out, it appears, because of the aggressive wooing of its governor" Collins, who made a number of "last-minute" concessions to the company to seal the deal (1990:76). Thus, extralocal rules around both aggressive recruitment and the down-to-the wire competition were being shaped in through the mid-1980s.

3 The 1990s: fast-policy in Southern Climes

By the early 1990s, a cadre of mobile policy experts and consultants was consolidating around local economic development, slowly establishing fast-policy networks to facilitate knowledge transfers of policy processes. Today, "the expectation of businesses that interact with these [development] orga-nizations is to have someone that is knowledgeable, competent, and has been educated in the right skills to be able to facilitate the kind of trans-action that they're...looking for" (EDP06 2016). This aspect of the re-cruitment rule regime was likely fostered in the recruitment of the German auto firms who transplanted in 1992–1993, both of whom hired specialized site selection consultants. They did this in part because, as foreign firms, they did not have a foothold in the United States, but also because it allowed them out-source risk and impose process-control. An individual working with development partnership in North Carolina elaborated the impact these consulting firms had:

> 30–40 years ago, you...didn't have this sizable cottage industry of third-party advisors... I mean, now you have this very specialized inter-mediary party that typically represents about half the potential deals out there, and their job is to extract the very best offer they can for their clients. And that's often times one of the chief filters for which they're evaluating [prospects] so of course, that's going to put a much greater emphasis on incentives than there has been before. And if the state hasn't stepped up its game...in the short term that could really cost the state some chances to win deals. (EDP05 2015)

The professionalization of site selection pushed localities to professionalize their efforts, and while South Carolina recruited BMW in a less rationalized process, led primarily by the Governor relying on personal contacts and favors, Alabama had dedicated local development officials, led by the Secretary of Commerce Billy Joe Camp. This is a critical shift in the dy-namics of business recruitment, as the formation of a field of development professionals – drawn from existing organizations like chambers of com-merce, corporate or utility marketing firms, local booster associations – created the social infrastructure for communication of recruitment policy and best practices (e.g., rule regimes). Mercedes-Benz was key to shaping these rules, as the company sent out a large package of questionnaires to potential states. According to then-Secretary of Commerce Billy Joe Camp, potential states were informed that "Mercedes would be seeking incentives that were at least comparable to BMW. In fact, [they] suggested that Mercedes regarded itself as a much more attractive investment than BMW, and the implication was clear" (McDermott 2013:67). Thus, Mercedes Benz effectively demanded localities adhere to extralocal rules around comparative policy development and competitive recruitment. The more sensationalized bidding wars that took place in the above account of VW in Tennessee were not yet the norm, but this process was normalized throughout the early 1990s as well. One of the officials that worked in both the 80s and early 90s clarified "there was not [a bidding up at the end of the Toyota project in 1985]... Toyota when they came they were very, very detailed...they had questionnaires that we directed from their contractors, from their accountants...and I'm sure they compared the answers...I don't know that much about BMW but I do know that Mercedes-Benz narrowed down to three finalists, North Carolina, South Carolina, and of course Vance, Alabama. Those were the three final sites. Yes, they did go back and forth – I [it was] think a very competitive situation, as you can guess." (EDP09 2016). The recruitment of the two German firms in the early 1990s solidified the extralocal recruitment rule regime, as localities and transnational firms together laid the groundwork for fast-policy systems that would hum monotonously into the new millennium.

4   *1999 and beyond: boutique policy, right off-the-rack*

Changes in recruitment and incentives after the early 1990s are emblematic of the fast-policy processes, in which more or less derivative policies and practices bounce around networks of chummy local technocrats, professional consultants, and their attendant publications. While all of the professionals I spoke to proclaimed the uniqueness of their deals, what fast-policy "really means is the importation of off-the-shelf program techniques from other locations... as local administrators benchmark their performance against that of other localities and... learn from local success stories" (Peck 2002:344).[6] In this regard, the fundamental similarity in the substance of the incentives packages detailed in Table 1A and Table 4.1 after the mid-1980s is more important than the dollar-value attached to them, which clearly fluctuates and does not rise in a simple linear fashion. "With each automotive project, starting in the 90's, the incentives sort of stepped up to some degree with each project. You know a company would know about what the prior company got, and there'd be a lot of pressure of the competing locations to do *at least* that, if not better than that" (SEL02 2016).

The fact that the dollar values do not increase in each case is best explained by the fact that while fast-policy is ideally mobile, *quick* policy, it inevitably come up against the "stubborn reality... that *making policies work* very often remains a hands-on, messy, and very much 'local' affair" (Peck and Theodore 2015:xvii). To understand how local messiness produces differences in incentives packages, we need to consider both the way the packages themselves are constructed, as well as the dynamics of fast-policy spread. The first thing to consider is the variation in local costs of what the incentives are intended to cover; while two plants may have the same initial investment and both require connecting roads, the cost of building those roads may be much higher at one location than the other. For example, when Honda came into Lincoln, AL, the combined cost of utility connections and road improvements and connections was $20 million, but in Canton, MS, the cost of road improvements alone was almost $60 million, with utility connections adding an additional $33 million to the package. As one person involved in recruiting both Mercedes-Benz and Honda to Alabama recalled, "the overall total package was somewhat smaller than Mercedes, although not significantly smaller, and most of that was in terms of the training facility that would be constructed. That was the biggest difference. And the lay of the land, how much work was required, what kind of roads would have to be [put] in, certainly played into it also" (EDP09 2016).[7] One official from Mississippi who worked to recruit Toyota noted the lay of land required a good deal of work, "we were virtually showing Toyota hills n' hollers – so they had to be convinced" (EDP07 2016). It is also important to consider the relative size of the plants that are intended to be constructed and the number of people they project to employ, as these affect the cost of land, utilities, and materials, as well as the dollar value of jobs-based tax credits.

Thus, each of the projects after the 1990s looks basically similar: "as the same set of policy ideas migrate across markets, they become a neoliberal script, where the same 'toolbox' of ideas or 'cookie-cutter' solutions are presented as the solution to particular… ailments" (Cleave et al. 2017:1139). One critical effect the structuration of this fast-policy regime has had is to compress the overall process, something also driven by increasing use of computers, databases, and desktop analyses early in the recruitment process. Said one such consultant, "I've seen this certainly evolve over time. So, you go back even 10, 15 years ago, whether it's the site selection firm like ours or a company doing a search on their own, they would reach out to 15 or 20 communities right at the beginning of the process. In today's world, with so much information being available publicly…our firm we have our own database, and we also pay to subscribe to information from different databases…to help us with that process…until we're down to six or fewer communities" (SEL03 2016). A number of development professionals echoed this observation, stating that "the internet has been the biggest change [in economic development]… because the speed at which people can get information… now they can do desktop analysis" (BDP01 2016) and that "there's a lot more information, and quantifiable, that's driving the process now, than was the case a quarter century ago" (EDP05 2015). In the broader view, it is not simply that there is new technology and more information, but the employment of technology and the dissemination of information amongst policy elites that has compressed the process of industrial recruitment. One professional site selector describes how the siting of the Nissan plant in Mississippi raised the level of competition in siting projects and getting them up and running:

> If anything has changed dramatically [since the 1990s] it's the amount of time that companies give themselves to make a location decision, and… get product to market. We did the Nissan site search, we had our first meeting in the middle of May of 2000, and we gave them a final recommendation with incentives packages done at the end of October, basically slightly under five months. The typical project – Hyundai, Kia – before that were a year and a half, two-year projects. And subsequent to that, the time frame on these automotive projects stayed pretty tight…the biggest change is the time frame that companies have to make these decisions, and to get the project up and running…that is a big influence on the location and the properties you're looking at, because it's no longer "what do you have in terms of size and capacity?" it's "when can you have it ready?" (SEL02 2016).

The time-compression effects of fast-policy are a definitive feature of current recruitment practice (Cleave et al. 2017), and this, in turn, led the drive to certify and even predevelop sites. A development official who had worked on several automotive projects in Alabama reflected that "when I started out it was more about…cash incentives and what you're going to do from that standpoint, I think it has dramatically shifted, to where the driver in my opinion is 'do you have a site? Do you have a product? Are you ready for a project to come there?'" (EDP08 2016). Thus, since the early 2000s localities and states began to purchase and certify sites through various certification programs (offered by utility companies or site selection firms) prior to any specific project being negotiated. The simplest version of this involves conducting due-diligence (environmental surveys, workforce potential, etc.) and proving proof of ownership, while the more extreme cases involved actually prepping the site before a deal is in the works. Today, most states or state utilities certify their own sites and Megasites (very large acreage locales), and list these on development websites, and some local coalitions build websites specifically for the Megasite itself (a clear and simple example of fast-policy diffusion). The cyclical modeling and transmission of best practices through networks, publications, and organizations is evidence that fast-policy processes are now firmly guiding industrial recruitment, and it is merely a question of adjusting the off-the-rack model of incentives to the particular company and local circumstances.[8]

Conclusions: a race to the bottom?

Clearly, the simple narrative that localities are caught in a pernicious but inevitable race-to-the-bottom for capital and investment is inadequate. It is as much the local leaders and policy elites who happily meet companies' demands and adhere to their rules, rules which are shaped and reshaped by both companies and local elites. In this context then, the *narrative* that localities are caught in a race-to-the-bottom for mobile global capital needs to be reframed as a script which is circulated amongst development elites with greater or lesser instrumental intent to justify practices which are normalized in their technocratic field, but often difficult to sell to a public that did not elect them. "In this hyperglobalized scenario, markets determine the rules of the game... for neoliberal politicians and corporate leaders this script is an appealing one because it allows the presentation of their (sectional) interests as systemic, rationalistic, and naturalized realities" (Peck 2002:334).

In this chapter, I have elaborated the processes of industrial recruitment of major automotive plants, the incentives offered and by whom, and how this process and the actors involved have changed over the life of the neoliberal globalization project. I have argued that the changes in these processes reveal the rise of a regime of fast-policy for local development and particularly recruitment. It is worth reiterating that many of the particular details discussed are unique to Greenfield industrial sites (as opposed to appropriated old factory sites, though Hamtramck would fall into this category). And note well that major industrial projects are uncommon in terms of the scope and scale of the investment and the employment they entail. It is further worth pointing out that the above elaboration has taken place from largely *within* the perspective of the government and private actors involved in industrial recruitment efforts. What is striking is the number of topics that did *not* emerge from my interviews: there were almost no mentions of officials or the public more generally objecting to any plant in a locality. Resistance to incentives was not treated with any legitimate concern in the few instances in which it was discussed at all (I discuss this further in the next chapter). Labor, as anything more than a workforce (as opposed to a political force) was scarcely mentioned. In other words, the theoretical considerations of class power, globalized competition, and the conjunction of economic and political power framed in earlier chapters, are considered *de facto* realities and not remarked upon in and of themselves.

As will become clear in the following two chapters, these remarkable omissions are part and parcel of the professional knowledge and perspective of the individuals interviewed here, what I call the "partnership" perspective. In the following chapter (5), I show that beneath the changing size and shape of incentives, the relationships between governments and business have also begun to change. As economic development and industrial recruitment become increasingly routinized and professionalized, the way in which governments and firms relate to each other and see each other's role in business has changed. In the next chapter, I elaborate on this professional field of knowledge in local economic development and its attendant perspective, and show that the omissions above are constitutive of this field. In chapter 6, I show that this partnership perspective is not a neutral standpoint but a reconfiguration of power relations, one that diminishes the political space of local actors and workers by eroding the legitimacy of the discursive land-scape on which they stand. This discursive shift is part and parcel of a po-litical shift in class relations driven by neoliberal ideology and the interests of global capital. But first, we need to apprehend the partnership perspective itself, and this is the task to which I turn in the proceeding chapter.

Notes

1 In the following chapter, I will discuss the importance of conceptualizing place as a product and governance as marketing.
2 At the high end, this would amount to more than $800 million. Such a number may seem high, but this would be in line with the estimates of Toyota's incentives in Canton, MS, amounting to over a billion (Mattera and Tarczynska 2013).
3 For a fascinating take on the way speculation can take over a community, one can read Joe Sherman's *In the Rings of Saturn* (1993).
4 Hamtramck, interestingly, was also the site of an earlier Chrysler plant closure – notable for its particularly militant unions.
5 In many ways, the Toyota recruitment is prototypical of the recruitment process we see today, in part because Toyota struck the balance of competition and confidentiality we see today. "The Saturn project it was just huge, they were- every state virtually in the country made some kind of an effort for it. And Toyota was a more typical Japanese, more very low key, not wanting to let the world know all what was happening with them" (EDP09 2016).
6 In this regard, fast-policy is a bit like fast fashion, thinly veiled emulation parading under a banner of boutique character.
7 In fact, a training center was constructed for Honda in 2001, which reports place between ten and thirty million dollars.
8 One official working with the TVA described one way in which recruitment po-licies and best-practices were cultivated, as they stress to localities that corpora-tions are "doing a lot of desktop analysis. You know because they can get demographic information, they can get labor information. So, one of our things [at TVA] we offer our communities is making sure their websites are up to date. Because if they're not they may get overlooked just because of the accuracy of the information" (BDP01 2016). In other words, as firms develop more sophisticated analyses, localities have to become more sophisticated in their "marketing" of their "product" – by maintaining accurate websites, gathering data. This, in turn, has driven the need to network with site selection firms, and invest in site certification programs, and increasingly actually break ground on sites before there is even a prospect on the horizon. "So, you've got to have the product...so much now is data driven, so much is elimination driven, these professional site consultants are people who do this – they go through a process of looking through a lot of good communities and they're going to eliminate down from 30, to 25, to three or four. And your objective is you've got to be competitive enough to stay in the game" (EDP08 2016).

Bibliography

BDP01. 2016. "Business Development Professional 01."
BDP02. 2016. "Business Development Professional 02."
BDP03. 2016. "Business Development Professional 03."

Boudreaux, Christopher, R. Morris Coats, and Earl H. Davis. 2012. "The Dark Side of State Competition for Foreign Direct Investment: That Which Is Seen and That Which Is Not Seen." *Southern Business & Economic Journal* 35(1):35–52.

Cleave, Evan, Godwin Arku, Richard Sadler, and Jason Gililand. 2017. "Is It Sound Policy of Fast Policy? Practitioners Perspectives on the Role of Place Branding in Local Economic Development." *Urban Geography* 38(8):1133–1157.

Cobb, James C. 1993. *The Selling of the South: The Southern Crusade for Industrial Development 1936-1990*, 2nd edition. Urbana: University of Illinois Press.

Cooper, Helene, and Glenn Ruggenbach. 1993. "Alabama's Winning of Mercedes Plant Will Be Costly, With Major Tax Breaks." *Wall Street Journal*, September 30.

Cope, Cassie. 2015. "How South Carolina Won Volvo." *The State*. Retrieved June 2, 2015 (http://www.thestate.com/news/politics-government/politics-columns-blogs/the-buzz/article21195345.html).

DuPlessis, Jim. 2002. "BMW's S.C. Plant Stays on Fast Track." *State, The (Columbia, SC)*, September 26, FINAL, A1.

DuPlessis, Jim. 2008. "BMW Expansion to Create 500 Jobs - $750 Million Spartanburg County Project to Make Plant Hub for X-Cars." *State, The (Columbia, SC)*, March 11, FINAL, A1.

EDP01. 2015. "Economic Deveopment Professional 01."

EDP02. 2015. "Economic Development Professional 02."

EDP03. 2015. "Economic Development Professional 03."

EDP04. 2015. "Economic Development Professional 04."

EDP05. 2015. "Economic Development Professional 05."

EDP06. 2016. "Economic Development Professional 06."

EDP07. 2016. "Economic Development Professional 07."

EDP08. 2016. "Economic Development Professional 08."

EDP09. 2016. "Economic Development Professional 09."

Gelsanliter, David. 1990. *Jump Start: Japan Comes to the Heartland*. New York: Farrar Straus Giroux.

Gilbert, Stuart C. 1994. "Observations on the Saturn Project: Site Selection, Financial Incentives, and Impact." *Economic Development Review* 12(4):35.

Good Jobs First. 2018. *The New Math on School Finance: Adding Up the First-Ever Disclosure of Corporate Tax Abatements' Cost to Public Education*. Good Jobs First.

Goode, S. 1992. "Two Special Incentives Given to BMW." *Spartanburg Herald-Journal*, June 24.

Hülsemann, Karsten. 2001. "Greenfields in the Heart of Dixie: How the American Auto Industry Discovered the South." Pp. 219–254 in *The Second Wave: Southern Industrialization from the 1940s to the 1970s*, edited by P. Scranton. Athens, GA: University of Georgia Press.

Jacobs, A. J. 2012. "Collaborative Regionalism and Foreign Direct Investment The Case of the Southeast Automotive Core and the 'New Domestics.'" *Economic Development Quarterly* 26(3):199–219.

Kebede, Allene, and Sylvain Ngandu. 1999. "The Economic Impact of the Mercedes Benz Investment on the State of Alabama." *Journal of Agricultural and Applied Economics* 31(2):371–382.

Luger, Stan. 2000. *Corporate Power, American Democracy, and the Automobile Industry*. Cambridge, UK; New York: Cambridge University Press.

Mattera, Phillip, and Kasia Tarczynska. 2013. *A Good Deal For Mississippi? A Report on Taxpayer Assistance in Canton, Mississippi.* Washington: Good Jobs First.

Mattera, Phillip, Kasia Tarczynska, Leigh McIlvaine, Thomas Cafcas, and Greg LeRoy. 2012. *Paying Taxes to the Boss.* Washington: Good Jobs First.

McDermott, Michael C. 2012. "Hyundai Automotive Group's Investments in the U.S. South: Competition and Decisions." *Southern Business & Economic Journal* 35(1):11–34.

McDermott, Michael C. 2013. "Mercedes-Benz, Tuscaloosa, Alabama: Drivers and Processes in the International Plant Location Decision." *Southern Business & Economic Journal* 36(1):57–73.

Meadows, Andrew. 1998. "New Auto, New Jobs at Bmw $600 Million S.c. Expansion to Bring 1,000 More Workers." *State, The (Columbia, SC)*, May 13, FINAL, A1.

Milward, H. Brinton, and Heidi Hosbach Newman. 1989. "State Incentive Packages and the Industrial Location Decision." *Economic Development Quarterly* 3(3):203–222.

Monk, Fred. 1992. "BMW Courtship Long and Rocky." *The State*, June 24.

Patterson, Dennis. 1993. "N. Carolina Balked at Huge Tax Breaks." *Huntsville Times, The (AL)*, September 30, 2, A 2.

Peck, Jamie. 2002. "Political Economies of Scale: Fast Policy, Interscalar Relations, and Neoliberal Workfare." *Economic Geography* 78(3):331–360. doi: 10.1111/j.1944-8287.2002.tb00190.x.

Peck, Jamie, and Nik Theodore. 2010. "Recombinant Workfare, across the Americas: Transnationalizing 'Fast' Social Policy." *Geoforum* 41(2):195–208.

Peck, Jamie, and Nik Theodore. 2015. *Fast Policy: Experimental Statecraft at the Thresholds of Neoliberalism.* Minneapolis: University of Minnesota Press.

Perrucci, Robert. 1994. *Japanese Auto Transplants in the Heartland: Corporatism and Community.* New York: Aldine de Gruyter.

Rubenstein, James M. 1992. *The Changing Us Auto Industry: A Geographical Analysis.* London England; New York: Routledge.

Schaffer, Susanne M. 2012. "BMW to Add 300 Jobs with $900 Million S.C. Expansion." *State, The (Columbia, SC)*, January 13, 14.

SEL01. 2016. "Site Selection Professional."

SEL02. 2016. "Site Selection Professional."

SEL03. 2016. "Site Selection Professional."

Sherman, Joe. 1993. *In the Rings of Saturn*, 1st edition. New York: Oxford University Press.

Spindler, Charles J. 1994. "Winners and Losers in Industrial Recruitment: Mercedes-Benz and Alabama." *State & Local Government Review* 26(3):192–204.

Thomas, Kenneth. 2011. *Investment Incentives and the Global Competition for Capital.* London: Palgrave Macmillan.

5   The business of partnerships

Installing neoliberal ideologies: recruitment within ideological perspective

On the surface of it, growing incentivization of private investment and socialization of associated costs and risks seems contradictory to the neoliberal project and its free market ideology. In practice, however, neoliberal policies often run counter to the core narratives of self-regulation and state retrenchment. As Harvey notes in his seminal text on neoliberalism, the neoliberal state (writ large) "twists and in some respects even reverses neoliberal theory in its practice" which in part arises "out of the need to create a 'good business or investment climate' for capitalistic endeavours..." (Harvey 2005:70). As we saw in the previous chapter, "neoliberal policy contradicts neoliberal rhetoric because political regulatory bodies typically expand alongside markets" and in some instances even "socialize the market" (Pacewicz 2013:434; Levi-Faur and Jordana 2005). This contradiction is deflected through an ideology of practice (governmentality) that is suffused with the language of entrepreneurial governance, a scalar narrative in which the words and silences equally give the lie to how the practice of local governance is deeply *classed* in the neoliberal era. I draw out these class processes more explicitly in the following chapter, but in this chapter my goal is to elaborate this ideological perspective of what local governance itself is, and how this is constituted within networks of fast-policy technocrats, in their own words.[1]

Economic development officials within different organizations and at different scales adapt recruitment and incentives policies according to their specific locality and the project at hand. However, site selection consultants and development professionals draw on a field of shared language, a specialized knowledge of expectations and best practices for businesses and governments in the process of development and recruitment. Indeed, many professionals who I spoke to had worked both for governments as economic development professionals, and as site consultants for private firms locating projects, and shifting between sides was fairly routine. While such professional intermingling is not necessarily unusual, it is reflective of the fact that

DOI: 10.4324/9781003107569-5

this professional field is articulated through a perspective that distinctly reflects the reality of private business. What this means is that as the field of local economic development grew, what took shape was an arm of local governments that acted *as* businesses; that dealt with private firms on their own terms, and from a shared perspective.[2] I will argue this manifestation of entrepreneurial governance is not simply government adapting to mobile capital, but government behaving *as* capital. The underlying theme that guides this chapter, and the actual entrepreneurialization of governance, is that of "partnership" – a concept that defines the way in which localities and businesses ideologically frame the appropriate function of government in private development and growth.

"The new entrepreneurialism has, as its centerpiece, the notion of a public-private partnership" (Harvey 1989:5). While sociologists and political economists have studied the structure and operation of formal public–private partnership arrangements, the partnership between the public and private realms is as much an ideology and theory of practice as it is an organizational form. The discourse of partnership reconfigures the role of subnational governments in relation to business from one of managers and regulators to that of the amenable business partner, whose potential benefit from job creation and economic growth makes them an equal entrepreneur in new capital investment ventures. This view of governance is different from understanding government as the manager of a locality, to use Harvey's term, which saw the role of local government as essentially "wards of the federal government and rely[ing] fundamentally on redistributions for survival" (Harvey 1989:4). Pacewicz's seminal ethnography of two local development organizations in Iowa highlights the fact that those who adopt the partnership perspective – *partners* as he calls them – typically also eschew public displays of partisan political harrumphing, which is viewed as unproductive (Pacewicz 2016:112). While localities in the southern United States have long had a more activist history in the promotion of business and local development, the partnership approach is different. In this view, governments are a distinctive *kind* of partner, one with a unique capacity to enhance a firm's locational capabilities (the ability of a firm to secure resources it needs) and reduce up-front and operational costs through public provision of incentives and infrastructure (Storper and Walker 1989:73). As Harvey points out "in many of the versions of public-private-partnership, particularly at the municipal level, the state assumes much of the risk while the private sector takes most of the profits" (Harvey 2005:77). Thus, as we will see, the changes and growth in incentives for business in the last 40-odd years, and the growth of the economic development profession, reflect a qualitative shift in the relations between local governments and private firms, from one of manager to one of business partner and fellow entrepreneur. The practice and discourse of partnership ties together three intertwined, but distinct, themes that emerged in the course of my interviews and coding (and are supported in literature more broadly): (1) the customer service experience, (2) place as product (development and marketing), and (3) business governmentality. Together, these themes constitute the partnership perspective and are the basis of shared knowledge that is formative of the economic development profession. Below I elaborate these three themes in order to add flesh to the bones of the partnership perspective, and then return to the theory of entrepreneurial governance and discuss how it frames contemporary governmental relations.

Partnership I: the Customer Service Experience (CSE)

Throughout my discussions with development professionals one clear theme that emerged was that businesses increasingly expect states to roll out the "customer service experience." The customer service experience (CSE) has both overt and subtle aspects, each of which can be reasonably compared to a luxury or boutique customer service experience. Overt aspects of the CSE include recruitment authorities treating the prospective firm and project as a distinct individual with particular needs and tailoring the incentives and site to meet those needs – much like a tailor fitting a bespoke suit. Note there are two interrelated aspects here, *getting to know* the needs, and *the tailoring* of the final product: for major industrial or headquarters projects, off-the-rack incentives simply will not do, no matter their scope. Given that the tools each locality can use to meet these needs differ from place to place, the CSE highlights the tendency of flexibility within uniformity characteristic of fast-policy. The subtler aspects of the CSE involve the overall tonality of the recruitment process, and the need for governments to impart the sense that they are *genuinely* invested and interested in the prospective client, inculcating a feeling in the firm that they are really wanted.[3] Together, these two aspects of the customer service experience serve to demonstrate the kind of partner the local and state governments will be, an unquantifiable but nonetheless critical aspect of business recruitment.

Ascertaining the needs of the particular project was a recurrent theme in discussions of successful recruitment efforts. As one city development officer put it, "the key to successful negotiation, in my opinion, is understanding what the company needs. It's not *all* about money. It could be marketing, it could be presence, it could be visibility, it could be workforce training…that is added value, that is money you don't spend – it's money I save you – so it's almost the same thing. [Q: *so, basically taking a kind of…customer service approach?*] You *have* to. To me, the most successful programs, that's what they do" (EDP02 2015). A development official with the Georgia Department of Economic Development (GDEcD) who worked to bring Kia to Georgia echoed this sentiment almost verbatim, "the most important thing I can do…in any negotiation…is develop a relationship…I have to know what you really want – what you really need…it doesn't sound like a lot, but it begins to create a bridge, and it says that 'you're acknowledging me – you're paying attention to me'" (EDP03 2015). This aspect of meeting the "customer's" particular needs was also central in the account of the VW recruiter in the previous chapter, who suggested that his tactic of saying "it would be more effective for us [the state] if we were able to know what you need…to see if we're in a position of being able to support what you need" (EDP06 2016) was what shifted the scales in winning the project over the "blank check" approach of the Alabama team. This strategy of addressing the specific needs of the incoming project is found throughout the cases I studied, and leads to several important outcomes, one obviously being that companies end up with incentives packages tailored to their project. Hence, in addition to common elements among incentives packages (site purchase, rail connections, etc.), there are typically perks and small gestures: states may increase the visibility of a plant through landscaping around the connecting highway, free advertising, stadia and streets are renamed, college education is provided for executives' children. There are larger individual elements for each package as well that reflect the tailoring of incentives, such as the Welcome Center constructed for Mercedes-Benz, or Toyota in Blue Springs, MS, receiving $30 million to encourage supplier relocation, or Georgia promising not only to construct a training center for Kia, but also to maintain the center for five years at an estimated cost of $5.5 million. Thus, central to the CSE is the process of getting to know the needs of the projects and using the tools available (jobs programs, extant legislation, and new provisions) in the particular localities to meet those needs as best possible.

Beyond the incentives packages themselves, companies are also looking for the appropriate mindset or attitude from governments, one that "pays attention" and demonstrates consideration of the uniqueness of the firm and its needs. Being creative in constructing incentives packages is a key aspect of the CSE not only because it meets relevant needs, but because it demonstrates the tone of relationships that companies like to see – namely one in which they are made to feel special. Said one state official of the incentives package they offered

Mercedes-Benz "I think we demonstrated we were really hungry for this [project], and would be the kind of partner Mercedes-Benz was looking for" (EDP08 2016). A similar sentiment was expressed directly to the lead Tennessee recruiter by the VW executive working on the project, "Stephan Jacoby…[who] said to us 'one of the biggest and most impressive things you did was clear that site before you even had a project – that was impactful to VW because it sent the message you're going to be a good partner'" (EDP06 2016). As should be clear from these examples, the sentiment of specialness conveyed by the CSE is essential to perceiving/conveying the government *as* a partner. Conversely, a former Commerce Secretary from North Carolina observed that the state's cool tonality may have impacted its competitiveness on some projects, "I used to say 'we're good enough not to have to be really good at economic development'…I think it was the tenor that I discovered [at the Department of Commerce], and it wasn't that we weren't working hard and we didn't have people engaged and recruiting, it's that we felt didn't have to be on the cutting edge of initiatives for recruitment...the hunger was not there, like it was in other places" (EDP04 2015). Thus, the importance of the CSE is not simply in approach and package, but in making the company feel special – as frivolous or adolescent as that might sound. Indeed, as early as Saturn's pursuit of its southern site, tenor and tonality were critical, as the professional who worked on that project for Tennessee recounted "[the] first choice for Saturn was around in the Lexington [Kentucky] area, and they came on down to Knoxville next. And I asked them later, 'well, why didn't you guys kind of get up in Kentucky?' They [Ed Dilworth and George Fox, with GM] both told me 'well, we just didn't feel like we were—like this was something they really wanted up in their bluegrass. They didn't want smokestacks and whatever'"(EDP09 2016). This same professional worked on the recruitment of Mercedes-Benz years later, and related a telling story, "governor Campbell, Carrol Campbell, who was an excellent economic development governor in South Carolina, I believe late at night that [the head of the Mercedes Benz team] said that Governor looked at him and said, 'look, let's put it this way, whatever they're giving you, we will match it in South Carolina' and I think that—his comment was 'well, that's nice, but that's not very creative.' I don't think that went over all that well. It was an interesting comment" (EDP09 2016).

The importance of the CSE helps us explain not only the individualized perks attached to each project, but also why incentives packages do not grow in a simply linear fashion in terms of dollar value. One former Alabama official explained why the incentives offered to Honda appeared somewhat smaller compared to previous and subsequent packages,

> Honda approached this in negotiating, and incentive package, that [*sic*] they felt was appropriate, and what they needed for their project. And that was the approach they took...the discussions we that had with them it was 'here's what we need, here's why we need it' and then Alabama responded and said 'here's what we can do, and here's how we will go about doing it.'...So that was the business approach that I remember us going through...the incentives are not always the driver that wins or loses projects, in my opinion, it's a lot more than that. It's the partnership. (EDP08 2016)

This anecdote highlights precisely the way in which localizing effects are negotiated through fast-policy processes, as both the actual locality and the particular project require the policies emulated to be grafted to the bodies found at hand. The importance of the CSE is also in part driven by site consultants, who bring the focus on their client's needs to the forefront of the negotiation. When I asked one site selection consultant about whether states were driving the shift in incentives towards offsetting up-front costs, he replied "I think partly, in the negotiation process. But I think it's incumbent on site selection firms, you know, corporate decision makers themselves saying 'okay, here's what's important to us – here's why these three issues are pain points for us, and why we need you to partner with us on that'" (SEL03 2016). He later continued, discussing the negotiation process in particular, effectively summing up the importance of the CSE to the partnership perspective,

> most communities and most states view it as a collaboration or a partnership. There's a lot of good interactions to say 'ok, well here's the tools we have – here are some ideas and ways we can deploy those tools to help your project, now tell us what's most meaningful to you.' And our job [as site consultants] is to quarterback that process…again, one, it helps support our clients need for the project, but at the same time it results in a structure where the city, the state, and our client feel like it's a positive outcome and everybody's equally invested and protected. (SEL03 2016)

The CSE noticeably depends upon the narrative of asymmetry between localities and capital, as localities behave like retailers trying to lure ever fickle customers to their fixed location. "In neoliberal scalar narratives, highly exposed localities are pitched in an asymmetrical competitive battle against an unyielding global market, their only realistic response being to adapt" (Peck 2002:334). The asymmetry of this narrative noticeably remains implicit for most of my participants, largely because it is as much a rationalizing *tale* as it is an empirical reality; but this purported asymmetry is important, because central to the partnership perspective is that age old adage of retail: the customer – capital – is always right.

Partnership II: place as product

The view of the relations between government and business as one of boutique customer service belies a particular relation to locality and place: as a product to be marketed and sold by the state (or more accurately, development officials). Scholars both critical and uncritical have noted in neoliberal cities in particular the tendency towards *place-branding* – or the marketing and selling of the idea of a place (Cleave et al. 2017; Jacobsen 2009; Kavaratzis 2005). The perception of *place as product* – the second key aspect of the partnership perspective – is both broader and deeper than place-branding, because it gets to the very conception of what *place* is. If place branding spurs local officials to (re)package the locality in a way that appears attractive and special, conceiving of place as product encourages changes to the place itself, to make *be* more attractive to potential corporate partners. If incentives policies must adapt to local conditions, so too must localities change themselves to be more easily adaptable *to*: people, politics, and all.

As with the CSE, there are several levels to crafting a good product, one concerning the broader business climates of the state and locality, the other concerning the development and preparation of a particular site. An official with the Economic Development Partnership of North Carolina (EDPNC), in discussing the different experience of working with a public-private partnership (PPP) – made clear the relationship between the customer service experience and the development of the place as product:

> I don't think [spinning off recruitment functions of the Commerce Dept. into the EDPNC] matters that much to the business community out there. A company out there that's getting ready to deal with North Carolina, they really don't care whether they're getting ready to deal with a private non-profit like us, or if they're dealing with the Department of Commerce. What they want is a customer service experience, that gives them the information they need in a timely fashion, and with discretion on anything that's confidential…what we can control [as a development and recruitment agency] is that customer service experience that a company has…what's not within our control is how the state is perceived as a business location…[which] is a function of tax policy, regulatory climate, workforce statistics and even [overall attractiveness]. (EDP05 2015)

The conception of place as a product demonstrates the way in which the perspective of capital is central to the partnership approach to governance, as the needs and wants of business are understood to be axiomatic in the formation of local policy. As the same developer with EDPNC phrased this notion of the fundamental place-product, "keep in mind, I think a lot of the success of any economic development network – whether that's local, re-gional, or state – has to do with how your product is perceived" (EDP05 2015). Throughout my interviews with experts in the field there were typi-cally efforts to downplay the role of incentives, and this discussion typically revolved around the product: "workforce and education, is now in my opinion – in addition to sites – the biggest driver [of site selection]. If you ask site consultants they will tell you that incentives are way down the list… incentives can make a good site better, but they can't make a bad site good. So you've got to have the product, and you've got to have the workforce and the ability to train that workforce" (EDP08 2016).

On one level, then, the *product* refers to overall business climate a state offers, including regulatory climate and tort reform laws, tax profile, and the labor force. One site selector noted that this level of the place as product features in the early phases of site selection in which many localities are filtered out:

> Some of those earlier screens…you know, right-to-work is a screen that comes up pretty early, especially with industrial projects. Looking at the tax structure, I mean, no longer is the–and this has been a change is last

10, 15 years as well—no longer is the least expensive location the best, because you know, you have to have quality. So, people want to look for things that look like a fair, and [a] manageable tax structure, and also where there's good human capital, good infrastructure. It's more about how...tax money is being invested than it is the lowest tax rate that's out there. Again, how I view it is the number one factor, 85% of the time is going to be human capital; the quality and cost of that human capital in a marketplace. And then taxes, real estate, those types of issues. (SEL03 2016)

Thus, the conception of place as product affects the way in which politicians and elites shape and craft policy well beyond the recruitment of a particular company. As the site selector above clearly stated, laws and regulations surrounding business and labor are understood not as a complex set of local management and regulatory relations, but as dimensions of a product under the consideration of capital investors. Consider the words of the governor I spoke to, who wanted to improve the product in his state:

I always say industries don't pick a state so much as they pick a location and community in order to site their facility...my first year as governor in the Spring, I went by the Toyota office in New York while I was up there on other business. I had read an article by Dennis Cuneo – in one of the economic development publications – about how important lawsuit abuse was to companies when it comes to siting facilities...and I was working very hard on tort reform in [my state]. And I wanted to see, based on what he'd written in this magazine, if he'd want to make a statement or make it plain that lawsuit abuse was a real problem if you're trying to recruit good industries. But the other reason I wanted to be there was I wanted to get our name on the list when they did build their next North American assembly plant...

Well I told him why I thought [my state] was an ideal location for him, and also we talked about tort reform and in fact he wrote a letter to the speaker of the...house, to me and to the president of the senate... explaining why tort reform was really important if you were a site selection officer for a big company. We passed, not long after that, what the Wall Street Journal called "the most comprehensive tort reform bill any state had passed" (GOV01 2016)

Importantly, understanding place as product moves consideration of capital investment to the center of local political concerns, to the extent that industry consultants become political consultants for local actors. While this sort of industry consultation is not the case with every piece of legislation, it does point to the *de facto* centrality of business in partnership governance, which also helps explain the shift discussed in the previous chapter towards governments pre-developing sites and Megasites for businesses looking to (re)locate. One of the key architects of the Tennessee Valley Authority's Megasite Designation Program made this clear in his elaboration of how the public corporation came up with the idea, saying the TVA decided "if we're going to be successful [in recruitment] let's talk to some people who know something about [the auto] industry. So, we jumped on a plane and talked to a couple automotive manufacturers and said 'if we did this [Megasite designation] what would it look like?' And they go 'well this is what you need to do.' Guess what? That's what we did" (BDP01 2016).

Thus, in a more material sense conceiving of place as product means actually developing and marketing products in terms of actual sites, rather than treating potentially available land as enticing enough. One business development professional emphasized this point, "there's a difference between land and a site…a site you actually have a plan as well as infrastructure, as well as everything else. So, government entities – beyond owning things – put investment into those properties, on a speculative basis many times, infrastructure, due diligence…so it just goes to show economic development is very competitive." (BDP03 2016). It is also clear from these professionals that the CSE and the notion of place-as-product develop hand in hand, the logic of partnership justifying speculative investment of public money as necessary for the competitive provision of product. Another development professional emphasized this point, saying "the world is changing and it's a matter of competition. The first time that somebody comes, they're looking for product, and it's something you either have or you don't. The question is going to be: 'alright…what sites? Or what kind of buildings do you have that will meet my needs?'…that's a must…more and more that you have to have prepared sites, makes the whole sell a lot easier" (EDP09 2016).

The final touch on this conception of place as product is the *marketing and sales* of the product at all levels, "[there has] got to be a good balance of strong product as well as strong promoting effort" (EDP06 2016). At the state level, this has been the case since the early 1980s, as Governors or development often take impromptu tours of automotive companies overseas to hawk the values of locating in their state. For example, upon hearing reports that a Japanese auto company could potentially locate a new plant in the United States, then Governor James Rhodes flew to Japan to court different firms – unsure which ones might be the actual prospect (if any) (Gelsanliter 1990:17–18), and Martha Layne Collins made eight trips to Japan in pursuit of Toyota (Gelsanliter 1990:77). These practices continue today, as when the Governor I spoke to who mentioned that he "went to Japan in 2005 and visited Toyota, [and] met with the chairman of the board at Toyota City. The trip was designed to coincide with the…kind of like the World's Fair – but we had a Mississippi exhibit and we put on a Mississippi Day, and then I went over and visited…the chairman of the board. I went back in 2006 and spoke at their Third Annual Science and Technology Exposition, put on by the Japanese government" (GOV01 2016).

While major projects receive such in-person attention in the name of the customer service experience, marketing also employs the tools of modern technology, as most Megasites have their own glossy websites, and all potential sites are listed on government and third-party websites which market all range of sites, list their capabilities, local workforce capacity, etc. This information gathering and publishing is both demonstrative of the CSE and helps the negotiations themselves. More than this, for localities marketing and publishing of product information is necessary to get on the map of site selectors; when I asked another professional if localities have to be competitive before you know you are even in the running he confirmed "that's exactly right, if you don't get on their radar...we may never know they were looking at us" (EDP08 2016).

Partnership III: partners in governance

What unifies the partnership perspective shared among development officials and their private partners is an underlying perspective on government and governance, of what local government is and should be – particularly in development. In addition to providing potential firms with a customer service experience, and treating place and locality as products to be developed, marketed, and sold, the partnership perspective understands governments and their development agencies as another kind of business entity – and the deals negotiated between governments and private firms simply as a kind of business deal. This is the case for both the private firms and the public actors – that is, for all the partners involved – as both sides perceive their role (their relationship to one-another and to the market) in terms of a business' needs and *as* business decisions.[4] What is fundamental to the economic development profession and the partnership perspective is the imperative that governments as partners not only understand the pressures and vicissitudes faced by businesses, but also share their concerns and act as partner in addressing them. In some instances, this can take on a bizarre role reversal, such as the episode discussed in the introduction in Tennessee when the state government was vehemently opposed to a unionization vote of which Volkswagen – a company familiar with corporatist bargaining – was actually supportive. The state itself had taken on the perspective of a business potentially locating in their locality, and treated the notion of unionization accordingly. I develop this notion further in the following chapter, but here it is worth noting that this episode is also indicative of the state understanding their place as product, since having a union shop in the state would hurt their image and brand with other prospective clients; hence, it was the state and not the firm that was most opposed to unionization.

Typically, this expectation that the local or state government behave like – and adopt the perspective of – business was expressed in the limitations that some developers ran into when trying to close or seal a deal. This came across clearly when I spoke with a former commerce secretary of North

Carolina about the decision to spin recruitment efforts off into a public-private partnership (PPP):

> Privatizing...allows for a little nimbleness...things like being able to take a trip privately to visit with a company or firm, the way public reporting is of expenses, that's immediately known. Where privatizing it, when that happens all that information will be disclosed...but it gives you some flexibility to manage through that process without concern for public scrutiny. Public accountability, for sure, but not so much visibility to what's happening...

> So part of it was that, and part of it was speed. Even booking...the process the state required for booking flights were just–it took forever, so it just allows them [at the PPP] to operate as a more *professional* sales and marketing organization, as private enterprise would do. (EDP04 2015)

Note here that the term *professional* is equated with the operation of private enterprise – indicating that a key aspect of professionalizing economic development is precisely adopting the partnership perspective. This notion of operating as a professional private enterprise was common in my interviews, but was typically expressed more subtly, in that public officials simply spoke of concerns about the market and labor as though they were a private business. Harvey notes this is fundamental to neoliberal governance, where capitalist class bias in governance "arise[s] in particular out of the treatment of labour and the environment as mere commodities" (Harvey 2005:70).

As partners, rather than as managers, it is also incumbent on development officials to cultivate business relationships, and demonstrate that they can act with the professionalism and alacrity expected of a private partner. This language of relationships – *business* relationships – is common in my interviews, such as one official who had worked on the Kia deal noting "my training had been from Georgia Power company, working as head of Government Affairs, and [*sic*] with an understanding that in order to get things done that you need – in the external world – you have to find...what they really want, but you have to be up front with people, and you have to develop relationships" (EDP03 2015). The language here is telling: "getting things done" in the "external world" – for example, the world outside of government – requires developing business relationships and delivering the customer service experience. From the partnership perspective, the relative transparency of government activity and the limited speed of action within a democratic and bureaucratic structure are seen as limitations on effective action by a partner, rather than constitutive of its nature as a public entity. From this view, then, states and local officials need to communicate and demonstrate that they are not delimited by their technically public nature, that they are able to "get things done." This is further reflected in two accounts of the moment in the Volkswagen recruitment, when Chattanooga officials set up the webcam for VW executives to view site predevelopment in real time: "that said a lot of things – that said, first of all, the locals can get stuff done quickly. Which is important to companies. You know, 'am I going to have the leadership that's going to have the capability to get things done?'" (BDP01 2016). This language, from a development official at the TVA, is echoed in the account by the state recruiter who pointed out that "that was a massive undertaking, that showed our ability to get things done" (EDP06 2016). Thus, the state as partner contrasted to a slow, bureaucratic structure; the government as partner is nimble enough *to get things done*, to deliver the customer service experience, and has leadership (governors and mayors) who understand their role as private partner in economic development.

Thus, since the 1980s the partnership view of governance has become increasingly institutionalized in local economic development and local government networks, and shared amongst an increasingly professionalized strata of local development elites through fast policy processes. It is through this lens that industrial recruitment policy and competition is made sense of, both by the elites themselves and *for* the public at large – but behind this common sense is a more profound shift in the nature and perception of governance.

Entrepreneurial governance: contradictions and contingencies

The diffusion of the partnership perspective among local government elites and their private counterparts is a manifestation of the turn towards entrepreneurial governance Harvey noted, that turn itself a manifestation of the larger neoliberal globalization project. While the entrepreneurial turn was remarkable in 1989, what is important to understand here is that partnership has become normalized, and among partners it is unproblematic and self-evident. The understanding that state and local governments should be active and amenable partners to private businesses is simply good common sense. And more than simply changing the way we think of local development activity, this entrepreneurial shift fundamentally changes what local governments *are* and *do*. Simply put, the shift to entrepreneurialism is not simply a shift towards a more superficial if spectacular approach to economic development, but a shift *from* government *to* entrepreneur.

In making this shift, local and state governments are increasingly occupying a contradictory terrain, as governors and development professionals push beyond norms and laws that served to regulate the behavior of public office. The terrain is contradictory because it constitutes a liminal space between public office and private business – as becomes clear when the dictates of business recruitment come into tension with the necessities of public governance. These contradictions become apparent when the most public aspects of governance conflict with the private business model; specifically, when transparency conflicts with confidentiality and when the contentious and changing nature of electoral politics conflicts with the need for predictability in business (Ritzer 2012).

Confidentiality and conflict as contradiction

Confidentiality, as has been noted, is central to the process of industrial recruitment and retention. While the final phase of negotiations becomes very public – at a point when competitors cannot take advantage of the knowledge of the site consideration – much of the negotiations process takes place under a cloud of confidentiality so thick that states and localities do not know the identity of their prospective client. While doing a deal in confidence may seem straightforward, there is a clear conflict with the re-quirements governments have for openness and transparency. "Companies like to maintain…keep their search confidential. Some states you know, have open records laws etc. and sometimes some states might be taken out early in the process because companies don't want to disclose what they're doing" (SEL01 2016). A city development official from Atlanta said much the same thing, referencing the process of requesting Urban Enterprise Zone designation, "some business will not want to go through it because it's very public and very open, but we won't go through it unless it's big enough" (EDP02 2015). A development professional with Fulton county in Georgia showed that the county government was well aware of the concern for confidentiality, saying "there's a lot of secretive— you don't want to blow it—if some company…we've actually had some companies that left, I mean that were coming here and decided 'you can't keep a secret and we're leaving.' At least that's what they said" (EDP01 2015). It is clear that companies will use their leverage to force confidentiality and secrecy on local officials.

The conflict around confidentiality is probably most apparent in the case of North Carolina, where sunshine (open records) laws permitted publica-tion of communications before the completion of negotiations on incentives deals. As the former Commerce Secretary noted

> it used to be that it was required legislatively in North Carolina that if you did not get a recruit but you were in conversation with a recruit you had to disclose that once the deal was determined. So, let's say we were recruiting Land Rover – they didn't choose to come to North Carolina – prior to legislation that we had enacted, we would have had to disclose *all* of the conversations. And that was problematic for us because it put all of our cards…made all of our cards public. And now you don't have to do that unless you win the deal…if you don't win the deal then there's nothing gained by making that public, and there's a lot lost because other companies looking at you know you're willing to offer and they may conclude, 'you know, we don't have any interest in going with them' or vice versa. (EDP04 2015)

As is clear, confidentiality is important to all actors in the incentives negotiation, as states and localities are acting *as* business partners, they also need confidentiality – in this sense from *themselves as* governments – to keep their hand hidden. The disjuncture here is telling: the conflict within the government of North Carolina is between the Commerce Department and the legislature, or between the representative body and the arm of the government trying to market and sell the state as a product. One of the leaders of the Economic Development Partnership of North Carolina made it clear that this transparency went both ways, and was an important aspect of forming the PPP – noting:

> Previously the Commerce Department had to turn over all correspondence under open-records rules, whether they wanted a deal or not. And that could be really…have a bit of a chilling effect on candid discussion between a company and the state, if they knew that win or lose that company would have its information put out in the open, because of the state's open records law. When they set up our organization…they modified those provisions of open records law, basically saying – if we lose the deal then there's a very narrow category of communication that are subject to open-records rules…narrow enough where it wouldn't really wrap up any of the conversations that the company itself was having…at the state level. (EDP05 2015)

The need for confidentiality in negotiations is, from the perspective of businesses and economic development professionals, common sense. And indeed, the underlying attitude regarding the conflict between transparency and confidentiality from the partnership perspective is one of bemusement at folks who do not understand how to get things done in the external world. It is worth pointing out that this common sense only makes sense if we accept the premise that governments *should* behave more like private organizations to begin with: this is the fundamental axiom of the development profession, the partnership perspective, and the shift towards entrepreneurial governance.[5]

The issue of confidentiality is emblematic of a deeper contradiction manifest between the professional development activities and the public managerial functions of government. More accurately, the problems arising from confidentiality represent conflicting views of the role and function of government, and its relation to private business. Consider, for example, the words of the former Commerce Secretary: "when it comes to those incentives…North Carolina just has a hard time, our legislative colleagues have just had a hard time letting loose of that control. And again, it goes back to this fundamental difference in understanding how this works… there's a limit to what can be offered without additional legislative action" (EDP04 2015). As she points out, the point of contention is a "fundamental difference in understanding" of how this – governance – works, and I would note this observation was intoned with a certain exasperated and even patronizing befuddlement – the legislature just don't *get* it. What they are failing to grasp is the partnership perspective itself and what they are failing to embrace is the view of private businesses. The Atlanta development official made this perspective quite clear, saying "the company doesn't want the headache of 'look, I don't know what your politics are' – and they don't care, and they shouldn't have to" (EDP02 2015). The practice of politics, the mediation of different interest groups and community concerns, is constructed as antipathetic to the practice of good partnership and entrepreneurialism. "Companies want to…see a political environment – especially at the local level – where the entities of government are working together, because the last thing they want to do is come into a place where there's chaos and conflict" (EDP06 2016).

As Pacewicz (2016:113) has pointed out, the partnership view of government as ideally non-conflictual extends to a conception of what constitutes strong leadership: a leader who is not embroiled in the vicissitudes of party politics and understands the imperatives of economic development. One site selector marked out this shift temporally, telling me,

> I think what's been good about economic development, generally speaking, across the US, is that it's a pretty bipartisan issue…generally speaking everybody recognizes that economic growth…is a good thing for an area…We don't see—I would say, generally, back fifteen years ago you would see the potential for bigger swings if you were from one political party to another, but I think the gaps have narrowed between those two groups, except on the fringes on both sides, you don't see any dramatic swings that generally take place in public policy…in a lot of states, there's not, when it comes to fiscal and economic development-type issues, huge gulfs of differences between political parties. (SEL03 2016)

Another site selector referenced the importance of the fringes elements of political parties and the effects they had on development, noting that "some states – South Carolina, Alabama, Mississippi – are consistently aggressive [in recruitment], but even a state like South Carolina lost a little bit of edge when Mr. [Mark] Sanford was governor. He was much more- he was Republican by name but he was a hardcore libertarian – and he wasn't interested in government participation in anything. Now, they still won projects and such, but they weren't as competitive for a little while as they used to be" (SEL02 2016). Indeed, transmitting these notions of leadership, and the partnership perspective more generally, is one of core aspects of the Tennessee Valley Authority's development training program for local communities. As one TVA official told me, this training "it's everything you would…need to be successful from an economic development standpoint. For example, do you have the right leadership? Do you have the right leadership at the table when a prospect comes? Do you have a mayor that really understands how this economic development process works, and can check his ego at the door? Do you have the right people there that can answer all your infrastructure needs?" (BDP01 2016). The reference to "egos" is more or less code for the differing agendas and interests of communities involved, differences that from the partnership perspective should be side-tracked in order to meet the needs of private companies. This is clear in another development official's statement that "egos get involved...and people try to, out-ego each other...it is just, you know, they have different agendas, different tax bases, different constituents and so everybody is trying to...[get] a better deal" (EDP03 2015).

Hence, showing leadership means discouraging contention and downplaying communities' disparate political imperatives in order to demonstrate one's quality as an amenable partner. As the former Mississippi governor emphasized, regarding the delay in breaking ground on Toyota's plant following the Great Recession, "one of the interesting things about [the Toyota delay in Mississippi], it's surprising in hindsight, not one legislator or state official ever complained about Toyota's delay or ever questioned whether or not they would keep their end of the deal. That's a pretty good partner" (GOV01 2016). Another official with a local chamber made it clear that it was comprehension of the partnership role, rather than party affiliation, that constituted strong leadership, elaborating that the "climate and aggressiveness for economic development projects – incentives, marketing, you know, all these things – vary greatly with leadership...so the political side of the spectrum is interesting, but I don't know that it weighs as much...as the current factors in play, even more so than party" (BDP03 2016).

Given the importance of leadership in establishing the partnership role, it is unsurprising that the cyclical electoral changes in leadership and governance are understood as problematic for effective economic development efforts. One official who worked with the Metropolitan Development Board (a business alliance in the Birmingham area) said that "between changing administrations...what's going to change is whoever's over at that agency is going to change...and the governor is going to change, and some of the legislature. So you do want to have some continuity" (EDP08 2016). This perspective was fairly common among development officials working in joint public-private or fully private development organizations: that a benefit of such a position was that it provided a stability for businesses amidst the electoral cycle. Said the leading official at the EDPNC,

> when you consider the fact that often the governing boards of these nonprofits [development agencies] tend to be appointed by elected officials, there's always going to be some degree of politics that's taken into account. The idea that, in the public sector you have a change of administration every four to eight years...you have a change is who's in the Governor's Mansion. Even during administrations you have changes...and with those changes comes a lot of potential disruptions...I think it disrupts the

continuity that any executive marketing and sales campaign needs to have over the longer term. The hope is that you can buffer yourself [in a PPP] from these periodic changes of administration…you have a better shot at that sort of continuity…that is very beneficial for the marketing and business development efforts that states are trying to accomplish. (EDP05 2015)

This sentiment is echoed by the official working with the TVA, itself a public corporation, who pointed out "one of the advantages of the TVA is we're probably the only consistent economic development agency out there… when we have a new governor, we don't leave, we're still here…we don't have the turnover…so we're very consistent." (BDP01 2016). Thus, from the perspective of pseudo-private organizations, their partial status as a private agency is a boon because it insulates them from electoral cycles. The core assumption here is that pace and prescriptions of private business activity are fundamentally correct and appropriate – even for the sphere of democratic public life and government. But this assumption also contains problematic propositions – such as the technocratic assumption that professionals know what is best for communities (see the discussion in footnote five in this chapter), and that the unpredictable nature of pluralistic participation should suborned and sublimated to emulate the corporate ethos of partnership. I develop the implications of these propositions, and the contradictions outlined above, in the following chapter.

Conclusions

The maturation of the economic development profession has expanded as the entrepreneurial approach to local governance spreads and becomes more normalized, though this process is contradictory and uneven – particularly in the United States where industrial policy is largely a matter of local legislation. Because states and local governments command relatively large budgets and can take on large sums of debt, these entities are crucial players in the new landscape in which public actors are supposed to play the role of entrepreneurial partner in new business projects. Indeed, this logic has extended well beyond industrial projects alone, and is typical even of small development projects – though the scale of incentives and effort government agencies show towards smaller projects is not the same. And some site selectors suggest that governments have become more savvy in pursuing businesses most relevant to the "product" their locality has to offer, as one noted, "I think in the last 10 years in particular, you've seen cities, regions, states, become more sophisticated, but also wisely say 'hey, we have the assets, whether it's people or infrastructure, real estate – for *these* types of industry sectors, we're really well positioned for these five to seven industry sectors. So let's not go out a chase something that we don't have the assets for'" (SEL03 2016). In other words, states and cities have become more informed business operators. Having outlined the partnership perspective and its essential contradictions in this chapter, I will in the next chapter take a further step back from the perspective itself, and critically evaluate the growth of the local development field and its partners in light of the theory and global political economic context laid out in chapter 2.

Before moving on to discuss the theoretical implications of these findings, it is worth noting that the partnership perspective is not wholly one-sided, though it does perforce imply more changes for government actors and perspectives than businesses. Partnerships, after all, go two ways: "We want to make sure we're doing an investment and that it's paying off...at the end it's taxpayer money, and I'm not just gonna' give away taxpayer money, where at the end we get horrible returns. I mean...would a business person do that?"(EDP02 2015). A number of officials noted that cost-benefit analyses were central to getting a good deal for their locality or state, one recruiter saying that "the press and public don't actually believe this but...on large projects be they headquarters, be they automotive plants...whatever it may be that we're chasing, we would do economic impact analysis. We'd want to have a pretty good idea of, 'what's the value of this to the state of Tennessee?' And then we would back up from that and say 'Okay, how much sales tax and other tax revenues are created from the construction of this project?'...And then we would look at 'Okay, what's reasonable to invest to get that?'" (EDP06 2016). Moreover, to some extent the partnership perspective itself mitigates some aspects of the race to the bottom in that, in a real partnership, "you can't have a situation where the company feels like they've won and a local state or community feel like they've lost. It really has to be a partnerships and really viewed as [such by] both entities investing in a project" (SEL03 2016). But while the partnership view may lessen the speed of a race to the bottom, is does not mitigate its essential contradictions: the shift from managerialism to entrepreneurial governance, and the treatment of territory and people within it as inputs for the process of production. These are the themes I explore in the following chapter.

Notes

1 It is of little consequence if these experts *believe* what they say to be true or are merely spouting party propaganda, nor am I concerned with whether or not their actions adhere to their stated positions (often, they do not). Rather, what is important is what is understood as plain, axiomatic, and what is omitted.

2 For more on why this field developed as it did throughout the 1980s see chapter four of Pacewicz's *Partisans and Partners* (2016).

3 During interviews, I was recalled of my experience as "team member" at Whole Foods Market, in which employees are trained not simply in tasks or skills, but also in appropriate demeanor and tone. As a high-end grocery store, we were instructed, people want to feel we are really invested in making their experience the best possible.

4 I note here that it is ultimately irrelevant whether partners truly believe in this view of governance (though see Pacewicz (2016:112–5)) or are espousing mollifying

discourse for purely instrumental purposes, ultimately the partnership view of governance forms the common sense that drives business recruitment efforts.

5 The need for confidentiality and assumption that governments should behave like states is one reason why in some states – particularly with more stringent spending and sunshine laws – recruitment activity and funds are shunted into pseudo-private entities and PPPs. Things such as spending money on flights for business recruitment or wining and dining interested executives – expected practices in business, but ones that might raise eyebrows when conducted with public funds – can be conducted without the same level of scrutiny. Again, the former North Carolina commerce secretary put the matter clearly,

> Privatizing it allows for a little nimbleness – but, let me give you an example. Things like being able to take a trip privately to visit with a company or a firm, the way public reporting is of expenses that's immediately known. Where privatizing it, when it happens all that information will be disclosed, or disclosable, but it gives them a bit of flexibility to manage through that process without concern about public scrutiny. Public accountability for sure, but not so much visibility to what's happening…the whole issue of confidentiality, the ability to be able to meet and to have dialogue with these folks without public visibility – that's really important. (EDP04 2015).

These words were echoed verbatim by a development official with a multi-county chamber, who clearly ties together the threads of confidentiality and operating as pseudo-private organization:

> [as a private organization] we have an opportunity to interact with clients in a confidential way and they can tell us things that they would not normally be able to tell a governmental entity. You know – their viewpoint on the state's public policy, let's say HB2 [House Bill 2, the so called bathroom bill in North Carolina]…so "I will come for HB2" or "I will not come for HB2"…So those are perceptions of public policy that have affected their business decision. They can tell us those things in a confidential way without having their personal or company politics splayed across the front page. So [being private] allows you to have a closer relationship – and to understand what they're doing much better. It also allows you as a private entity to do the normal business development things, under less scrutiny by people saying that [it is] their dollars going into that. So, for example, if I wanted to go and buy a steak dinner for the CEO of this company. Great. You know if that's 'gonna get the deal done, great. Versus people saying well "why did you pay 5$ for that steak and not 3$?" So it allows you to have the broader vision for what needs to be done in order to catalyze and accomplish the deal.

> Let me give you one more example…the CEO of GE Aviation "said hey…come to Paris with me, I'm going to announce ground breaking for this…technology in Asheville." We said…"we'll be there." Quite a hubbub around travel to Paris, but as a private entity, that's our prerogative…with just purely public dollars… everybody scrutinizes those actions. So, it allows us to be more nimble. (BDP03 2016)

The relative freedom of states to engage in business deals without oversight is dependent upon each state's laws – with North Carolina having more stringent transparency requirement pushing development officials in that state to form the PPP, 85% of whose funding still comes from the Commerce Department. In this push to outsource recruitment is apparent a deeper contradiction in the imperatives that dictate the pace and propriety of government and businesses processes and behaviors, a contradiction essential to the partnership approach to governance.

Bibliography

BDP01. 2016. "Business Development Professional 01."

BDP03. 2016. "Business Development Professional 03."

Cleave, Evan, Godwin Arku, Richard Sadler, and Jason Gililand. 2017. "Is It Sound Policy of Fast Policy? Practitioners Perspectives on the Role of Place Branding in Local Economic Development." *Urban Geography* 38(8):1133–1157.

EDP01. 2015. "Economic Development Professional 01."

EDP02. 2015. "Economic Development Professional 02."

EDP03. 2015. "Economic Development Professional 03."

EDP04. 2015. "Economic Development Professional 04."

EDP05. 2015. "Economic Development Professional 05."

EDP06. 2016. "Economic Development Professional 06."

EDP08. 2016. "Economic Development Professional 08."

EDP09. 2016. "Economic Development Professional 09."

Gelsanliter, David. 1990. *Jump Start: Japan Comes to the Heartland.* New York: Farrar Straus Giroux.

GOV01. 2016. "State Governor."

Harvey, David. 1989. "From Managerialism to Entrepreneurialism: The Transformation in Urban Governance in Late Capitalism." *Geografiska Annaler. Series B, Human Geography* 71(1):3–17. doi: 10.2307/490503.

Harvey, David. 2005. *A Brief History of Neoliberalism.* Oxford: Oxford University Press.

Jacobsen, Bjcobsen 2009. "Investor-Based Place Brand Equity: A Theoretical Framework." *Journal of Place Management and Development* 2(1):70–84. doi: 10.1108/17538330910946029.

Kavaratzis, Mihalis. 2005. "Place Branding: A Review of Trends and Conceptual Models." *The Marketing Review* 5(4):329–342. doi: 10.1362/146934705775186854.

Levi-Faur, David, and Jacint Jordana. 2005. "Globalizing Regulatory Capitalism." *The Annals of the American Academy of Political and Social Science* 598(1):6–9. doi: 10.1177/0002716204272612.

Pacewicz, Josh. 2013. "Regulatory Rescaling in Neoliberal Markets." *Social Problems* 60(4):433–456. doi: 10.1525/sp.2013.60.4.433.

Pacewicz, Josh. 2016. *Partisans and Partners: The Politics of the Post-Keynesian Society.* University of Chicago Press.

Peck, Jamie. 2002. "Political Economies of Scale: Fast Policy, Interscalar Relations, and Neoliberal Workfare." *Economic Geography* 78(3):331–360. doi: 10.1111/j.1944-8287.2002.tb00190.x.

Ritzer, George. 2012. "The Weberian Theory of Rationalization and the McDonaldization of Contemporary Society." Pp. 41–59 in *Illuminating Social Life*, edited by P. Kivisto. Thousand Oaks, California: SAGE.

SEL01. 2016. "Site Selection Professional."
SEL02. 2016. "Site Selection Professional."
SEL03. 2016. "Site Selection Professional."
Storper, Michael, and Richard Walker. 1989. *The Capitalist Imperative: Territory, Technology, and Industrial Growth*. New York: Basil Blackwell.

6 The political and economic in partnership

In the last two chapters I outlined the qualitative changes in industrial recruitment and economic development strategies at the local level in the southeast United States, and how that shift is undergirded by deeper changes in the practice and perception of local governance as partnership. In this chapter, I situate my findings in the broader theoretical and historical context laid out at the beginning of this work. I argue that the form of entrepreneurial governance that has taken shape in the cases studied here is part of the broader shift in the world political economy I call the neoliberal globalization project. I stress that the particular form of entrepreneurial governance is in many ways shaped by the history of southern states pursing an expanded role in industrial and economic development and the political relations discussed in chapter 3 (Cobb 1993; Hülsemann 2001). Furthermore, returning to the perspective of critical geography and the political Marxism of Wood among others, I argue that the economic development profession and the partnership perspective are a part of this larger project to change the geographic scale of class dynamics and political relations.

The class project

In chapter 2, I outlined the conceptual framework of the neoliberal globalization project as a hegemonic class project intended to rearticulate class relations on both global and local levels, transcending the entrenched national framework for mediating class antagonisms (Gough 2004; McMichael 2000; Peck 1996). This scalar shift in production and accumulation processes enhanced the importance of supra- and sub-national territorial frameworks for increasingly global capital flows. The ideology behind this project that is used to justify and explain its current realities is neoliberalism: "globalization as a political project, concerns the attempt to institutionalize the neoliberal agenda of market reform by removing public constraints on economies. The premise is an ideological assertion that markets are 'self-regulating' and that the visible hand of the state is a recipe for inefficiency" (McMichael 2000:110). Hence, the neoliberal "globalization project is a

DOI: 10.4324/9781003107569-6

movement to institute market rule by a powerful global managerial class" (McMichael 2000:113) or hegemonic bloc (Gramsci 1971; Robinson 2005).

As noted previously, in light of the increasing mobility of capital, and a dominant narrative establishing, emphasizing, and exaggerating that mobility, local governments felt pressured to engage in more entrepreneurial strategies to attract inward investment. This pressure was enhanced by re-oriented national government agendas (Scholte 1997:444), but also driven by the localities and development professionals themselves. The past 40 years have seen an increasing competition among localities, and "underpinning this acceleration [of competition] is the politics of neoliberalism. Local strategies – aimed particularly at securing mobile (public and private) investment…are in fact about selling the local to the global" (Peck and Tickell 1994:318). This dynamic of global capital abrogating entrenched class relations and localities entrepreneurializing their efforts to secure investment took a particular shape in the United States South, molded by that region's particular historical and institutional structures. The particularly repressive labor control regime that was and is a major draw for corporations seeking malleable workers (Cobb 1993:1–4; Hülsemann 2001:224; Jacobs 2012:201–202; Rueschemeyer, Stephens, and Stephens 1992:121), and the characteristic aggressiveness in their pursuit of private investment among southern states gave rise to the particular form partnership we see today (Cobb 1993:4; Hülsemann 2001). Indeed, elites involved in this partnership project were well aware of this regional specificity; one site selector, for example, noted "the South Atlantic, the southeast – which is where this idea of economic development and recruitment took hold…still tend to be the most aggressive states, and by many measures the most pro-business states in terms of overall government policy" (SEL02 2016). If we are to truly understand the nature of the changes in local economic development and governance in this study, we need to step back and examine the class struggle at the heart of the matter.

Risk shifting

If we step back from the normative logic of the partnership perspective, recent efforts by local and state governments to develop as well as pre-certify and pre-develop sites show that it is not simply costs that are being shifted to local governments but also risk. This is because investment in fixed capital is among the riskiest aspects of most business endeavors. As Harvey notes, fixed capital is distinguished by the slow, piecemeal process through which it is used up, "the machine remains behind after the production process is completed…the value equivalent of the fixed capital circulates 'piecemeal, in proportion as it passes from it to the final product'" (Marx *cited in* Harvey 1982:206). As opposed to other investments made in production, such as metal or glass or energy, fixed capital is not used up in one production cycle but over the lifetime of the machinery and plant/office space. Due to such lengthily turnover, "capital tends to underinvest in sectors of long turnover time...and this is exacerbated by the increased risks of a period of stagnation" (Gough 1996:2184). The important point here is that fixed capital entails very large investments whose value is only slowly realized "over several turnover periods" (Harvey 1982:206) or business cycles. While investment in fixed capital is necessary and beneficial to any industrial operation, it is the most inherently risky part of the investment insofar as its fixed, slow circulation entails greater risk of devaluation over time through competitive technological change or an economic slump. Thus, localities are not only taking on a greater portion of the overall investment in entrepreneurial ventures, they are absorbing part of the riskiest portion of the sunk costs in fixed capital. Moreover, to the degree that the agreements between partners includes measures such as those in Alabama with Mercedes, where states allow the corporations the right to essentially tax employee incomes, the entirety of the cost of new fixed capital – the plant – is covered by taxpayers and employees (see Mattera et al. 2012 for a deeper look at *Paying Taxes to the Boss*).[1]

Development officials rarely directly acknowledge the risk involved in entrepreneurial partnership, and on those occasions those I spoke to did so it was rather contradictory. For example, the recruiter who initiated the pre-development of the Tennessee Volkswagen site said it as "a sort of low-risk strategy because if Volkswagen did not come, that site still needed to be prepped for future use. If they did come, it was a very small investment in making sure that it was a win" (EDP06 2016). In other words, the recruiter frames the risk of pre-development as mitigated by the competitive necessity to predevelop sites – the competitive behavior of states is justified by competition itself. Yet, later in the same interview, and referring directly to a probing inquiry on the shift towards Megasite pre-certification efforts, he explained that "our economy has changed and will continue to... decision cycles are shorter. Risks are higher, and the ability to de-risk any aspect of a project vis-à-vis anyone else gives you an advantage. So any way you can de-risk a project is going to differentiate you" (EDP06 2016). Thus, while clearly attempting to downplay the risk involved in development and recruitment efforts, this individual also pointed out that shifting risk is precisely what local incentives and investments do (there is, after all, no such thing as de-risking in a competitive market). Pre-development only increases this risk-shifting insofar as localities take a major risk in developing *potential* sites without any committed investors.

It is also worth noting that the up-front costs absorbed by localities serve not only to lower the amount paid by private firms but also to quicken their time to profitability – or turnover time. Though this cost shifting does not in fact speed up the turnover time of fixed capital, to the degree that localities take on the slow circulating fixed capital costs the private partner is freed from its stultifying effects. Additionally, localities are shortening the time to market for investors by eliminating the time that goes into site purchase, certification, and development. As one site selector looked at the question of site pre-certification, "when everyone in a company decides they're going to spend five hundred million to a billion dollars, every month you're not producing is pretty costly...so I think that's where it came from...generally speaking it's speed to market and the competitive aspect and cost aspect of that" (SEL02 2016).

As McMichael notes, the neoliberal globalization project "implies transformed states...this transformation involves a shift from states managing national economies, to states managing the global economy...facilitating global circuits of money and commodities, and resolving the contradictions of global capitalism" (McMichael 2000:110). What we see local governments doing in this entrepreneurial partnership approach – reducing costs and absorbing risks, minimizing time to market – is precisely turning *outward* towards management of the imperatives of global capital and facilitation of its circulation. As noted by the above development official, and numerous scholars, global competition has increased the pressure to turn a profit in ever shorter time frames, increasing the already heavier risks associated with investment with the uncertainty of global markets (Harvey 1989). By partially defraying the costs and absorbing the risks associated with fixed capital investments in particular, local governments act to minimize this potential disincentive to invest by exorcising the specter of devaluation, and thus work to facilitate the circulation of capital. This facilitation is of course further seen in the removal and reduction of various taxes that feature in incentives agreements at all levels of government (detailed in chapter 4) that serve to free up capital to circulate through local institutional structures by significantly reducing tax barriers, and in the standardized stipulation of incentives arrangements that minimize regulatory burden and streamline the permitting and regulation activities of local governments. Thus, the transformations of the state under neoliberal globalization that McMichael discusses in the southeastern United States takes on the partnership approach to entrepreneurial governance outlined in the previous chapters.

Im / mobility

In addition to facilitating the circuits of global capital, the partnership approach also works to resolve a central contradiction for capital: the contradictory impulses towards fixity and mobility. Put in Marxian terms, local partnership works to resolve – albeit partially and unequally – the contradictory capitalist drives to "annihilate space through time" and "time through space" (Harvey 1982, 1989). In other words, the imperative to accumulate attempts to remove spatial barriers to accumulation (such as fixed capital, borders, taxation, etc.) by speeding up the process of production and exchange (the movement of money, commodities, and services through space at an ever increasing pace – space *through* time), while at the same time capital is able to speed this process up by creating infrastructure and spatial networks to facilitate this accelerated movement (time *through* space).[2] For many firms, and for capital in general, there is then a dual impulse toward mobility and fixity *in situ*:

> In order to produce surplus (value), firms must build up a productive apparatus consisting of fixed capital, workers, land, political alliances, and so forth – all with a local base. This process renders capital temporarily immobile, making it subject to some leverage by workers, communities and governments…thus capital is in a bind…mobility and immobility both offer advantages, but each has costs. (Storper and Walker 1989:47).

These contradictory impulses are just what localities are in practice mitigating where they attenuate the fixing effects of capital sunk into development in place, and by socializing what were previously private fixed capital investments and their associated risks. The effect here is to at once facilitate the circulation of privately-owned capital while reducing its circulation through fixed investments, attenuating the connection of firm to place and speeding up time to market and profitability. To the degree that localities simply pay the costs of fixed capital investment, the amount of privately invested capital circulating slowly through infrastructure and means of production is directly diminished. To the degree that taxes are redirected to defray fixed capital costs, the time in which these sunk costs are recovered is diminished. Hence, local partnership can actually weaken the connection of firms to a locality, not only because they reduce the private capital directly circulating in that locality (itself, as a physical place), but also because they diminishes the barriers to locating a new site insofar as workforce training and site pre-development streamline the process of relocation.

Certainly, major industries that rely on agglomeration are still connected to localities through supplier networks, and social and political relations formed in place. And the growth of lean, just-in-time production processes only serves to further tie firms to one another by deepening social and material relationships between them within a region. Nonetheless, as incentives are offered to suppliers and major assembly plants, the overall effect of the local partnership is to attenuate the fixing effects of local investment on capital. GM's recent decision to close its Hamtramck plant, the beneficiary of one of largest early incentives deals, is indicative here – the company was still very profitable when the closure was announced. Moreover, many firms that are not tied to place by large fixed capital investments and agglomeration effects benefit from the same incentives. One site selector noted that "our clients are typically looking at a ten, fifteen-year cost model when they make a decision to go somewhere, because when they do a project they're going to be there for a long time" (SEL03 2016). Yet other projects such as headquarters, smaller service providers, sports stadia, are treated as partners just the same as a long-term industrial project, and these types of businesses do not have the same supplier networks and agglomeration effects that characterize industrial production. These lower infrastructure projects to a much greater degree have the fixing effects of investment in place reduced through local partnership. Hence, as McMichael argues, as the neoliberal globalization project facilitates the formation local government partnerships, this relation serves not only to facilitate the circulation of capital through space but also ameliorates (though not entirely resolves) the contradictory impetus towards mobility and fixity.

Uneven effects on local policy

As they work to facilitate global capital circulation and accumulation, local and state governments are in this sense turning outward towards those transnational firms and flows, and this is precisely what being a good partner implies: facilitating the circulation of global capital (Brenner 1999:439). Beyond the more abstract considerations of the spatial configuration of capital flows, the entrepreneurial turn has an immediate impact on- and implications for – local and regional policy. The imperative to be – or at least appear to be – a good partner has had multiple effects at different levels of governance. Two primary effects I would argue are most important are the contention incurred by the differential spread of the partnership perspective at different levels and localities of governance, and the chilling effects on disparate forms of legislation that might detract from the image of performing as a good partner.

While partnership has becoming hegemonic among local governments, particularly in the United States South, it is not completely dominant, and its uneven spread in many ways follows the channels of fast-policy diffusion. That is, it spreads among elites and technocrats hooked into these networks but not necessarily to locally elected legislators. While it is difficult to firmly state the different levels at which specific localities have taken on the partnership perspective, contention over economic development decisions at different levels of governance can be taken as indicators of such disparities. Policy contention within southeastern states typically takes the form of a conflict between the partnership views of governance, and policies that reflect local concerns and initiatives that conflict with the actual or perceived interests of business (and perforce, partners).

A prime contemporary example of this is recent contentions around laws "protecting religious freedoms" and policies that would affect Lesbian, Gay, Bisexual and Transgender (LGBT+) individuals. A number of conservative state legislatures in the South have taken up Religious Freedom Restoration (RFR) policies, whose ostensible goal is to codify the right of individuals and business to refuse services or contracts based on religious beliefs. Such RFR laws are popularly understood to affect LGBT+ individuals in particular, discrimination against whom would theoretically be legally protected if it had religious bases. The most vocal objections to such laws comes from gay and human rights organizations, as well as businesses who wish to be seen as non-discriminatory (Jurney 2016). In Georgia, the contention over such a bill broke out between the business-friendly Governor Nathan Deal, and the socially conservative legislature, and the governor ultimately vetoed the bill. Note that the governor and legislature belong to the same Republican political party. When Indiana passed a similar law, the legislature and governor were in lock-step, but many businesses openly condemned the law and several cancelled planned expansions or events in the state (Bender 2016). In North Carolina, in a variation on this theme, the state adopted legislation that would limit local governments' ability to pass legislation protecting LGBT rights, superseding an ordinance in Charlotte, a major banking city. With the governor and legislature again in lock-step, several major businesses cancelled expansions, and several collegiate athletic associations' planned events were moved to other states (Jurney 2016). The contention led to a heated battle for governorship, in which the governor who signed the law was narrowly voted out. In the ensuing political battle between the new governor and the conservative legislature (as (Pacewicz 2016) would put it, between partisans and partners), a compromise bill ultimately emerged in which the law (House Bill 2) was repealed, but it also barred new local ordinances protecting special statuses. This compromise, one might note, works well for businesses who may not have liked increased regulations but who also wanted to be seen as non-discriminatory. Indeed, while Price and Bell noted that the "compromise on the controversial House Bill 2 law drew a fiery response from across the nation, with both conservatives and liberals calling it a failure," businesses and athletics associations approved, with the latter reinstating events that had been threatened to move to other states shortly after the compromise bill became law (Price and Bell 2017).

Another prominent example of the contention caused (in part) by the differential acceptance of the partnership perspective are recent instances of states superseding progressive localities who have attempted to raise the minimum wage in their jurisdictions. A number of states, such as North Carolina (in the above mentioned compromise legislation), Ohio, Michigan, Missouri, and others have passed legislation specifically intended to supersede local minimum wage ordinances and maintain the business friendly atmosphere of the state. For example, in 2013 Tennessee state legislature brought a "U.S. Chamber of Commerce-backed bill that would strip local governments' ability to set wage standards, family leave and insurance requirements for businesses seeking local government contracts" (Sher 2013). A similar law was passed in Florida around the same time, and the congressmen who sponsored it quote extensively from the book of partnership. According one news report, "Rep. Jimmie Smith... said local governments have it all wrong. 'We want people to be successful so they can hire more people,' he said. 'We should not destroy or interfere with the free market system'...Rep. Steve Precourt [said] 'Some counties'...ordinances are really distorting the current economy and there is a need for uniformity,' Precourt told the House Local and Federal Affairs Committee. He said the laws have suppressed the state's ability to generate jobs" (Klas 2013). The rationalizations offered here are clearly articulated in language of partnership, and Representative Precourt even refers to the state as itself a job-creator, in other words, referencing the ability to be a good partner to business. Ironically, voters in the state would later approve a statewide increase in the minimum wage in the general election of 2020, perhaps indicating the conflict between the rarefied partners and elites and the local constituency the supposedly serve.

There are, of course, other factors at play here besides the understanding of partnership, in particular rural/urban disparities in social and political beliefs, which have only widened as some urban areas – such as Charlotte – become more tied to flows of global capital (Sassen 2012).[3] But the policy conflicts that arise in the above mentioned cases are not centrally about the underlying ideological worldviews nor about party politics, though these may be important. They are at core about local partners who "understand the role of government" in business, and who does or does not accept the partnership perspective. The key difference between North Carolina passing ostensibly LBGT unfriendly legislation, and Georgia not doing so, is not as much an ideological difference, but that the Georgia governor "gets it" as the former North Carolina commerce secretary put it. As one site selector noted, Georgia governor "[Nathan] Deal...CEO's really like him, they feel comfortable with him and they know they'll have access to him after the deal" (EDP03 2015). The difference between localities pursuing wage ordinances and the state government in Florida is not about political parties, but that the "local governments have it all wrong" – they do not *get it*. They do not understand that the locality is product and the state a potential partner. And businesses clearly recognize what good leadership here entails, as a BMW executive told McDermott about South Carolina, "Some governors understood their role in economic development...others did not" (McDermott 2011:86). Thus, as the complex networks of actors at various scales of governments differentially turn outward in entrepreneurial pursuit of investment and partnership, conflicts arise from policy imperatives that are differentially responsive to local initiatives and pressures.[4]

One side-effect of such local kerfuffle has been that development agencies and third-party actors actively train and instruct locally elected officials in development and partnership. For example, a development official in Tennessee stressed the importance of *alignment* among localities, "TVA has a community development team, [Tennessee Department of Economic and Community Development] has a community development team, and we cross trained them...on community leadership, on infrastructure...[it] helps community leaders and alderman understand economic development...it made [development efforts] less burdensome" (EDP06 2016). Plainly, the goal of alignment and economic development training is to impart the partnership ethos more uniformly across localities and facilitate more uniformity in adherence to that perspective. The minimization of conflict between localities and the pursuit of localized interests serves to realign and reorient localities towards the needs and impulses of global capital (Pacewicz 2013). And this reorientation is not simply a turn from the local to the global, but as argued above, a shift toward business and capital. And this shift has important consequences for the political position of labor.

The elision of labor

I have noted already the labor repressive legacy of the South and its widespread antipathy towards organized labor, even among the workforce (Cobb 1993:259), yet despite this there has hardly been a complete absence of labor organization or political activity. Unions have consistently been involved in contesting plant construction as well as issues within plants since the very beginning in the 1980s (Gelsanliter 1990:65, 110). And although no major assembly plants in the South have unionized, the UAW has consistently led unionization campaigns throughout the region. Moreover, while the populist campaigns throughout the South in the 1890s were not strictly *labor* movements, Cobb notes that the response to this populist challenge was in part the reason why southern political leaders embraced a more activist approach to recruiting businesses (Cobb 1993:3). The point here is that labor, as an organized political force, is and has been present for the past 40 years and beyond in the southeast – the specter of organized labor looms over the region – though in the attenuated form characteristic of the South's labor control regime.

It is striking, then, that throughout the course of my interviews, the question of labor as a political force with distinct interests was almost entirely absent. Jobs, of course, were central to many discussions with development professionals, and were crucial in decisions about incentives. Discussing the trade off on incentives negotiations in dealing with Kia, one recruiter pointed out "when there's a real need to reduce your unemployment rate, you're looking at a real motivation to bring hundreds if not thousands of jobs." (EDP03 2015). And an Atlanta official emphasized that "we really…I have every interest to make sure that as many jobs as possible, that are hired locally by city of Atlanta residents, they have a chance to get that job" (EDP02 2015). And site selectors and professionals routinely discussed the importance of the labor force, or of having a *quality* workforce, or a large enough workforce. But this is not the same as regarding labor and workers as a *political* force with particular and legitimate interests. The single time the politics of labor were brought up was by one site selector, in discussion of the locational factors under consideration, who noted that during desktop analysis "some of those earlier screens, you know right-to-work is a screen that comes up pretty early, especially with industrial projects" (SEL03 2016).

This conspicuous absence of labor as a political factor from the economic development profession and the partnership discourse is in part reflective of the fact that, as mentioned in the previous chapter, governments adopting the partnership perspective are eager to appear as strong potential partners – and the presence of organized labor is problematic to the presentation of that image. An account of efforts to unionize an independent auto part supplier in Alabama in 2015 relates this sentiment, noting that "opponents argued that unionizing would damage the state's competitiveness, and repeatedly raised the specter that unions helped bring about the problems in Detroit's automobile industry" (Cohen 2015). But the invisibility of labor's interests is also due to the fact that, like the so-called egos of local officials, the interests of workers that run counter to business partnerships are also seen as irrational resistances to the epistemologically primary interests of capital. In this perspective, labor is not a legitimate political actor with legitimate interests, in much the same way local governments lose legitimacy upon aversion to the partnership view. As Jessop said of hegemonic projects in chapter two, "those particular interests which are inconsistent with the project are deemed immoral and/or irrational and, insofar as they are still pursued by groups outside the consensus, they are also liable to sanction" (Jessop 1983:100).

However, unlike local political figures, labor is fundamentally incapable of *becoming* a *legitimate* political force – because labor is not understood as separate from the needs of business and much needed jobs for the government partners. Thus, labor is here *properly* viewed as an input, a production factor of variable quality that should be enhanced and marketed as with any other property of a locality that affects entrepreneurial decisions. And the underlying assumption of economic development professionals and officials who accept the partnership view is a moral-political predicate that the unimpeded (but by no means unassisted) activity of private firms in the marketplace is good and correct.[5] As Peck and Tickell put it, "in a situation of continuing global crisis and deregulation, in which there is not enough investment to go around, localities are resorting to beggar-thy-neighbor strategies. The prevailing orthodoxy of neoliberalism provides a political rationalisation (of sorts) for these strategies through the faith which it places in the immutability of global economic forces and the virtues of competition" (Peck and Tickell 1994:319). Or, as the former governor pithily summarized the view, "this is all a business."

Two caveats must be added here. First, this view of labor is not so much communicated through clear and conscious articulation as much as by the consistent and deliberate omission of any discussion of the concerns of labor by officials and professionals in the field. Insofar as the field omits consideration of labor beyond a perfunctory discussion of right-to-work as a preliminary screen for local competitiveness, the organized interests of labor are discursively elided from the professional and official field of economic development and the partnership perspective.[6] And this elision occurs not through Machiavellian maneuvers so much as a bland, uncritical acceptance of an unarticulated neoliberal ideology. "The new religion of neoliberalism combines a commitment to the extension of markets and logics of competitiveness with a profound antipathy to all kinds of Keynesian and/or collectivist strategies" (Peck and Tickell 2002:381). The second caveat is that this approach to the question of labor is not a reflection of particular businesses or even a particular segment of capital. In other words, the partnership perspective is not constituted around a particular firm, project, or investment, but rather an abstraction of business or "capital in general." Hence, local and state governments *as* partners can deviate from the interest of particular firms (such as Volkswagen) while maintaining an entrepreneurial approach to governance, as they may be giving broader consideration to being a good partner to businesses in general.[7] Certainly, when delivering the customer service experience, the partnership approach takes account of the particular needs of businesses, but in constructing place as product localities are taking account of the needs *businesses in general*, and these are derived primarily from the neoliberal project itself and its ideology.[8]

All of these implications of entrepreneurial governance and the partnership approach – the attenuation of spatial fixity, the partial outward turn of local policy, and the practical and discursive marginalization of labor from politics – are part of a deeper, more fundamental shift in the relationship between the public and private, the political and economic spheres of power in neoliberal capitalism.

Public and private? Decoding the political and economic

The elision of labor as a legitimate political actor is not simply a matter of appearances or discourse, but reveals a particular configuration of class relations and political power at the core of the partnership approach to entrepreneurial governance. It is worth a brief reiteration of the approach I use to understand the state, and the relation between the political and economic spheres of capitalism, because it is precisely the relation between these spheres that is distinctive of partnership. Many theories of the state view it as a more or less autonomous realm of power, distinct from economic or class power in some form; most accept some form of a pluralistic approach that treats governance and the state as in some way responding to a plurality of competing interests among private actors/groups. Mann (1986), for example, sees the political realm as a particular type of power resource (specifically coercive domination) distinct from economic power. Most sociologists and political economists would be familiar with the debates among Marxist perspectives on the state in the 1970s around the relative autonomy of the capitalist state from the economy (Berberoglu 2013:40–52; Clarke 1991b). These views assert a basic distinction between the political and economic realm, whether this takes the form of a convoluted structuralist distinction between an economic base and political superstructure (Poulantzas 1975), or an instrumentalist approach that asserts "different forms of state have different degrees of autonomy. But all states enjoy some autonomy or independence from all classes, including the dominant classes...the relative independence of the state does not reduce its class character" (Milliband *cited in* Berberoglu 2013:43).

In this work I take a view of the state and markets as mutually constitutive institutions, and governance not as an autonomous or external practice of regulating markets and class struggle, but as constitutive of the form and shape of class relations, conditioning and conditioned by class struggle (Brenner 1977; Clarke 1991a; Gough 2004; Wallerstein 1974; Wood 1981). The importance of this perspective for the current discussion of the erasure of labor from legitimate political discourse is that it marks an important shift in the role of public institutions in class struggle. As Ellen Wood has argued,

> From an historical point of view even political institutions like the village and state enter directly into the constitution of productive relations and are in a sense prior to them (even where these institutions are not the direct instruments of surplus-appropriation) to the extent that relations of production are historically constituted by the configuration of political power that determines the outcome of class conflict. (Wood 1981:80)

As Wood argues at some length, the apparent separation of politics from economics is in fact the differentiation of the "social functions of production and distribution, surplus extraction and appropriation, and the allocation of social labour" (Wood 1981:81) from the public or political dynamics of coercion and consent. But those dynamics are still central to the function of a capitalist society, as "on the one hand, the 'relatively autonomous' state has a monopoly of coercive force; on the other hand, that force sustains a private 'economic' power which invests capitalist property with an authority to organize production itself—an authority probably unprecedented in its degree of control over productive activity and the human beings who engage in it... the direct political powers which capitalist proprietors have lost to the state they have gained in the direct control of production...at the same time, the powers of the appropriator no longer carry with them the obligation to perform social, public functions" (Wood 1981:81). The apparent separation of political and economic power in capitalism is in fact a differentiation of distinct *moments* of political domination, and the shift towards partnership is precisely a shift in these differentiated moments of domination: a shift in the discursive and practical constitution of the public and private spheres.[9] This comes across most clearly in the state Supreme Court cases which legitimated public spending on private industrial projects. Probably the first instance of this occurred in 1980, when city and state officials in Detroit evicted the population and razed some of their neighborhood for a new factory, and the residents challenged the city in court. To reiterate Luger's account: "the heart of the legal challenge hinged on the meaning of 'public use' in eminent domain law. The basic issue, according to the Michigan Supreme Court, was whether the proposed condemnation was for the primary benefit of the public or the private user, in this case GM. The courts ruled (5–2) that the primary benefit from the taking of the neighborhood was for the public... regardless of the fact that there was an 'incidental' private gain" (Luger 2000:110). As noted in previous chapters, the real break in economic development and recruitment practice occurred around the recruitment of Toyota in Kentucky, which was also challenged and ended up in the state Supreme Court. "The Kentucky Supreme Court ruled 4-3 that the Collins incentive package was constitutional. At issue had been whether the state had the power to raise and spend money for the benefit of a private business. Proponents argued ...the potential benefits to be derived were so great that the constitution must be judicially amended" (Gelsanliter 1990:128; Perrucci 1994).

The logic of those rulings essentially stated that a private investment could be justified as – and *understood* as – a public good or service, insofar as that investment enhanced the local economic profile and provided employment and a stronger tax base. And this logic lies at the core of the partnership approach to governance, which reconfigures the political and economic – the public and the private – by situating private investment as a larger public good and insisting that the "primary benefit [of private investment]...is for the public" (Luger 2000:110). From this view, private investment and gain is not an indirect social good, but a real public service. Thus, taxpayer funds are justifiably invested directly in private ventures, because what had previously been characterized as "backward linkages" or "beneficial externalities" of private enterprise are now argued and understood to be intrinsically a social boon.

This is a distinctly skewed view of business and investment, but it is hardly a new one. Indeed, in the process of coding my interviews and developing a framework for the partnership perspective, I was reminded of a wry, caustic passage from Volume I of Marx's *Capital,* that it took me a moment to put my finger on. The passage is from his chapter on "The Labor Process and the Valorization Process" and comes out of his investigation of the origins of surplus value; in it, Marx drolly mocks the assumption that the capitalist entrepreneur is ennobled by the public good at the root of her investments:

> Our capitalist...may perhaps say that he advanced his money with the intention of making more money out of it. The road to hell is paved with good intentions, and he might just as well have intended to make money without producing at all. He makes threats. He will not be caught napping again. In the future he will buy the commodities in the market, instead of manufacturing them himself...He recites the catechism:...'have I not

rendered society an incalculable service by providing my instruments of production...and the worker too, for have I not provided him with the means of subsistence?'" (Marx 1976:298–299)

The catechism of the capitalist might well be written above the door of every economic development authority and chamber of commerce. The point that Marx is making is that the capitalist is investing not for the public good, but for the ultimate goal of private enrichment through production. This ironic recital is offered by way of making the ultimate point that capital is internally related to labor – capital needs labor to produce a surplus and profit. From the Marxian view, roughly speaking, the greater the degree that direct producers work for the dominant class – and not for their own needs – the greater the amount of surplus.[10] This is precisely why Marx and most prominent Marxist sociologists and economists use the term class *relations*, and why Wright notes that these relations are fundamentally *asymmetrical*, in the sense that the material interests of one class are diametrically and dialectically opposed the those of the other (Wright 1997:10). The partnership perspective ignores these fundamental connections between classes; indeed, the Supreme Court justices may as well have read Marx's ironic catechism from the bench: "have businesses not rendered society an incalculable service by providing [their] instruments of production...and the worker too, for have [they] not provided him with the means of subsistence?" This is precisely the reasoning behind the partnership perspective and the economic development field and its array of best practices and rationalizations thereof. The entrepreneurial activities of private companies and their government partners are fundamentally in the public interest, and both sides of the partnership ultimately are benevolent benefactors bestowing jobs on the populace.

This reasoning and ideology have reconfigured local power relations by blurring the distinction between the public and private sphere – but in a distinctly one-sided way. Wood argued above that the separation of the political and economic in capitalism saw an increase in the domination of capital over labor *within* the private sphere of production, while it marked a certain abstraction of the power of coercion to the public realm of the state. At the same time, capitalists sloughed off the public obligations attached to feudal relations of production. In the partnership obligations between classes are restored, but again in one-sided fashion: the obligation is on the part of the *worker* to her benevolent employer. Taxpayers' money – recalling again that these private corporate citizens are given immense tax relief – is then spent on private enterprise, and the justification is that the corporate investor is providing employment and wages, and perforce tax revenue for the region. Private employment *becomes* public in this sense; *doing business* is no longer simply private economic activity but an incalculable social service. At the same time that private citizens in this perspective now have an obligation to offer up public funds to benevolent employers, the discursive elision of labor from the public political discussion marks an extension of the domination of capital over labor from the private to the public sphere. As local governments differentially take up the reasoning and ideology of the private firm, the more or less absolute power over labor *within* production is – through this discursive and political aversion – extended to the realm of local politics, not as the power of a single firm over its employees but in the form of the abstract or public state acting in the name of prospective businesses (capital in general). In a certain sense, then, the direct power of surplus appropriation is split – as was the political moment of coercion in Wood's argument – between the public and private. While many have argued that appropriation of tax revenue is a kind of social appropriation for the social provision of capital (Bowles and Gintis 1982; Teeple 2000:45; Tilly 1992), the partnership approach now sees this revenue contributing directly to private enterprise, through the public partner. And in cases such as Alabama and Mississippi, where the power to tax employees' income devolves directly on the private enterprise, the public power of taxation is reconfigured to apply within the production relation.

This marks an important reconfiguration of class relations, and thus relations between the public and private sphere in neoliberal globalization, one that can be best apprehended through Marxian theory. The partnership approach and the reconfiguration of political economic relations leads to an erosion of the political legitimacy of labor because the perspective understands development to originate with capital investment and not the relations of production between classes. This is the fetishized view of capital at the core of neoclassical economics and the neoliberal project. To again quote Marx, "*capital appears as a relationship to itself*...it appears to consciousness as if capital creates this new value in the course of its movement... and appears to derive from hidden qualities that are inherent in capital itself" (Marx 1981:139). For my purposes here, the critical point to take away from Marx is that when capital appears as a relation to itself, it does not appear related to labor dialectically. When this is the case, it appears that there *is no power relation at all*: there is no domination of labor, there is no dialectical relation between capital and labor, and there is no appropriation of surplus. From this fetishized viewpoint, labor *cannot* make legitimate political claims because this view denies the fundamental opposition of capital and labor, and thus where labor organizes (or threatens to) and accordingly makes plain that dialectic, the soundness of its claims is epistemologically precluded by the partnership perspective.

Thus, in the partnership approach capital appears as a relation to itself, but this is merely the form of appearance. Where the essential class relationship between capital and labor is apprehended through analysis, we see partnership reconfigures the political constitution of relations between classes. On the one hand, the state no longer appears as relatively autonomous, as its public functions are now directly related to – and constructed as – coterminous with the interests of private investors. On the other hand, the power to control

labor is no longer confined to the private economic realm of contractual relations, but is now exercised (more explicitly) by the public partner in the
political realm through the erasure of labor's political legitimacy and outright
suppression. While labor still exists and struggles within the class relation, its
political potential is further stultified through the epistemological erosion of
its political legitimacy.[11]

It is worth noting that partnership is not intrinsic to firms themselves, but
to the nexus between transnational corporations and local governing officials and development professionals. Indeed, after reciting the catechism of
capitalism, Marx notes "the capitalist... with a hearty laugh, he recovers his
composure. The whole litany he has just recited...he himself does not care
twopence for it. He leaves this and all similar subterfuges and conjuring
tricks to the professors of political economy, who are paid for it" (Marx
1976:300). In other words, while the partnership approach to entrepreneurial governance does not change the essential dialectic between
capital and labor, what it does do is alter "the shape of specific social de-
terminations, the particular modes of organization and domination and the
forms of property in which relations of production are embodied" (Wood
1981:80), in such a manner as dictated by the dominant hegemonic bloc
driving the neoliberal globalization project.

Conclusion

States have always supported and facilitated capitalism and worked to mitigate its contradictions, and many scholars have shown the growth of capitalism and the nation-state to be internally related historical processes
(Brenner 1977; Harvey 1982; O'Connor 1973). Under the development
project of the postwar era, governments undertook massive social investments in infrastructure and welfare to facilitate and encourage mass production and consumption (Harvey 1989; O'Connor 1973:23–25), and while
these larger social projects directly facilitated the circulation and accumulation of capital, the apparent separation of political and economic spheres
of power remained more or less intact. In the current study, these spheres
break down and the political leaders come to take on the perspective of
businesses, and act directly as investing partners in private economic activity. This is part and parcel of a deeper shift in the political formation of
class relations, one that differentially works to further the project of dis-
empowering labor vis-à-vis capital in the neoliberal globalization era. The
particular form this change in power relations takes depends numerous local
factors, including the spread of the economic development profession and
partnership, the degree of alignment between scales of governance, and the
particular practices of governments and firms within the confines of the
ideological class project.[12] Hence, the elision of labor's political legitimacy is
in most cases incomplete and highly contested, as recent unionization efforts
by Amazon warehouse workers Alabama evidence. The last point I might

make here, is that while neoliberal ideology drives the partnership perspective, and this ideology is characterized by faith in markets and competition, it should be clear that the partnership approach involves ever more direct government involvement in private investment and entrepreneurship. As David Harvey has argued, a central yet ironic feature of neoliberal practice and policy, is the "principle, which flew in the face of the non-interventionism that neoliberal theory prescribed...put crudely...was: privatize profits and socialize risks" (Harvey 2010:10). Peck and Tickell make much the same observation, that "while rhetorically antistatist, neoliberals have proved adept at the (mis)use of state power in the pursuit of [their] goals" (Peck and Tickell 2002:381).

Partnership and the neoliberal globalization project are internally related processes, and thus the future of such processes depends on the fate of neoliberalism as a class project – and this fate is decidedly uncertain. Between a global surge of an authoritarian populist right that has fractured some critical institutions of globalization, and a global pandemic in which government interventions have given the lie to neoliberalism's antistatist refrain, it is possible neoliberalism as a class project has suffered a fatal blow (though these bells have tolled before). I turn to the current moment, and to the future, with my remarks in the following chapter.

Notes

1 An interesting theoretical and practical question is how this process affects firms' perception of circulation and turnover. While firms would reach profitability quicker through these public investments, the actual rate at which the fixed capital circulated would not change – the costs and risks would simply be shifted to public authorities. However, this would not be apparent to the firms themselves.

2 This is perhaps nowhere more evident than in Amazon (and increasingly its competitors) sprawling networks of distribution centers that appear to abolish the limits of time (same-day delivery!) through massive infrastructure networks. The limits of time are overcome through building and investing in place.

3 These disparities were only exacerbated by the Trump presidency which played to rural voters in particular, and his loss in the 2020 presidential election, in which cities with large black populations were demonized by the failed President.

4 It is worth noting that the same outward turn could not only have a chilling effect on some legislation, but could also create an impulse towards meretricious legislation that makes the locality *appear* to be an effective partner, while not really accomplishing anything. An example of this might be an educational reform bill pushed by business friendly Georgia Governor Nathan Deal. The first iteration of this bill, written in 2016, consolidated control of failing schools with the state, but had no real practical impact (such as increasing much needed funding) beyond that centralization.

5 As a number of scholars have noted, what is distinct about *neo*liberalism is the more activist function of the state in maintaining and encouraging accumulation and circulation of capital. I discuss this further below.

6 In this regard, I would raise some skepticism to Pacewicz's assertion of political agnosticism among partners: "My analysis runs counter to academic criticisms of "neoliberal" urbanism, which portray community leaders as ideologically opposed

to federal social programs, union-friendly policies, and putative corporate reg-ulations, in part because I found some partners to be privately supportive of polices ranging from the libertarian to nostalgia for New-deal style union protections, regulations, and social programs" (Pacewicz 2016:112). This is in part confirmed in my discussions, as some are ostensibly in favor of clawbacks and great transpar-ency, to make development more honest and popular. Yet this argument belies the fact that the very nature of partnership displaces the community and labor in its direct incorporation of the views of business and capital into its *common sense*. The flexibility, entrepreneurialism, and such at the core of partnership (Pacewicz 2016:115) are the views that center business and are fed by – and demanded by – global capital.

7 Interestingly, this is distinct from the political economy of US regulatory capture articulated in previous chapters. Rather than particular segments of capital "capturing" the regulatory apparatus to benefit a particular segment of labor, here we see governments pushing labor from the picture and appealing to capital in a general sense.

8 Though as we have seen, some developers will send out surveys and ques-tionnaires to the business community and such efforts also inform the view of capital or businesses in general.

9 "In a sense, then, the differentiation of the economic and the political in capit-alism is, more precisely, a differentiation of political functions themselves and their separate allocation to the private economic sphere and the public sphere of the state" (Wood 1981:81).

10 For example, the more the feudal lord extracts tithes from the peasant, the less the peasant has for herself and the richer the lord. For Marx, the wage relation in capitalism disguises the appropriation of surplus value.

11 Nowhere is the illegibility of alternative viewpoints clearer than in the kerfuffle over Amazon's HQ2 in New York state, whose massive incentives deal was re-buffed in a rare alliance of right and left community forces. In an Op-Ed released by New York Governor Andrew Cuomo on his website in response to critics of his incentives deal, where he called the opposition to their deal with Amazon either "extreme right" or "socialists" (Cuomo 2018), implying resistance of whatever political stripe has a tenuous grip on reality.

12 Of particular importance is the regional context of the southeastern United States, a region with long history labor repression and a "closed political system [that has] produced public officials disinclined to regulate but eager to protect the interest of industry, particularly in labor-management conflicts" (Cobb 1993).

Bibliography

Bender, Andrew. 2016. "Indiana's Religious Freedom Act Cost Indianapolis $60 Million In Lost Revenue." *Forbes*. Retrieved May 12, 2017 (https://www.forbes.com/sites/ andrewbender/2016/01/31/indianas-religious-freedom-act-cost-indianapolis-60-million-in-lost-revenue/#722f7b222e2a).

Berberoglu, Berch. 2013. *Political Sociology in a Global Era: An Introduction to the State and Society*. 1st ed. Boulder: Routledge.

Bowles, Samuel, and Herbert Gintis. 1982. "The Crisis of Liberal Democratic Capitalism: The Case of the United States." *Politics & Society* 11(1):51–93.

Brenner, Neil. 1999. "Globalisation as Reterritorialisation: The Re-Scaling of Urban Governance in the European Union." *Urban Studies* 36(3):431–451. doi: 10.1080/ 0042098993466.

Brenner, Robert. 1977. "The Origins of Capitalist Development: A Critique of Neo-Smithian Marxism." *New Left Review* 104(1):25–92.

Clarke, Simon. 1991a. "State, Class Struggle, and the Reproduction of Capital." Pp. 183–203 in *The State Debate*, edited by S. Clarke. Hampshire: Palgrave MD.

Clarke, Simon. Ed. 1991b. *The State Debate*. Hampshire: Palgrave MD.

Cobb, James C. 1993. *The Selling of the South: The Southern Crusade for Industrial Development 1936-1990*. 2nd ed. Urbana: University of Illinois Press.

Cohen, Patricia. 2015. "Alabama Vote Is Rare Win in the South for the U.A.W." *New York Times*, September 24. Retrieved May 3, 2017 (https://www.nytimes.com/2015/09/25/business/workers-at-alabama-truck-parts-factory-vote-to-join-uaw.html).

Cuomo, Andrew. 2018. "Op-Ed from Governor Andrew M. Cuomo." *Governor Andrew M. Cuomo*. Retrieved January 6, 2019 (https://www.governor.ny.gov/news/op-ed-governor-andrew-m-cuomo).

EDP02. 2015. "Economic Development Professional 02."

EDP03. 2015. "Economic Development Professional 03."

EDP06. 2016. "Economic Development Professional 06."

Gelsanliter, David. 1990. *Jump Start: Japan Comes to the Heartland*. New York: Farrar Straus Giroux.

Gough, J. 1996. "Not Flexible Accumulation -- Contradictions of Value in Contemporary Economic Geography: 2. Regional Regimes, National Regulation, and Political Strategy." *Environment and Planning A* 28(12):2179–2200.

Gough, Jamie. 2004. "Changing Scale as Changing Class Relations: Variety and Contradiction in the Politics of Scale." *Political Geography* 23(2):185–211. doi: 10.1016/j.polgeo.2003.11.005.

Gramsci, Antonio. 1971. *Selections from the Prison Notebooks*. International Publishers Co.

Harvey, David. 1982. *The Limits to Capital*. Chicago: University of Chicago Press.

Harvey, David. 1989. *The Condition of Postmodernity: An Enquiry into the Origins of Cultural Change*. Oxford: Blackwell.

Harvey, David. 2010. *The Enigma of Capital: And the Crises of Capitalism*. New York: Oxford University Press.

Hülsemann, Karsten. 2001. "Greenfields in the Heart of Dixie: How the American Auto Industry Discovered the South." Pp. 219–254 in *The Second Wave: Southern Industrialization from the 1940s to the 1970s*, edited by P. Scranton. Athens, GA: University of Gerogia Press.

Jacobs, A. J. 2012. "Collaborative Regionalism and Foreign Direct Investment The Case of the Southeast Automotive Core and the 'New Domestics.'" *Economic Development Quarterly* 26(3):199–219.

Jessop, Bob. 1983. "Accumulation Strategies, State Forms, and Hegemonic Projects." *Kapitalistate* 10:89–111.

Jurney, Corrine. 2016. "North Carolina's Bathroom Bill Flushes Away $630 Million In Lost Business." *Forbes*. Retrieved May 12, 2017 (about:reader?url=https%3A%2F%2Fwww.forbes.com%2Fsites%2Fcorinnejurney%2F2016%2F11%2F03%2Fnorth-carolinas-bathroom-bill-flushes-away-750-million-in-lost-business%2F%232699d4254b59).

Klas, Mary Ellen. 2013. "Bill to Block Local 'Living Wage' Ordinance Gets Push in Florida House." *Badenton Herald*. Retrieved May 12, 2017 (http://www.bradenton.com/news/business/article34573482.html).

Luger, Stan. 2000. *Corporate Power, American Democracy, and the Automobile Industry*. Cambridge, UK; New York: Cambridge University Press.

Mann, Michael. 1986. *The Sources of Social Power. Volume 1, a History of Power from the Beginning to A.d. 1760*. Cambridge: Cambridge University Press.

Marx, Karl. 1976. *Capital: Volume 1: A Critique of Political Economy*. Vol. 1. London: Penguin Books in association with New Left Review.

Marx, Karl. 1981. *Capital: Volume 3: A Critique of Political Economy*. Vol. 3. London: Penguin Books in association with New Left Review.

Mattera, Phillip, Kasia Tarczynska, Leigh McIlvaine, Thomas Cafcas, and Greg LeRoy. 2012. *Paying Taxes to the Boss* | Good Jobs First: Washington D.C.

McDermott, Michael C. 2011. "BMW, Spartanburg, South Carolina: Drivers and Processes in the International Plant Location Decision." *Southern Business & Economic Journal* 34(1/2):73–94.

McMichael, Philip. 2000. "Globalisation: Trend or Project?" Pp. 100–113 in *Global Political Economy: Contemporary Theories*, edited by R. Palan. London: Routledge.

O'Connor, James. 1973. *The Fiscal Crisis of the State*. New York: St. Martin's Press.

Pacewicz, Josh. 2013. "Regulatory Rescaling in Neoliberal Markets." *Social Problems* 60(4):433–456. doi: 10.1525/sp.2013.60.4.433.

Pacewicz, Josh. 2016. *Partisans and Partners: The Politics of the Post-Keynesian Society*. University of Chicago Press.

Peck, Jamie. 1996. *Work-Place: The Social Regulation of Labor Markets*. New York: Guilford Press.

Peck, Jamie, and Adam Tickell. 1994. "Jungle Law Breaks out: Neoliberalism and Global-Local Disorder." *Area* 26(4):317–326.

Peck, Jamie, and Adam Tickell. 2002. "Neoliberalizing Space." *Antipode* 34(3):380–404. doi: 10.1111/1467-8330.00247.

Perrucci, Robert. 1994. *Japanese Auto Transplants in the Heartland: Corporatism and Community*. New York: Aldine de Gruyter.

Poulantzas, Nicos. 1975. *Classes in Contemporary Capitalism*. 2nd ed. London: NLB.

Price, Mark, and Adam Bell. 2017. "National Reaction Divided over HB2 Repeal." *Charlotte Observer*. Retrieved May 12, 2017 (about:reader?url=http%3A%2F%2Fwww.charlotteobserver.com%2Fnews%2Flocal%2Farticle141823074.html).

Robinson, William I. 2005. "Gramsci and Globalisation: From Nation-State to Transnational Hegemony." *Critical Review of International Social & Political Philosophy* 8(4):559–574.

Rueschemeyer, Dietrich, Evelyne Huber Stephens, and John D. Stephens. 1992. *Capitalist Development and Democracy*. 1st ed. Chicago: University Of Chicago Press.

Sassen, Saskia. 2012. *Cities in a World Economy*. 4th ed. Thousand Oaks, Calif: SAGE/Pine Forge.

Scholte, Jan Aart. 1997. "Global Capitalism and the State." *International Affairs* 73(3):427–452.

SEL02. 2016. "Site Selection Professional."

SEL03. 2016. "Site Selection Professional."

Sher, Andy. 2013. "Tennessee State Laws Supersede Local Rules." *Chattanooga Times Free Press*. Retrieved May 12, 2017 (http://www.timesfreepress.com/news/local/story/2013/mar/17/state-laws-supersede-local-rules/102704/).

Storper, Michael, and Richard Walker. 1989. *The Capitalist Imperative: Territory, Technology, and Industrial Growth.* New York: Basil Blackwell.

Teeple, Gary. 2000. *Globalization and the Decline of Social Reform: Into the Twenty-First Century.* 2nd ed. Ontario: Garamond Press.

Tilly, Charles. 1992. *Coercion, Capital, and European States, Ad 990-1992.* Rev. pbk. ed. Cambridge: Blackwell.

Wallerstein, Immanuel Maurice. 1974. *The Modern World-System I.* New York: Academic Press.

Wood, Ellen Meiksins. 1981. "The Separation of the Economic and the Political in Capitalism." *New Left Review* (I/127):66–95.

Wright, Erik Olin. 1997. *Class Counts: Comparative Studies in Class Analysis.* Cambridge: Cambridge University Press.

7 Axiomatic? A weird, blurred line

This research began with a puzzle, an apparently bizarre reversal in the state of Tennessee where local lawmakers raised voices aloud and threatened to pull state-funded incentives if the workers and managers of the Volkswagen plant agreed to unionize the shop, claiming it would bring harm to the community. I posed the question of just what community these lawmakers were referring to, if not that of the workers whose jobs all of their economic development efforts were intended to create? We have seen that this community is in fact that of the business and economic development professionals, of the site selectors and government elites who *get it* – partners (Pacewicz 2016). The neoliberal globalization project opened up nation-states to global flows of capital and saw localities embrace an entrepreneurial approach to governance, turning ever more outward towards management and facilitation of global capital flows (Brenner 1999:439), and turn towards each other in competitive policy mimesis. This same project ruptured the rigid structures of Fordist organization of production, and brought new firms into the arena of American automotive production. The dual developments of global changes and inter-local competition pushed Japanese and German firms towards the southeast, where eager officials tested and transformed the boundaries of the public-private divide in their efforts to draw inward investment. As we have seen, the picture is more complex than the journalistic accounts of local and state governments powerless before transnational corporations that are hell-bent on squeezing every penny from recruitment deals.

The case studies presented here build on a rich field of sociological and geographical literature dealing with local development, governance, partnership, and class dynamics. These cases show that localities and officials have taken on the role of co-investor and business entrepreneur, all while treating global corporations as prized customers of their public services (and funds). My research shows how localities are absorbing the heaviest risks associated with capital circulation and accumulation, in particular those long-term fixed capital investments that otherwise would serve to *fix* a corporation in place. Geographer Neil Brenner has made similar observations about municipal governments in Europe:

DOI: 10.4324/9781003107569-7

governments…[are] directly embracing…supply-side strategies that entail the demarcation, construction and promotion of strategic urban places for industrial development…as Harvey indicates, such state-financed mega-projects are designed primarily to enhance the productive capacity of urban places within global flows of value, rather than to reorganise living and working conditions more broadly within cities. At the same time, however, the locational capacities of these urban places necessarily depend upon a relatively fixed infrastructure of territorial organization through which value can be extracted and valorised at globally competitive turnover times. (Brenner 1999:446)

While my findings concur with Brenner and Harvey who made similar observations, they differ in at least one crucial way (at least, in terms of emphasis). I argued in the last chapter that the blurring between the spheres of political economic activity – between the public and the private – marks an important reconfiguration of class relations as they are constituted through property relations and political institutions.[1] In other words, while industrial recruitment efforts have certainly "enhanced the productive capacity" of localities, in the South this has taken on precisely a reorganization of living and working conditions insofar as these are constituted by and through the relations of (re)production. This reconfiguration erodes the legitimacy of both local concerns vis-à-vis businesses and enervates the legitimacy of labor as a political actor. And this blurring of public and private is not merely a theoretical abstraction, but plays out through the everyday relations and practices – the living and working conditions – of development officials and site selectors. As one business development official in North Carolina told me,

> there's a great debate within our state…right now…as to dollars – if you have contract with governmental entities, does that essentially make you a *de facto* a public entity? And [whether or not] people would have the ability to weigh in on those decisions, or weigh in on those expenditures whatever it might be, *acting* as a public agency?…So what used to be a very clear understanding of "oh, I'm public" or "I'm private" is not-that line is becoming blurred…So the [Economic Development Partnership of North Carolina] as a public-private partnership, some would say "Ok it's a private…" but when the media ask for his emails or for his communications, they are responding to the media…as if they were a public agency. So it's this weird blurred line. (BDP03 2016)

Apprehending this reconfiguration of power relations through the hegemony of partnership under neoliberalism is arguably crucial to understanding the strange political landscape we find ourselves in as I write these concluding remarks early in 2021. In these last pages I offer a few final thoughts on the question of whether partnership is really a bad deal, what the implications are for the future of partnership, and offer some broader suggestions for theorizing and researching class, states, and power in the curious time of the COVID-19 crisis.

Losing on local deals?

Most critics of the entrepreneurial approach to governance have often worked within a line of questioning whether or not major public investment in private activities are a "good deal" for the taxpayers footing the bill (Baade, Baumann, and Matheson 2008; Boudreaux, Coats, and Davis 2012; McDavid 2010). For example, a prominent watchdog group that tracks incentives – *Good Jobs First* – titled their report on the Nissan plant in Mississippi, "A Good Deal for Mississippi?" (Mattera and Tarczynska 2013). And indeed, this is how development officials themselves have framed their efforts throughout my interviews, claiming that careful cost-benefit analysis is done to make sure investments ultimately pay off and taxpayers get a good deal.

But these questions about "what's a good deal?" fundamentally miss the mark, for they beg the question of why localities are making deals in the first place – of why it is now considered necessary, if not reasonable and right, to invest public funds in private enterprise? One of the officials I interviewed laid out the contradictory thinking behind his normalization of incentives, reasoning that, "it's an investors game, they can go anywhere. So where do they go? Yes, they have to have the right land. Yes, they have to have the right—all of that. But they want to know...'are these the kind of people we're going to be able to work with?'" (EDP03 2015). The contradictions contained in this statement are instructive, for in the same moment that he notes that companies have certain locational specifications ("they have to have the right _____") he also says "they can go anywhere." Here we see that the partnership view and its underlying ideology fetishize the mobility of capital by assuming capital can invest anywhere, even though in a number of interviews the same professionals noted that there are just not many sites capable of hosting major industrial projects. This is a fundamental contradiction within the partnership approach to governance, in which the professional field of knowledge of local economic development dictates, on the one hand, the need to cater directly to the interests and requirements of particular incoming businesses while, on the other hand, placing ideological limits on the customer service experience where demands of particular businesses could appear to contradict neoliberal orthodoxy.

What is interesting about this contradiction is that in many ways it appears to replicate the debate around the relative autonomy of the state from capital, which suggested that the state represents the interests of "capital in general," establishing a relative autonomy from *particular* interests of individual segments of capital or capitals. While I agree with Clarke (1991) that that there is no such thing as "capital in general," in the sense that there is no general interest empirically expressed "out there in the world," through the formation of partnership practices in economic development there is created a policy space that does indeed consider the needs and expectations of *potential* business partners and investors (place as product). Thus, what appears to be a contradiction in the statement of the development official above is in fact a duality within partnership itself, the twin needs of developers to market themselves as an attractive product to businesses in general *and* deliver a customer service experience that caters precisely to those locational specifications that limit the mobility of particular capitals, the former necessity informed by the ontological assumption (or assertion?) of the pure mobility of capital.[2] Moreover, in addition to the implicit assumption of pure mobility, itself a core tenant of neoliberal ideology, regional inter-local competition is enhanced by the underlying morality of that ideology which valorizes market rule and espouses the virtues of competition.[3] In many ways, then, the current competitive climate among states and localities throughout the Southeast is as much a product of the partnership perspective as it is the cause. This is what is most important to consider when asking whether these states are in a race to the bottom or getting a raw deal, for if there is a race among localities, they themselves have mapped the course and fired the starting gun.

Where does partnership go from here?

If local governments and corporations are dance partners waltzing out of step to a neoliberal tune, where does this dance take us in the future? This question is of course speculative, and the current moment in the United States following the chaotic presidency of Donald Trump and the crisis brought on by the COVID-19 pandemic makes any speculation borderline scientifically heretical. However, it is possible to outline some potential suggestions in contemporary trends, if we partially bracket the upheaval that the crisis of COVID-19 has wrought. In particular, by following the logic of partnership, we can trace a path in which capital extends its dominion over local public life, where the blurring of the public-private distinction can be tied back to the sacred substance for which capital is fetishized: jobs.

One clear logical extension of partnership currently observed has been pushing incentives proposals beyond business recruitment to *retention*. As the governor noted in chapter 4, not long ago the idea that localities would be willing to offer incentives simply for a corporation not to leave, or to minimize the number of jobs eliminated, would have been lunacy. Yet, just days after his election in 2016, U.S. President Donald Trump proclaimed his incredible success in negotiating a deal with Carrier in Indiana that saved 2,000 jobs! The deal, of course, had been in the works at the state level for a while, and aggrandized numbers aside (it was more around 800 jobs), the "success" here was offering up millions of dollars for a firm *not to move jobs overseas.* This story is anecdotal evidence of a broader trend in which localities increasingly consider the potential threat of disinvestment and job flight to be a legitimate justification for publicly funded incentives. Hence, throughout my interviews individuals spoke about efforts to recruit *and* retain jobs and businesses. This shift suggests that where development professionals and firms seek to extend the reach of incentives and investment efforts, it will likely be directly relatable – as far as possible – back the ostensible justification of the whole local development enterprise: jobs. This is one area as well in which we can guess that the impact of the COVID-19 economic crisis and the widespread unemployment it has brought, which *could* bolster partnership and recruitment efforts for some time into the future. Economists currently are offering tentative estimates that employment figures in the United States may not recover until 2024.

We can also follow this logic of partnership to see how the expanding dominion and influence of capital in the realm of local governance may progress in ways not immediately related to recruitment and retention. One clear way in which the state-class nexus could develop in the future is through further forms of local socialization in which businesses seek to actively create ties to a locality and enhance local development. In Atlanta, alongside the stadium constructed for their associated football team, the city and other developers built a $45 million dollar park with heavy investment from the owner of the football team, ostensibly intended to start redevelopment of the West Side, a district of that city marked by its visible poverty (Trubey 2017). This is an instance of a "strategy [of] *local integration* of economic actors that aims to ensure...crucially, the construction of political consensus between sections of capital, labour, and residents" (Gough 2004:196). While the park could be seen as promoting consensus insofar as it was intended to mollify public outcry about the billions going into a stadium right next such visible poverty, it is again a clear blurring of the civic landscape and private interests. And like most things under neoliberalism which ostensibly benefit the poor, the park reclamation and maintenance depended not on the systematic reappropriation of wealth through taxation, but on the charity of a billionaire. In another more troubling example of this local integration, in South Carolina "Clemson University [located near the sprawling BMW production facility in Anderson] received $10 million from the German automaker BMW in 2002, [and] the money helped jump-start a $1.5 billion automotive research and educational center. It also led to a partnership that both the automaker and the university acknowledge has grown extraordinarily close" (Browning 2006). This latter example is telling of the ways in which the deepening of local ties by a corporation can mark a further blurring of the public and private, in this case by directly extending corporate control over curricula in the state university system. As Browning points out, "in return for the largest cash donation ever received by the school, Clemson gave the company some unusual privileges, including a hand in developing a course of study" (2006). Thus, we can see that, as part of these territorial socialisations, active cooperation of labour and residents with capital is promoted alongside, and founded on, the disciplines imposed by value. This is reinforced by measures to reproduce better labour power (local initiatives for reproduction [...]). The sharper imposition of value...and the defeats of trade unions in the 1970s and 1980s have allowed capital to develop weak, tentative forms of cooperation with labour at both the local and [supra-national] scales, avoiding the over-politicised national scale. (Gough 2004:205)

The Clemson-BMW example points to both the possible future deepening and broadening of the partnership approach as well as its likely limits. On the one hand, we see the extension of corporate power into areas not directly related to recruitment or retainment of jobs, but on the other hand this form of socialization is directly linked to the interests of the firm in cultivating labor power within its own region and directly related to its corporate interests. At the same time, it is also justifiable from the side of local governance for the exact same reason: that this extension serves to further enhance the quality labor power and therefore create more jobs. Thus, we are likely to see the further deepening of local partnership – and blurring of the public and private – where it is both directly related to the immediate interests of businesses within a locality or region while also defensible in some way as related to job creation or retainment (or perhaps upskilling etc.) and creating weak forms of local cooperation.[4]

One potential avenue of future research which follows from this logical extension of partnership would be to examine patterns in public work and spending that may be indirectly tied to private partner's needs and interests. One of the most recent and absurd recruitment deals in recent memory involved Wisconsin offering Taiwanese electronics giant Foxconn three billion dollars to locate a flat-screen manufacturing complex in their state. The project has completely fallen apart (the 13,000 jobs and $10 billion investment has not manifested, nor will it be a manufacturing center) but it is perhaps instructive in that, after the deal was announced, a long neglected infrastructure improvement suddenly found itself funded and underway. "Dubbed the *I-94 North-South Freeway Project*, the reconstruction plan was approved in 2008, and was originally supposed to be completed by 2016. But the highways project didn't get funded until the Foxconn agreement was signed by Governor Walker in November, 2017" (Hill 2019). This case is only anecdotal, but if the need to market place as product implicitly shapes patterns of legislation as suggested in chapter 5, it is reasonable to hypothesize that public infrastructure spending not directly tied to a particular recruitment effort could balloon around those projects. Thus, such patterns of spending and unequal development could be yet another way in which partnership bleeds outside the borders of public and private, giving firms implicit and indirect control over infrastructure spending where they find amenable partners in local government. The evidence at this point is, however, only suggestive, and more research is needed.

Theoretical implications: class, state, and the neoliberal now

These practical and local considerations of how partnership plays out in the future must of course take into account the current upheaval of the COVID-19 pandemic and the economic crisis it represents for workers, corporations, and governments at every scale. To do so first requires we directly consider the theoretical implications in the previous chapter for theorizing the state and relations of production as they actually exist. We have seen that one outcome of the partnership approach *seems* to be that local governments internalize "the contradiction between the autonomy of the state acting for capital as a whole and its response to the demands of particular capitals" (Gough 2004:204). But this is not quite right, on two counts. First, as we have seen, the appearance of the local state acting in a relatively autonomous manner is in essence a manifestation of a contradiction between different aspects of the theory and practice of the partnership approach to governance itself. Rather than representing some form autonomy from capital though, this duality is a result of localities behaving more directly *as* capital and *as* a business. Secondly, it is incorrect to suggest that local governments internalize exogenous contradictions, for in fact this is a political expression of the concrete forms of class struggle as they are differentially articulated through local and regional institutions and structures. For example, we saw in the Saturn case U.S. auto firms attempting to impose their regional articulation of production relations on Japanese firms in the South and notably failing to do so, and in Tennessee we saw Volkswagen consider cultivating its corporatist form of production relations only to be rebuffed by state officials working ever so hard to maintain neoliberal class relations. Theorization of the state and class thus requires not only consideration of the different institutional scales at which class relations are politically constituted, but also the national-regional institutional lineages of class actors and segments of labor and capital. These findings also suggest that we pay attention to the tension *between* the political articulation of relations of production and the political basis of class power, *and* the structural development of classes in the material practice of production and capital accumulation. Put more concretely, we above saw the erosion of the space for the legitimate political expression of the interests of labor, but we have also witnessed in four decades of neo-liberalism the expulsion of large numbers of workers from the labor market and the increasing polarization of wealth, power, and classes. This creates a tension in which deepening class polarization is caught up with the erosion of political space for the expression of class conflict. It is precisely this tension in the neoliberal project which has played out before our eyes in the polarized politics in the latter half of the 2010s, and that has possibly reached its breaking point in the crisis of COVID-19 and the global pandemic.

Thinking through partnership in the neoliberal now: in these uncertain times...

It might seem a tenuous thing to connect this little study to the resurgence of openly far-right politics, quasi-populist leaders, and movements for racial justice – and I will certainly limit my observations. The point to make here is that the hegemonic project that justifies partnership by epistemologically centering the perspective of capital, creates the polarization of political activity that has so captured the public narrative over the last decade or so. It does so precisely because it shapes the common sense which delimits *reasonable* thought, rendering unquestionable the power structure that benefits the project architects. Arlie Russell Hochschild's ethnographic study of socially conservative Louisiana residents left behind by neoliberal globalization vividly highlights the contradictory successes of this project to win consent among white working and middle classes in that state:

> feeling betrayed by the federal government [elsewhere described as "a more powerful, distant and untrustworthy version of *state* government"] and turning wholeheartedly to the free market, the right is faced with realities the deep story makes it hard to see or focus on. Giant companies have grown vastly larger, more automated, more global and more powerful...but it is very hard to criticize an ally, and the right sees the free market as its ally against the powerful alliance the federal government and the takers...in the undeclared class war. (Hochschild 2016a:150–151).

For the Louisiana residents Hochschild got to know, the "deep story" is one in which the free market and competition (assumed to be morally good things) are disrupted or distorted by an often ethnicized or racialized Other who hitches a free ride on government subsidies, or even crony capitalists who do not compete fairly in the market.[5] Hochschild's profile shows that among some groups the ideological project of neoliberalism has been very successful indeed, and that this success is inherently contradictory. Where the project is successful, it is so because it directs the anger with the insecurity and immiseration of neoliberal reality away from the ruling bloc which is its cause. The success is contradictory because there is no real answer to that anger, like all the contradictions of capitalism it is not resolved but displaced (Harvey 1982, 2010). Importantly, consent to – and normalization of – partnership is secured on the same ideological grounds that consent to the rule of the neoliberal bloc in general is won.[6] But that consent is never truly *won*, because where it succeeds in precluding class antipathy and consciousness, it provides no meaningful alternative. The thin fiction of individual effort and responsibility is a flimsy barrier to the massive inequalities that neoliberalism reproduces daily, and so consent – where it is even sought amongst the working masses – is constantly renegotiated on increasingly thin terrain. And this is only where consent has been sought, which is to say nothing of the poor and Black communities in the United States which have been subjected to a massive carceral project for 40 years. This subjugation has forced many into a prison system where their labor is extracted for pennies (Alexander 2012; Vitale 2017), while those who get out are effectively forced into a marginal underclass, a peripheral necropolis of liminal existence which is somehow still better than the brutal inhumanity of the prison industrial complex that looms over them (Bhattacharyya 2018). The difference between those who search for answers in the exclusion of a racialized Other from a nonexistent market utopia, and those who organize for the validation and flourishing of Black lives, is that the latter is based in the harsh realities of racial capitalism, the former in its self-flattering fantasies.

In this sense then, the polarized politics of the latter half of the 2010s is the flipside of partnership governance. It is in part the manifestation of the anger and pain of a class war that dare not speak its name, does not have the words to name it, nor the air to breathe life into them if it did so.[7] The polarization of politics and the loss of the political center here is not adjacent to partnership but an extension of the same project. The fact that figures like Trump enact policies that are at once utterly neoliberal (violent suppression of dissent, rampant, and uncontrolled deregulation) and fundamentally undermine that project (withdrawal from – and deconstruction of – global institutions) becomes more comprehensible once we understand that, despite his apparent peripatetic idiocy he is savvy enough to tune into the contradictory emotions and impulses of those who have completely bought the lie of a system that let them down.

All of these political pressures were pulling at the corners of the neoliberal globalization projects core contradictions when the COVID-19 pandemic showed up with its scissors. The COVID-19 pandemic presents a unique crisis, for neoliberalism certainly, but for partnership specifically. As a force exogenous to both markets and individuals it defies by its existence the logic of rational choice. By making the most mundane and purposefully ignored work a literal question of life or potential risk of death, it has forced aggressively submerged questions of labor to the forefront of the popular imagination and collective conscience. By exposing the much diminished (in some localities nearly extinguished) capacity of public institutions, the pandemic has raised new questions around austerity and taxation at same time that it has made plain the necessity of those institutions. By affecting the whole globe and lasting over a year, the pandemic has created natural experiments in political practice, both through the inevitable cross-national comparisons of policy and effectiveness of COVID-19 responses, and in the United States through a major election which replaced an effectively *no* government president with a pro-government one. All of these tensions pull the displaced and submerged tensions of neoliberalism's contradictions to the surface, and in shouting the quiet part out loud they present the potential to disrupt the ideological basis upon which local recruitment practices are justified. *If* the effects are truly profound and long lasting on the collective consciousness – if the common sense of partnership is ruptured – *then* there could be implications for alternatives to both neoliberalism as a project and partnership as a mode of local governance. I limit myself to a few potential hypotheses about the future partnership and recruitment here:

Change will be slow, local, and uneven

If the lugubrious madness around masks and public health regulations is any indication, then the effects of the COVID-19 crisis on the collective consciousness will be dependent on how *conscious* (of reality, anyway) some of the collective are. Nevertheless, we can hypothesize ways in which the current intersecting crises might change some of the fundamental dynamics of the public consciousness in ways that could challenge recruitment activities and partnership more broadly. First, however, it is worth emphasizing the barriers that efforts to disrupt partnership face. As I have highlighted in the last three chapters of this book, one of the core tenants of being a good partner is insulating partnership activity in general, and especially recruitment efforts, from public oversight and the cycles of electoral politics. If any of the efforts to challenge recruitment activities hypothesized below do arise, they will likely have to work slowly through various legislative and organizational measures intended to prevent them. Moreover, if the tensions discussed in the previous chapter in Florida and other states are any indicator, efforts that challenge partnership directly or indirectly (e.g., minimum wage laws) will likely be caught in tensions between different scales of government where partnership is more or less accepted. The spectacular debate around Amazon's HQ2 in New York was in part a product of such a disjuncture between local and community politicians and organizations, and the emphatically pro-business state government. While it would be unwise to draw many general conclusions from such a singular case, both the presence of state-level legislation which streamlined (i.e., cut out local political oversight) structuring the incentives deal, and the discord between state and local politicians, may be indicative of the difficulties in problematizing incentives in the future. So why, then, might the COVID crisis also create new pressures which challenge partnership?

Starved local governments

Whatever challenges and changes to recruitment efforts do occur, it will most certainly be due to purposive and explicit efforts at the local level to re-politicize recruitment activities that have long been normalized and routinized. Some unique aspects of the COVID crisis mentioned above may, however, serve to problematize recruitment and partnership in more structural and systematic ways. First, the crisis has highlighted the general dearth of funding for public institutions, and the failure of starved public health agencies and struggling school systems in particular may create a more general awareness and concern for public funding and revenue streams. In such an environment, granting tax breaks and public funds to profitable corporation could potentially become optically challenging. There may also be more demand for local politicians and leaders who promise to fortify these institutions. On the other hand, unemployment, ever the friend of penurious employers, may well be a counterbalance to any such weight on the imagination of the public. Second, and perhaps more importantly, the pandemic has raised in the mind of many the problem of work and labor, and its centrality for profitable companies. The pandemic has at once highlighted the wide disparity between the upper and lower strata of services employees – as the former have been able to safely work from home only because the latter absorbed the riskier aspects of domestic life through expanded provisions of services – while at the same time demonstrating how crucial lower-paid services are for the higher end service workers to function where they were curtailed for public health reasons. Certainly, many of the parents I know will never take childcare services for granted again. There is thus potential that in some localities (and perhaps somewhat more broadly) that a kind of class consciousness may breathe anew, or at least begin to claw its way out from the grave Reagan dug. Indeed, there are some early signs that this may already be occurring, with Amazon workers currently voting on unionization in Alabama, and a boarder discussion in national media about a livable minimum wage. Alternatively, the desperation for some sense of normalcy amongst many in the upper strata of service workers may foster enmity towards workers' collective action where it impedes the patterns of consumption they hold most dear. If localities *do* see increases in unionization and union activity, this may serve not only to question some of the unspoken assumptions of recruitment policy, but also to create additional bases for political organization which could politicize and problematize incentives. Third, and related to unionization, where communities have had to organize and support one another amidst the lack of public institutional response, we may emerge from the pandemic with more active and involved community political organizations. These groups, along with local leaders and unions, may form in some localities and states coalitions which can challenge the assumptions that underpin recruitment and public subsidies for corporations.

The National Scale and beyond: a new "double movement?"

All of the above points are locality specific, and will likely take different paths dependent upon the local articulation of each issue, and the dynamics of resistance that they face. On a broader scale, resistance to public investment in private enterprise will be more successful in so far as the implicit logic spoken to at length here is undermined by the seriatim crises through which the public has lived. Partnership and recruitment depend upon the uncritical acceptance of the (at times contradictory) neoliberal narratives about the inefficacy of public administration, the moral centrality of the individual (and her freedom), and practical superiority of competitive markets as a mode of organization. Simply put, the COVID-19 pandemic and the unequally effective responses to it have turned all of these propositions on their head. Centralized coordination, government led research, and aggressive regulatory intervention, all now look somewhat more appealing than they did in January 2020. More interestingly, most wealthy and even middle-income nations have just gone through some version of a massive experiment in universal basic income provision, and even in places where this was relatively small in scale the impact of not only the benefits of such a program, but also seeing the capacity of governments to administer it, could be very long lasting. Conversely, the many leaders who continue to dance to the tune of neoliberal ideology look increasingly like parodies of themselves, caricatures extracted from 1931 political cartoons. Texas politicians, in particular, seem to have an astute sense of morbidly absurdist humor here, openly saying that going to one's death or sacrificing vulnerable elderly citizens is preferable to halting the daily churning of markets or federal oversight of their failing power grid. With such an incredible conjunction, could we be witnessing the final straw which fatally fractures the neoliberal project?

On a recent evening I was watching (or really listening to) a recurring Friday segment on the *PBS Newshour* where commentators from the right and what passes for the left in America discuss the implications of the past weeks' political events. It happened to be that the main event they were discussing was the signing earlier that day by President Joe Biden of a pandemic relief bill that cost nearly two trillion dollars. The right-leaning commentator (whose insights I often find to be meretricious, though he seems like a nice man), noted the bipartisan public support for the legislation, remarking that it seemed like the era of austerity and small government was over. Then again, he's often wrong.

Polanyi famously characterized the developments of modern society as shaped by a "double movement:" one towards market expansion outward (international markets) and inward (commodification), and a countermovement to restrict the commodification of "fictitious" commodities of land and labor (Polanyi 1957:138). This double movement, the intervention into economic life to partially decommodify land and labor, is a result of the fact that "no society could stand the effects of such a system of crude fiction even for the shortest stretch of time unless its human and natural substance as well as its business organization was protected against the ravages of this satanic mill" of market regulation and the law of value (Polanyi 1957:76–77).[8] If neoliberal globalization is a project to re-institutionalize a self-regulating market at a global level, are we not likely to witness another double movement? Will a post-COVID demand for governance and the prior fracturing of globalizations institutions by populist stooges fatally fracture the hegemony of the neoliberal globalization project?

From my theoretical position, the establishment of the national-state and capitalist markets are coterminous developments based in class struggle and the attempt to establish hegemonic domination. The double movement in society is Polanyi's pluralist take on this dynamic, though it should be noted that his definition of class is one that is decidedly Weberian and quite different from mine. The problem is that the terms on which hegemony is sought have changed: the neoliberal globalization project is wrought in a different context wherein the scale at which a double movement might be sought, and under what auspices, is fundamentally unclear. The neoliberal project is global not because it encompasses the whole world – for markets achieved this in Marx's time; it is a globalization *project* precisely because it is an effort to disentangle capital flows from the institutional framework of the nation-state, even as the state is re-oriented towards instituting global capital accumulation processes and a "self-regulating" market on a supra-national scale. Moreover, the hegemonic project at the core of the national development period was informed by the fact that both capital and labor were variously capable of articulating their interests by and through national institutions, and the fact that the ideology of this project was fashioned in the context of a competing ideology of socialism that in various forms dogged capitalist orthodoxy since its inception. It's hard to say that either of these holds true today – but there are some potentialities.

While Hoschchild's research suggests that even those members of the working class sloughed off by neoliberal competition accept the sacrality of private property, competition, and markets, more recent social and political movements have begun to carve out space in the political landscape. Black Lives Matter and affiliated movements for racial justice have at their core deeply progressive politics which extend beyond local police forces and their ubiquitous violence. Indeed, the current U.S. President – who was himself an architect of the neoliberal state – has said he is open to discussions of reparations to Black Americans; these may be mere political peans, but it should be clear to anyone who has glossed racial inequality in America that this problem cannot be addressed without a significant and systemic reallocation of wealth and sustained investment in Black communities and institutions. Moreover, amidst the predominance of center-right politics in the Democratic party there has emerged in recent years a growing group of senators and congressional members who promote genuinely leftist policies. While far from a majority in either party, these political figures have shifted the terms of mainstream political discourse and brought leftist – if not genuinely socialist – political propositions into the public debate. All of these suggest that neoliberal project's hold on the public imagination – and particularly on the common sense of the American public – is at least beginning to fracture beneath the weight of the material reality that project delivers, particularly among younger generations terrorized by the precarity of a market organized life.[9]

A more fundamental – if obscure – question is, if there is some new double movement, or even a more anti-capitalist turn, at what political scale and through which institutions would such regime be articulated? Prior to the pandemic there were already troubled attempts – supported in part by the rise in far-right xenophobic sentiments in core nations – to withdraw from global institutions in the United Kingdom and United States. The pandemic itself has short circuited a number of global commodity chains as production has shut down in some countries, and in other areas (such as vaccine production) nation-states have prioritized domestic production. But there does not seem to be any real *systematic* attempt re-nationalize global production chains, nor is it clear this could be done even if such political sentiments materialized outside far-right white nationalist circles. While it seems likely that Brexit and the U.S. withdrawal from NAFTA are more spastic reactions to far-right demands than signs of any systemic changes in the global political economy, they do serve as a reminder that globalization is in fact a project actively instituted by nation-states and their elites. It is thus possible that as nation-states respond to the COVID-19 pandemic, there could be a partial reorientation inward to manage domestic discontent, particularly where institutions have had to be fortified and expanded to deal with the pandemic. The key word here is *partial*, as whatever turn nation-states take will likely be guided by those who implemented the neoliberal globalization project in the first place, and any inward turn seems as likely to be repressively authoritarian as progressive. If a real a double movement does manifest in the wake of COVID-19, it is much more likely to be instigated at sub-national levels, where the circulation of capital flows more slowly through embedded networks of material and social relations that can, perhaps, be shaped into a social safety net, or even something more. I am tempted to say: after a year like 2020 nothing would…but then, committing those words to the page seems like a colossally bad idea.

Limitations and a last few words

In this book I have conducted a focused, comparative case study of a unique region of the United States, itself a unique nation in terms of industrial policy and labor relations. Hence, I think it is fair to say that the findings as they are written here are not generalizable in a quantitative sense far outside of that context. E.U. regulations on incentives limit comparisons in the most structurally similar countries (Thomas 2007, 2011); the best comparative cases are likely found in the semi-periphery, particularly in countries that have less authoritarian leaning governments (such as India). There is good research, for example, suggesting that there may be similar patterns to what I account for here in Latin America, in particular that local government partners are the key drivers of incentives provisions (Danzman and Slaski 2021). Counter to this suggestion, there is also some evidence that the central government in China purposefully stimulates inter-locality competition (Lee 2018).

This study has also focused on the nexus between government and industry, and while these findings have large implications for both workers and businesses, my interviews have not taken these latter views directly into account.[10] This is a definite limitation of my study, but also leaves clear potential for future research. My findings are also likely specific to large, greenfield industrial projects and investments, and should be generalized outside of this context only with caution and careful qualification. Indeed, as the site selection professionals noted above, the automotive industry in particular seems to have been the catalyst in the mid 1980s for changing the landscape of development and governance discussed in this research.

These limitations, however, should not be considered to limit the theoretical developments and generalizations I have laid out in this and the previous chapter, as all scientific theories are only properly understood as applicable within an historically delimited and clearly specified theoretical domain. Moreover, this research has only scratched the surface on an entire world of economic development and partnership governance that contains myriad possibilities for future research. One need only to look at the wide world of economic development and incentives to see opportunities for future research into the complex and interwoven layers of incentives and development efforts. For example, the State of Georgia offers no fewer than nine different specific tax credits that target industries, areas, projects of different sizes, and these beg for careful analysis into their efficacy and the ways in which different incentives relate to each other. Another opportunity is to examine how the partnership approach creates different forms of spatial agglomeration given the specifications of different industries and their relative ascendency. Georgia, for example, has become known as "Hollywood of the South" because its Film and Television incentives program has been successful in luring companies in and encouraging them to invest in studio space and the formation of labor power relevant to the industry. In response, there have been numerous local initiatives to create education and training programs to foster such labor power in the region, and local schools have developed or expanded film and television programs. Many research questions arise here, particularly why Georgia succeeded in facilitating the growth of this industrial center when Louisiana and North Carolina also offered tax incentives for film projects? Or one might research how the competition between localities for film production differs from that of automotive, given the difference in the processes and relations of production, and the product itself.

My research has made some important contributions, but these examples show that there is still a lot of research left to be done. Nevertheless, my findings provide valuable insight into how the neoliberal globalization project has shifted the terrain of local governance and affected the configuration of political class relations. Given the apparent fragility of the global economy, I think these findings should present a political imperative as well as scholarly insight. Given the rise of the far right, and the observation that "contemporary states have shown little disinclination to apply armed violence inwardly, against people who rank among their citizens" (Scholte 1997:447), the erosion of ground for legitimate opposition to business interests contains dark implications for democracy. If public resistance to the essential inequality of neoliberal capitalism is indeed growing, so too are the authoritarian tendencies of that project, of which Donald Trump and his ilk are merely one potent example. As I write this, Republican lawmakers across the United States are moving to limit access to voting, and the brutal suppression of racial justice demonstrations in the summer of 2020 showed us the West is willing and capable to put down resistance to neoliberal misery. If the neoliberal project is fracturing, the most conservative elements of that bloc have shown us a glimpse of what alternatives to much needed progressive changes might look like. The neoliberal project is, after all, famously founded on the proclamation of an "excess of democracy" (Teeple 2000:46).

Local government elections, however, can often offer a much greater diversity of platforms and political views than national or federal platforms, and perhaps the increasing importance of local governments in global capitalism presents an opportunity for formulating real alternatives to the current agenda at the local level. History has shown that even as the development project and nation-state centric patterns of accumulation were being created, working class formations shaped the nature and patterns of those institutionalizations of class relations (Hicks 1999; Huber and Stephens 2005; Rubinson and Sokolovsky 1988; Wallerstein 1979). As Gough notes, as local governments become increasingly important "systems of local dependence may give rise to arrangements within which labour's cooperation and welfare play a significant role. This is partly because labour can find particular strengths and resources for resistance at the local level" (Gough 2004:189). Local governments have, after all, been the site of new regulations and limitations on businesses even in the South of the United States, and despite the dominance of the ideas of a market-governed society, the practice of governance and the failure of markets consistently challenge this orthodoxy. For those that value even the attenuated democracy of global capitalism, the political imperative is clear.

Notes

1 Put differently these class relations are constituted through the nexus of what Sassen calls territory, authority, and rights (Sassen 2008).
2 Marx notes that this tendency towards abstraction is inherent in capitalism, which is constantly driving towards the accumulation of wealth in the abstract – exchange value – but is tethered to reality through the necessity of producing use-values.
3 Indeed, the political economic literature devoted to competitive federalism discusses (and to some degree espouses) the effect of such competition on economic development.

4 It is worth noting that the impetus for this sort of local socialization is "greatest where capital seeks to use 'strong competition' based on innovation and quality" (Gough 2004:190), and thus where labor is of relatively high skill and scarcity. Such local socializations can only serve to deepen the rural-urban divide characteristic of American and European societies discussed below. In this sense, we should not expect the political divisions of current moment to dissipate through such efforts, as they will have little effect on the working classes left behind by neoliberalism.

5 In an interview on this research, Hochschild elaborated this attitude towards markets and the local state:

> What's really happening in Louisiana, which I think may exaggerate what's happening in a lot of states, is that the oil companies really dominate the state. The state is a servant to oil and the petrochemical industry. And the state is saying, "Oh, please come and settle here in Louisiana, not Texas. We will give you $1.5 billion in 'incentive' pay, 'incentive' benefits." With that money, these companies make a donation to the Audubon Society and to a bird sanctuary, and so people think, "Oh, the company is so generous…plus it's offering us jobs, "…and so, the company looks good.

> Meanwhile, the state is doing the bidding of the companies. It is not a regulated state, but there are regulators who are not doing their job. So, in a way, the state had become like the compliant clerk for the companies [!]…It was saying, "Well, we're—you know, you deserve to be regulated," but it doesn't do it. So, the [folks] of Louisiana were saying, "Why am I paying taxes to a state that's not doing its job?" (Hochschild 2016b).

6 If one wanted to use technical language in an untechnical way, the same moral logic of business = good, government = bad establishes the internal and external validity of partnership and local economic development efforts. Internally, the perspective is shared among partners and is the lens through which they make sense of their activity. Externally, this moral logic works to explain and justify, where needed, the necessity of incentives and recruitment.

7 Lest I stretch too far, I am *not* suggesting that Black Lives Matter nor the racial horrors of American life are reducible to mere expressions of a deeper class struggle. The issue is far more complex.

8 Ruggie has argued the post WWII era is characterized by a balance of "markets and authority," what he calls embedded liberalism, a compromise between instituting a global or international trade infrastructure (or multilateralism) while maintaining a domestic safety net that relatively mitigates the worst effects of market regulation on human life and the environment (Ruggie 1982).

9 Ruggie pointed out over a decade ago that "the American public and its leaders appear trapped by their own ideological predispositions, which make it difficult for them to see the contradiction between their increasingly neo-laissez-fair attitude toward government and the desire to safeguard the nation for the adverse effects of increasingly denationalized market forces" (Ruggie 1997:9–10)

10 Though site-selectors do represent the interests of major firms, and a number of professionals turned out to have worked for automotive companies directly at some point.

Bibliography

Alexander, Michelle. 2012. *The New Jim Crow: Mass Incarceration in the Age of Colorblindness*. New York: The New Press.

Baade, Robert A., Robert Baumann, and Victor A. Matheson. 2008. "Selling the Game: Estimating the Economic Impact of Professional Sports through Taxable Sales." *Southern Economic Journal* 74(3):794–810. doi: 10.2307/20111996.

BDP03. 2016. "Business Development Professional 03."

Bhattacharyya, Gargi. 2018. *Rethinking Racial Capitalism*. Lanham: Rowman & Littlefield International.

Boudreaux, Christopher, R. Morris Coats, and Earl H. Davis. 2012. "The Dark Side of State Competition for Foreign Direct Investment: That Which Is Seen and That Which Is Not Seen." *Southern Business & Economic Journal* 35(1):35–52.

Brenner, Neil. 1999. "Globalisation as Reterritorialisation: The Re-Scaling of Urban Governance in the European Union." *Urban Studies* 36(3):431–451. doi: 10.1080/0042098993466.

Browning, Lynnley. 2006. "BMW's Custom-Made University." *The New York Times*, August 29. Retrieved June 10, 2017. https://www.nytimes.com/2006/08/29/business/worldbusiness/29bmw.html

Clarke, Simon. 1991. "State, Class Struggle, and the Reproduction of Capital." Pp. 183–203 in *The State Debate*, edited by S. Clarke. Hampshire: Palgrave MD.

Danzman, Sarah Bauerle, and Alexander Slaski. 2021. "Incentivizing Embedded Investment: Evidence from Patterns of Foreign Direct Investment in Latin America." *The Review of International Organizations*: 1–25. doi: 10.1007/s11558-021-09418-0.

EDP03. 2015. "Economic Development Professional 03."

Gough, Jamie. 2004. "Changing Scale as Changing Class Relations: Variety and Contradiction in the Politics of Scale." *Political Geography* 23(2):185–211. doi: 10.1016/j.polgeo.2003.11.005.

Harvey, David. 1982. *The Limits to Capital*. Chicago: University of Chicago Press.

Harvey, David. 2010. *The Enigma of Capital: And the Crises of Capitalism*. New York: Oxford University Press.

Hicks, Alexander M. 1999. *Social Democracy & Welfare Capitalism: A Century of Income Security Politics*. Ithaca: Cornell University Press.

Hill, Andrea. 2019. "How Much Does Foxconn Announcement Really Change Things for Wisconsin?" *Forbes*, January 31. Retrieved March 11, 2019. https://www.forbes.com/sites/andreahill/2019/01/30/how-much-does-foxconn-announcement-really-change-things-for-wisconsin/#19dbe384642d

Hochschild, Arlie Russell. 2016a. *Strangers in Their Own Land: Anger and Mourning on the American Right*. New York: The New Press.

Hochschild, Arlie Russell. 2016b. "What Drives Trump Supporters?: Sociologist Arlie Russell Hochschild on Anger & Mourning of the Right."

Huber, Evelyne, and John D. Stephens. 2005. "State Economic and Social Policy in Global Capitalism." Pp. 607–629 in *The Handbook of Political Sociology: States, Civil Societies, and Globlization*, edited by T. Janoski, R. Alford, A. M. Hicks, and M. A. Schwartz. Cambridge: Cambridge University Press.

Lee, Ching Kwan. 2018. *The Specter of Global China*. Chicago, Ill: University Of Chicago Press.

Mattera, Phillip, and Kasia Tarczynska. 2013. *A Good Deal For Mississippi? A Report on Taxpayer Assistance in Canton, Mississippi.* Good Jobs First.

McDavid, Kathleen E. 2010. "Giving State Tax Incentives to Corporations: How Much Is Too Much." *South Carolina Journal of International Law and Business* 7:257.

Pacewicz, Josh. 2016. *Partisans and Partners: The Politics of the Post-Keynesian Society.* University of Chicago Press.

Polanyi, Karl. 1957. *The Great Transformation.* Boston: Beacon Press.

Rubinson, Richard, and Joan Sokolovsky. 1988. "Patterns of Political Industrial Regulation: Railroads in the World Economy." Pp. 3–20 in *Rethinking the 19th Century,* edited by F. O. Ramirez. California: Greenwood Press.

Ruggie, John Gerard. 1982. "International Regimes, Transactions, and Change: Embedded Liberalism in the Postwar Economic Order." *International Organization* 36(2):379–415.

Ruggie, John Gerard. 1997. "Globalization and the Embedded Liberalism Compromise: End of an Era?" Working Paper 97/1, Max Planck Instiut, Cologn.

Sassen, Saskia. 2008. *Territory, Authority, Rights: From Medieval to Global Assemblages.* Updated ed. edition. Princeton, N.J.: Princeton University Press.

Scholte, Jan Aart. 1997. "Global Capitalism and the State." *International Affairs* 73(3):427–452.

Teeple, Gary. 2000. *Globalization and the Decline of Social Reform: Into the Twenty-First Century.* 2nd ed. Ontario: Garamond Press.

Thomas, Kenneth. 2007. *Investment Incentives: Growing Use, Uncertain Benefits, Uneven Controls.* Geneva, Switzerland: Global Subsidies Initiative.

Thomas, Kenneth. 2011. *Investment Incentives and the Global Competition for Capital.* London: Palgrave Macmillan.

Trubey, J. Scott. 2017. "Ground to Be Broken to Launch New Park on Atlanta's Westside." *Atlanta Journal Constitution*, May 18. Retrieved June 10, 2017. http://www.ajc.com/news/local/ground-broken-launch-new-park-atlanta-westside/K1h3BjlUqRIpK30qqeY4wM/

Vitale, Alex S. 2017. *The End of Policing.* London; New York: Verso.

Wallerstein, Immanuel Maurice. 1979. *The Capitalist World-Economy: Essays.* Cambridge: Cambridge University Press.

Appendix 1

Greenfield plant locations and incentives packages detail

Table A1.1

Greenfield plant locations and incentives packages detail

[Details provided as available from texts and materials]
[Borrowing Costs excluded from all estimations](number in parentheses are rough estimates of inflation, adjusted to 2014 dollars)

1980 Honda
Ohio | City: Marysville| County: Union
Initial Firm Investment: $750 million | Deal Announced: Late 1979 | Plant operational: 1982
Up Front Incentives:
•   Highway Construction
•   Site improvements
Sub-Total: $22 million
Tax-Based Incentives:
• $5 million unspecified tax incentives
Incentives Total: $27 million ($77.5 million)

1980 Nissan
Tennessee | City: Smyrna| County: Rutherford
Initial Firm Investment: $760 million | Deal Announced: November 1980 | Plant Operational: 1982
Up Front Incentives:
• $22m Road Improvements and Site prep
• $11m Employee Training
• $13m "indirect incentives"
Sub-Total: $46 million
Tax-Based Incentives:
• $10m unspecified tax incentives
Incentives Total: $66 million ($186.7 million)

1985 Saturn
Tennessee | City: Spring Hill | County: Maury & Williamson
Initial Firm Investment: $ 1.5 billion | Deal Announced: July 1985 | Plant Operational: 1991
• $30m worker training
• $50m road improvement and construction

Table A1.1
(Continued)

Sub-Total: $80 million
Tax-Based Incentives:
• PILOT agreements, amount not documented (no basis for estimates)
Incentives Total: $80 million+ ($176 million)

1985 Toyota
Kentucky | City: Georgetown| County: Scott
Initial Firm Investment: $800 million | Deal Announced: December 1985 | Plant
  Operational: 1988
Up Front Incentives:
• $20m site purchase & prep
• $10.28m Utilities (water and gas)
• $12.2m wastewater facility
• $47m road improvements
• $7.2m Training center
• $55–$65m worker training
• $5.2m Toyota families' education
Sub-Total: $147 million
Tax-Based Incentives:
• Unspecified Tax Incentives, amount not documented (no basis for estimates)
Incentives Total: $147 million+ ($318.4 million)

1986 Fuji-Isuzu
Indiana | City: Lafayette| County: Tippecanoe
Initial Firm Investment: $500 million | Deal Announced: December 1986 | Plant
  Operational: 1989
Up Front Incentives:
• $19m site purchase & prep
• $37m Road & Utilities (water and gas)
• $29m worker training
• $1m Japanese family transition
Sub-Total: $49 million
Tax-Based Incentives:
• $210m tax abatements and credits
Incentives Total: $260 million ($561.6 million)

1992 BMW
South Carolina | City: Spartanburg| County: Union
Initial Firm Investment: $300 million | Deal Announced: June 1992 | Plant
  operational: 1994
Up Front Incentives:
• $36m Site Purchase $[31.6 state;$5mn County]
• $22.5m Infrastructure & Site prep; road improvement; utilities and lines;
  expansion of airport runways
Sub-Total: $58.5 million
Tax-Based Incentives:
• $70.7m
    – Fee in lieu of property tax

(Continued)

Table A1.1
(Continued)

  – Job Tax credits
  – Creation of industrial park
Sub-total: $70.7 million
Incentives Total: $129.2 million ($214.7 million)

1993 Mercedes Benz of Alabama
Alabama | City: Vance| County: Jefferson
Initial Firm Investment: $300 million | Deal Announced: September 1993 | Plant Operational: 1997
Up Front Incentives:
* $30m–35m Site Purchase and development [Tuscaloosa City & Country + $5m From Birmingham city]
* $35m Training Facility [state?]
* $45m Worker Training and Pay while training [State]
* $5m Welcome Center
* $11m Alabama Power incentives
Sub total: $126 million
Tax-Based Incentives:
* $280m 25 Year Corporate income Tax Holiday [State [Law passed for both]]
    – Worker Income tax deferred to MBZ (5% of worker pay) [State and Local; 'Mercedes Benz Bill']
* $9m/yr Property Tax Breaks [Property tax break (Spindler 1994:198)]
    – No Timeline [assume 10yrs (low estimate) = $90m]
Sub-Total: $370m
Incentives Total: $ 496 million ($800,484,130)

1999 Honda Manufacturing of Alabama
Alabama | City: Lincoln| County: Multiple
Initial Firm Investment: $450 million | Deal Announced: May 1999 | Plant operational: 2001
Up Front Incentives:
* $16m Site Purchase [Counties: Jefferson, St. Claire, Talladega, Etowah, and Calhoun]
* $64m Site Prep
* $20m Road Improvements and Utilities
*   Worker Training [Unspecified]
Total: $102.7m
Tax-Based Incentives:
* $ 56m Tax Breaks/Abatements [Details Unclear – based on previous legislation]
*   [Estimated Property Tax Exemptions (10 years – low estimate): $90 million]
Incentives Total: $158.7 – $248.7 million ($222.8–$349.1 million)

2000 Nissan
Mississippi | City: Canton| County: Madison
Initial Firm Investment: $900 million | Deal Announced: November 2000 | Plant Operational: 2003
Up Front Incentives: (Initial Package)
* $93m site purchase and prep [State and local]
* $59m road improvements
* $33m water and sewer infrastructure

Table A1.1
(Continued)

- $17m "vehicle preparation" building
- $25m university-level automotive engineering center
- $80m for training
- $5m marketing plan to promote both the company and the state
- $8m miscellaneous expenditures

Sub total: $320 million
Tax-Based Incentives: (Estimates)
- $400 million Jobs tax Credits
- $72m Corporate income tax breaks
- $160m Advantage jobs subsidies
- $210m Property Tax abatements

Sub total: $842 million
Incentives Total: $1.162 *billion* ($2.2 billion)

2002 Hyundai Motors Manufacturing Alabama
Alabama | City: Montgomery| County: Butler
Initial Firm Investment: $1 billion | Deal Announced: April 2002 | Plant operational: 2005
Up Front Incentives:
- $55m site purchase and improvement [25m City and County & 34m State]
- $7m training center [State]
- $54.8m training [State I Think]
- $20m road/access improvements [State]
- $21m sewer and water line improvements [City & County]
- $18.2m utilities & railroad improvements [Private (Utility Companies)]
- $1m employee housing assistance [State]
- $12m Miscellaneous

Sub-Total: $170.8 million
Tax-Based Incentives:
- $ 82m Corporate income tax breaks (20yrs)
- Property tax breaks undocumented [very low estimate $100m property tax breaks based on equivalents]

Sub-Total: $82–$182 million
Incentives Total: $252.8–$358.2 million ($329.9–$467.5 million)

2006 Kia Motors Manufacturing of Georgia
Georgia | City: West Point | County: Troup
Initial Firm Investment: $1.2 billion | Deal Announced: March 2006 | Plant operational: 2009
Up Front Incentives:
- $60.5m site purchase and prep (includes resident relocation) [state]
- $36m road improvements & rail spur [State GA DOT]
- $21m infrastructure improvement
- $40.5m Training equipment and hard assets [Local & State]
- $31.4m Training Centre (5yrs) and maintenance [State]
  – Includes 5 years Operation Costs and Maintenance
- $5.7m Job Training [State]

Sub Total: $195.1 million

(Continued)

Table A1.1
(Continued)

Tax-Based Incentives: X
- $65.6–75.9mn Job-based tax credits ^{State & Local?}
- $14m (est.) sales tax exemption on equipment/other purchases ^{State}
- $130mn Property Tax abatements (15yrs)

Sub-Total: $209.6 million
Incentives Total: $404.7 million ($473,453,777)

2007 Toyota[Plant opening delayed by recession, opens 2011]
Mississippi | City: Blue Springs| County: Pontotoc, Union, Lee
Initial Firm Investment: $1 billion | Deal Announced: February 2007 | Plant
  operational: 2011
Up Front Incentives:
- $67m site purchase and prep ^{$30m Local Gov't}
- $136.6m infrastructure upgrades ^{State & Federal}
- $ 80m training ^{State}
- $10.3 miscellaneous ^{Local}
- $30m tier-1 supplier (earmarks)

Sub Total: $323.9 million
Tax-Based Incentives:
- Tax Incentives not Documented
- Estimates [based on 2000 Canton, MS deal]
  - $250m Jobs-based credits
  - $100m Job Advantage Subsidies [low estimate]
  - $100m Property Tax Abatements [low estimate]

Sub Total: $450 million [estimate]
Incentives Total: $323.9–$773.9 million ($368.6–$880.7 million)

2008 Volkswagen Group of America
Tennessee | City: Chattanooga | County: Hamilton
Initial Firm Investment: $1 billion | Deal Announced: July 2008 | Plant
  operational: 2011
Up Front Incentives:
- $81m site purchase and development ^{City and County}
  - Property a "gift" to VW
  - $93m roads and highway improvement ^{Federal and State}
- $30m worker training, screening, training center construction ^{Fed, State and Local}
- $3.5 rail upgrades ^{State, City and County; Hamilton County Railroad Auth.}

Sub-Total: $207.5m
Tax-Based Incentives:
- $200m job tax credits (20yrs)^{state?} [$5k/job/yr (20yrs) 'Super Job Tax Credit']
- $150-$350m property tax breaks (30yrs) ^{City & County} ["at least $12m/yr"]

Sub-Total: $350–$550 million
Incentives Total: $557.5 – 757.5 ($611.2 million)

2015 Volvo
South Carolina | City: Ridgeville | County: Berkely
Initial Firm Investment: $500 million Deal Announced: May 2015 Plant operational:
  TBD [2018 Est.]

Table A1.1
(Continued)

Up Front Incentives:
- $29m site purchase ^{Santee Cooper [Public Power Comp.]}
- $25m worker training ^{Santee Cooper}
- $5m ^{Berkley County}
- $120m economic development bonds
- $30m State development grants

Sub-Total: $209 million

Tax-Based Incentives:
- Not Reported ("Multi-Millions" in Credits and PILOT)

Incentives Total: $210 million+

2018 Toyota-Mazda
Alabama | City: Huntsville | County: Limestone & Madison
Initial Firm Investment: $1.6 billion Deal Announced: Jan 2018 Plant
  operational: TBD

Up Front Incentives:
- $68m site purchase ^{Local/City}
- $20m worker training ^{State Alabama Industrial Development Training}
- $20m reiumbursement for capital costs ^{State}
- $100m Road Improvements/Extensions ^{City/County}
- $9.4m Rail Extensions^{City/County}
- $2.8m Utility Extensions^{City/County}
- $9m Various Direct Expenditures

Sub-Total: $229.2 million

Tax-Based Incentives:
- 90.6m Jobs-based credits/10yr ^{State}
- $210m Investment Credit/10yr ^{State}
- $25m State Sales Tax Abatement ^{State}
- $14.3m Non-ed State Property Tax Abatement ^{State}
- $107m Property Tax Abatement/20yr ^{City/County}
- $24m construction sales tax abatement ^{City}
- $80m county property tax abatement/20yr ^{Limestone County}

Sub-Total: $550.9 million

Incentives Total: $780.1 million+

Appendix 2

Sample of prompts to business development professionals

Note – These questions are basically suggestions. In my experience the answers to these questions overlap – so I would not expect to ask all of them.

- Does the TVA *only* work with state-level authorities on development?
- Do state/local laws on economic development affect the role of the TVA in partnering in retaining/recruiting industry? (e.g., North Carolina's sunshine laws – Tennessee laws on giving subsidies to private corporations).
- Does federal "ownership" of the TVA affect its role in economic development?

    - What is relationship to EDA of U.S. Dept. of Commerce?

- How does the primary role of the TVA as a utility provider affect its economic development goals for the region?

    - Are there some prospects the TVA will not engage with (scale/scope)?
    - Are industrial projects of primary consideration?

- Does competition among states for companies affect the TVA relationship? How does TVA navigate competitive recruitment? (Is it a consideration?)

    - Does the TVA ever take part in the competition itself (does the Authority increase incentives etc. in negotiation – or simply offer non-negotiable packages)
      [Both final sites (Chattanooga and Limestone County, AL) for VW in 2008 were in TVA area]

- How has the role of the TVA in local economic development changed in your time there?

    - Has MEGASITE certification – and site *pre*-development in general – come to be of greater importance since the 1980s–1990s?

- Regional development bodies seem to have become more important since the 1980s…

- In what ways does working in economic development at a chamber of commerce differ from a government position?
- Would you say relationships between COCs and Development authorities has changed since the 1980s–1990s?
- Have expectations of private firms and industrial prospects changed in terms of what state/local authorities can/should offer? (In the past few decades).

Index

Note: Page numbers followed by 'n' refer to notes.